T&T Clark Studies in Systematic Theology

Edited by

John Webster, King's College,
University of Aberdeen, UK

Ian A. McFarland, Candler School of Theology,
Emory University, USA

Ivor Davidson, St Mary's College,
University of St Andrews, UK

t&t clark

WRATH AMONG THE PERFECTIONS OF GOD'S LIFE

by
Jeremy J. Wynne

t&t clark

Published by T&T Clark

A Continuum imprint

The Tower Building, 11 York Road, London SE1 7NX

80 Maiden Lane, Suite 704, New York NY 10038

www.continuumbooks.com

First published 2010
Paperback edition first published 2012

Jeremy J. Wynne has asserted his right under the Copyright, Designs and Patents Act, 1988, to be identified as the Author of this work.

British Library Cataloguing-in-Publication Data
A catalogue record for this book is available from the British Library

ISBN: 978-0-567-48854-1 (hardback)
      978-0-5671-0310-9 (paperback)

Typeset by Newgen Imaging Systems Pvt Ltd, Chennai, India
Printed and bound in Great Britain

CONTENTS

CONTENTS

ACKNOWLEDGMENTS

I have become convinced in the last few years that a responsible account of the triune God ranks among the most edifying (and patently unavoidable) of theological tasks. Like all theological reflection, it requires constant attentiveness to demands for confidence and modesty, breadth and depth, accountability to the authority of tradition, and the call to a genuinely contemporary restatement of Christian faith. It also provides, however, a rare and eminently focused space for reflecting on the glory of the Living One at the center of Holy Scripture and Christian tradition. This book, aimed at clarifying the wrath which belongs to God, is one contribution to this very old task.

The text was developed on the basis of my research studies at the University of Aberdeen culminating in 2009. Thanks are due first to John Webster. For his penetrating feedback, for his rare ability to nurture independence of mind and, of course, for his constant patience and encouragement, I am immensely grateful. Francesca Murphy and Philip Ziegler are master teachers. I am all the richer for the stimulating conversation, good humor, and wise counsel they have provided, as well as three enjoyable years teaching with them on the Critics and Defenders course. Katherine Sonderegger and Donald Wood examined the manuscript with tremendous care, identifying important opportunities for improving the text as well as fresh avenues for future research. Friends and officemates, finally, have made King's College a home away from home; I think especially of Andy Draycott, Darren Sarisky, David Gibson, David Gilland, Carolyn Kelly and, in the final hour, Justin Stratis.

Without the financial support of the Overseas Research Studentship Award Scheme and the University of Aberdeen College of Arts and Social Sciences, this research would not have been possible. The college is well attuned to both the needs of its students and the demands of the job and has been particularly generous in providing stipends to help with research in Princeton and Chicago as well as office space for the duration of the program.

I am grateful for the pastors and pilgrims of High Church Hilton, who embraced our family and ministered to us daily. The events leading us to Scotland were set in motion years ago. It was from my loving parents, Jim and Karen, that I first heard the words of the Gospel, and their support for this move overseas never wavered. In our final two years in Aberdeen, both Hannah Verity and Asher James were born. They have been for me as clear

ACKNOWLEDGMENTS

a miracle of God's grace as I have ever known and a wonderful distraction from research. I hope they can return one day to visit the place of their birth. My deepest love and gratitude, however, is reserved for Betsy, my wife and co-worker in the faith. This book is dedicated to her.

J. Wynne
Advent 2009

1

A SYSTEMATIC APPROACH
RECONSIDERED

From a survey of theological science in its many subdisciplines, it would seem that the matter of divine wrath is among the more elusive of scriptural themes. There is a substantial body of literature available on the topic, which spans the continuums of terse and expansive, wary and enthusiastic, impressionistic and analytic, ancient and contemporary. Despite the fact that the wrath of God has been a topic for these sundry occasional and thematic studies, the crucial question of its place within a more nearly systematic account of Christian theology—which is to say, an account of wrath self-consciously worked out in light of the whole—has largely been neglected.

More common is the strategy of analyzing a handful of persistent and thorny questions, not the least of which explore whether wrath is an affective dimension of God's character or an effect of God's working; whether it is more directly attributable to divine action *ab extra* or an outworking of structures immanent to creation; or, finally, whether there is assignable to wrath any properly redemptive, or perhaps pedagogical, end.[1] Inevitable as it is that such matters are touched upon in any extended essay on God's oppositional work, nonetheless, this general approach to the question fosters more confusion than clarity. Principally, it overlooks the complex manner in which the scriptures of the Old and New Testaments guide theological judgments concerning the character of the triune God. The purpose of this study, therefore, is to work out with greater *systematic* specificity the Christian claim that wrath belongs to God in his perfection.

The present chapter unfolds in three parts. To begin with, a modest overview of the kinds of studies which are already available—literary, historical, practical, and systematic—will suggest the importance of a constructive account of the fitting coordination between form and content in theological

---

[1] Cf. Stephen H. Travis, *Christ and the Judgment of God: Divine Retribution in the New Testament* (Basingstoke: M. Pickering, 1991), pp. 33ff.

consideration of divine identity descriptions. Second, we will suggest by way of transition that a renewal of interest surrounds the specifically theological task of the divine perfections, and so we will indicate at least one major resource for this investigation as well as a few key contemporary representatives. Development of these two observations—a representative overview of scholarly work on God's wrath as well as one provocative and innovative approach to this doctrinal locus—provides the background for the distinctiveness of this study. We will conclude by outlining, third, the goals and limitations that attend this constructive, biblical-dogmatic essay on wrath's place among the perfections of God's life.

I. *Theological Approaches to the Topic of Wrath*

One useful place to begin is with a representative overview of scholarly work on God's wrath. The subject has been variously treated as a biblical and literary theme, such that matters of terminological frequency, genre, intertextuality, and sociocultural context are pressed to render the most reliable semantic range for translation and interpretation. In the specific case of God's wrath, these kinds of studies have been executed with both painstaking attention to individual passages and an impressive grasp of the broad canon of testimony. As will be made particularly clear in the scriptural exposition of part two of our study, the background and insight which this kind of research offers can facilitate a higher order of theological engagement.[2]

We can note in this connection one particularly important decision for our argument. While a variety of terms are employed in the scriptural witness—most frequently אַף (e.g. Ex 4.14; Isa 5.25), חֵמָה (e.g. Nah 1.2; Ezek 5.15), ὀργή (e.g. Eph 5.6; 1 Thess 2.16), and θυμός (e.g. Rev 19.15)—all may be translated "wrath," and that is the procedure we have followed. One of the benefits of deciding in favor of a term, which is undoubtedly archaic in contemporary English language, is precisely its strange character. In this sense, for example, "wrath" may function as a semitechnical term in a manner unavailable to the more psychological concept of "anger." While not itself determinative, this seems a prudent choice where the burden of an argument is in every respect to identify wrath as it belongs uniquely to God. While it is quite true that this choice reinforces a certain noetic distance between

---

[2] For a thorough overview of the terminology, cf. esp. Stephen H. Travis, "Wrath of God (NT)," *The Anchor Bible Dictionary*, ed. D.N. Freedman, vol. 6 (New York: Doubleday, 1992), pp. 996–998; Gary A. Herion, "Wrath of God (OT)," *The Anchor Bible Dictionary*, ed. D.N. Freedman, vol. 6 (New York: Doubleday, 1992), pp. 989–996; and Scott A. Ashmon, "The Wrath of God: A Biblical Overview," *Concordia Journal* 31, no. 4 (2005): pp. 348–358. For statistical analysis, see Bruce E. Baloian, *Anger in the Old Testament* (New York: Peter Lang, 1992), esp. pp. 65–124.

biblical and everyday use—ostensibly making intelligibility the chief hurdle—it "has the advantage of reducing the risk that God's wrath be misunderstood as an arbitrary emotion."[3] In its relationship to the divine perfections, we will argue that wrath is neither a generally available nor intuitable notion, but rather that its veracity depends upon careful attention to the self-revelation of the triune God in concrete events.

Our own approach may be further distinguished from general, biblical investigations of the topic. In the first instance, the theological position for which we will argue requires one to look more broadly, and so beyond instances of individual terminological reference, across the testimony of God's dealings with his people in Old and New Testament alike. Understanding God's wrath is neither identical with an account of these writings in their broader sociocultural context nor, therefore, is it primarily a matter of the relation between these texts and extracanonical literary resources. Rather, as with all such identity descriptions, God's wrath is revealed in concrete acts of opposition to the human refusal to live in covenant fellowship. The requisite attention to the discursive and dramatic form of the self-revelation of the eternal God, and its place in theological exposition, will be addressed more fully in part one. Concern for the particular and concrete content of theological concepts will be a constant focus of this essay. Of course, acknowledging that theological judgments or presuppositions condition our argument does not imply, conversely, that the discipline of biblical study is a theologically neutral or unbiased enterprise. One finds this point in evidence most clearly where significantly divergent positions are considered alongside one another.[4]

Alternatively, the topic of the wrath of God has been treated in a historical perspective, though the distinction between biblical and historical approaches is not a tidy one. Ferdinand Weber, for example, has mounted an impressive historical analysis under the following thesis.

Die Historie der göttlichen Zornesoffenbarung ist also wesentlich der Nachweis der Objectivität des Versöhnungswerkes Christi als Sühnung [cf. ἱλασμός, 1 Jn 2.2, 4.4] des göttlichen Zorns.[5]

---

[3] Travis, "Wrath of God (NT)," p. 998.

[4] Both D.A. Carson's biblical analysis, cf. "The Wrath of God," *Engaging the Doctrine of God: Contemporary Protestant Perspectives*, ed. B.L. McCormack (Grand Rapids: Baker Academic, 2008), and the more extended work of R.V.G. Tasker, *The Biblical Doctrine of the Wrath of God* (London: Tyndale, 1951), are peppered with illuminating insights. As we will see, they nonetheless stringently oppose some of the key arguments of A.T. Hanson's rigorous study, *The Wrath of the Lamb* (London: SPCK, 1957), esp. ch. 8. Cf. also Ralf Miggelbrink, *Der zornige Gott: Die Bedeutung einer anstössigen biblischen Tradition* (Darmstadt: Wissenschaftliche Buchgesellschaft, 2002).

[5] Ferdinand Weber, *Vom Zorne Gottes: Ein biblisch-theologischer Versuch* (Erlangen: Andreas Deichert, 1862), p. 2.

While an historical study of sorts, what Weber proposes is clearly not an investigation of the history of interpretation but rather an interpretation of so-called biblical history through the lens of the manifestation of divine wrath. *Vom Zorne Gottes* is therefore a meticulous examination of the narrative stretching from the event of original sin, to the institution of the law and covenant, to the prophetic witness, to redemption in Jesus Christ [*der Wendepunkt*], and so finally to God's wrath as it is co-constitutive of final judgment.

By contrast, a genetic procedure focused upon continuity and/or development in interpretation will trace the influence and transmission of this theme through the work of individual thinkers, schools of thought, and distinct epochs in theological history. The relationship between God's wrath and debates over divine impassibility particularly characteristic of the patristic period—though certainly not unknown to contemporary theology—have in this regard received disproportionate attention. This is due partly to the fact that the first Christian theological treatise devoted entirely to the subject was composed by the gifted rhetorician, Lactantius (ca. 240–320 AD).[6] Central to the task of these kinds of studies is gaining purchase upon the particular contexts in which such thinkers lived and therefore the outside influences exerted upon Israelite and early Christian understandings of wrath.[7]

More recent is the historical study by Stephen B. Murray, *Reclaiming Divine Wrath: An Apologetics for an Aspect of God Neglected by Contemporary Theology and Preaching*.[8] Despite the stated intention of this encyclopedic 2004 doctoral dissertation, the actual constructive contribution is limited to the organization of historical views of wrath under six

---

[6] See, e.g., Ermin F. Micka, *The Problem of Divine Anger in Arnobius and Lactantius* (Washington D.C.: Catholic University of America Press, 1943), esp. pp. 7–17; and Sven Grosse, "Der Zorn Gottes: Überlegungen zu einem Thema der Theologie bei Tertullian, Laktanz und Origenes," *Zeitschrift für Kirchengeschichte* 112, no. 2 (2001): pp. 147–167. For a translation of the original work by Lactantius, cf. "De ira Dei," *The Ante-Nicene Fathers: Translations of the Writings of the Fathers Down to A.D. 325, vol. 7*, eds. A. Roberts, et al. (Edinburgh: T&T Clark, 1986).

[7] See esp. M. Pohlenz, *Vom Zorne Gottes: Eine Studie über den Einfluss der griechischen Philosophie auf das alte Christentum* (Göttingen: Vandenhoeck und Ruprecht, 1909); also Bertil Albrektson, *History and the Gods: An Essay on the Idea of Historical Events as Divine Manifestations in the Ancient Near East and in Israel* (Lund: Gleerup, 1967); Richard E. Creel, *Divine Impassibility: An Essay in Philosophical Theology* (Cambridge: Cambridge University Press, 1986); H. te Velde, *Seth, God of Confusion: A Study of his Role in Egyptian Mythology and Religion*, trans. G.E. van Baaren-Pape (Leiden: E. J. Brill, 1967).

[8] Stephen B. Murray, "Reclaiming Divine Wrath: An Apologetics for an Aspect of God Neglected by Contemporary Theology and Preaching" (unpublished Ph.D. diss.; Union Theological Seminary, 2004).

overlapping headings.[9] As an attempt at conceptual clarity, its success is therefore limited by a palpable lack of theological method. The dissertation is focused, on the one hand, upon ameliorating a broad tendency in contemporary theology toward abandonment of the theology of God's wrath through an overwhelming demonstration of wrath's thematic presence within the tradition and, on the other, upon rectifying certain mistaken concepts of wrath used to underwrite human acts of violence. While the work forcefully demonstrates broad, historical disagreement over the character and purpose of divine wrath, as well as a general lack of focused criticism, as a systematic-theological thesis it would more compellingly achieve its ends through analysis of primary rather than secondary sources as well as by more substantial first-order theological engagement with scripture.[10] It will be the burden of our own argument to demonstrate that these systematic issues and concerns are more constructively advanced through critical consideration of distinctly theological resources and criteria, and specifically through the coordination of theological form and material content.

Alongside these biblical and historical approaches, the topic likewise has been approached with distinctly practical concerns in view. Among such constructive interactions, Alastair V. Campbell's *The Gospel of Anger* is undoubtedly among those most lucid and compelling. At heart, it is a pastoral theology of anger that seeks to emphasize how God is "closer to us, more involved with us, than we might at first think."[11] Anger, Campbell argues, is not mechanistic in nature but a moral emotion which, in light of the Christian call to compassion and justice, leads us to sever "the link between anger and destructiveness and to find ways in which people's powerful reactions to life's dangers around them may be put to the service of human

---

[9] Specifically, wrath's capacity for: providing moral direction, impairing malign behavior, protecting the vulnerable, restructuring society, eliminating the conditions of original sin and, finally, for eschatological rectification—ibid., pp. 284ff.; cf. the thesis at pp. 9, 14.

[10] This evaluation pivots on the extent to which, e.g., either Friedrich Schleiermacher's theological disavowal of wrath (cf. ibid., pp. 185–189) or Karl Barth's incorporation (cf. ibid., pp. 196–208) may be adequately accounted for apart from a focused reading of and grappling with their major dogmatic works. All the more provocative is the fact that an intricate rethinking of the matter of the divine attributes characterizes the work of both theologians. See also the foundational chapter and its heavy indebtedness to the work of A.T. Hanson.

[11] Alastair V. Campbell, *The Gospel of Anger* (London: SPCK, 1986), p. 15. Another set of studies belonging to the broad category of practical concern was published in *Concordia Journal* 31, no. 4 (2005): cf. John W. Oberdeck, "Speaking to Contemporary American Culture on Sin and the Wrath of God," pp. 398–410, and James V. Bachman, Peter L. Senkbeil, and Kerri L. Thomsen, "God's Wrath Against Sin: Echoes in Contemporary Culture?," pp. 411–424.

wholeness."[12] At the same time, the author's fundamental assertion that a tension must be maintained between God's will for the destruction of creation and his will for its well-being lacks the material center, which we propose to offer. It is the unified drama of creation and redemption, in other words, centered on the life, death, and resurrection of Jesus Christ, which singularly reveals the meaning of wrath and so its salvation-determination. In this respect, our task will be to chase down and give greater clarity to the theological discussion which, Campbell admits, is "beyond the scope" of his own project.[13]

This leads us to a consideration, finally, of explicitly systematic-theological developments of the topic. Here we can be somewhat more discriminating and suggest these studies are distinguishable on the basis of the theological *locus* within which each is most nearly situated. As a dominant biblical theme at least partially constitutive of many of the episodes comprising God's variegated work of creation and redemption, and insofar as systematic theology defines its own subject matter as a unity in distinction, a number of options present themselves. Wrath may be situated, in the first instance, in relation to the providence of God, and so developed as an aspect of the sovereign Lord's ongoing provision for and governance over creation.[14] Second, the wrath of God may be given particular attention as a distinctly eschatological matter, and thus considered primarily in relationship to the final resolution of the history of perdition, first through death and resurrection and subsequently through judgment unto heaven or hell.[15]

A third critical option is to elucidate God's wrath as it belongs to the gracious and healing forgiveness by which God restores his sinful creatures. Such soteriological studies constitute perhaps the most common avenue of approach.[16] In point of fact, the present study grew out of a prior interest in

---

[12] Ibid., p. 31.

[13] Ibid., p. 88.

[14] See, e.g., Rufus Burrow, Jr., "The Love, Justice, and Wrath of God," *Encounter* 59 (1998): pp. 379–407; Jan Jans, "'neither Punishment nor Reward': Divine Gratuitousness and Moral Order," *Job's God*, ed. E.J. van Wolde, pp. 83–92 (London: SCM Press, 2004); Kōsuke Koyama, "The 'Wrath of God' and the Thai Theologia Gloriae," *Christ and the Younger Churches: Theological Contributions from Asia, Africa, and Latin America* (1972): pp. 42–50.

[15] See, e.g., William V. Crockett, "Wrath that Endures Forever," *Journal of the Evangelical Theological Society* 34 (1991): pp. 195–202; Eberhard Jüngel, "The Last Judgment as an Act of Grace," *Louvain Studies* 15 (1990): pp. 389–405; Niels Henrik Gregersen, "Guilt, Shame, and Rehabilitation: The Pedagogy of Divine Judgment," *Dialog* 39, no. 2 (2000): pp. 105–118; Stephen T. Davis, "Universalism, Hell, and the Fate of the Ignorant," *Modern Theology* 6 (1990): pp. 173–186.

[16] See, e.g., M. Aloysia, "The God of Wrath?," *Catholic Biblical Quarterly* 8, no. 4 (1946): pp. 407–415; Richard Mouw, "Violence and the Atonement," *Must Christianity be Violent?: Reflections on History, Practice, and Theology*, ed. K.R. Chase, A. Jacobs

wrath's place within a theology of the atonement. Insofar as these concerns turn upon inquiry into God's character, however—especially in the relationship between the Father and the crucified Son or in connection to God's disposition toward sinful, beloved creatures—it became increasingly evident that clarification and resolution depends more immediately upon matters decided within the doctrine of God. Thus the poignancy of G. C. Berkouwer's observation, namely that "the background of the doctrine of reconciliation is the doctrine of the attributes of God."[17] Our subject matter, in short, is directly relevant to recent debates over whether the gospels of the New Testament, and specifically the passion narratives therein, legitimately attribute an element of either *com*-passion[18] or violence[19] to God himself. At the same time, we recognize that because these are substantial theological questions in their own right, adequate treatment of either rests outside the purview of our study. Undeniable as these connections are—and particularly in chapters 4 through 6, it will be neither possible nor desirable to try and avoid completely the material overlap—our task is to remain as focused as possible upon the wrath of God as it belongs to the conceptual environment of the doctrine of God.[20]

(Grand Rapids: Brazos Press, 2003); Christoph Schroeder, "Standing in the Breach: Turning Away the Wrath of God," *Interpretation* 52, no. 1 (1998): pp. 16–23.

[17] G.C. Berkouwer, *The Work of Christ* (Grand Rapids: Eerdmans, 1965), p. 266.

[18] In this regard, Jürgen Moltmann's *The Crucified God: The Cross of Christ as the Foundation and Criticism of Christian Theology* (New York: Harper & Row, 1974), has become a standard work. Among the direct and indirect influences on Moltmann see, respectively, Abraham J. Heschel's highly regarded *The Prophets* (New York: Harper & Row, 1962), and Kazō Kitamori's *Theology of the Pain of God* (London: SCM Press, 1966). Regarding the latter, lesser-known work, the Japanese original dates from 1946. Taking his cue from Jeremiah 31.20, Kitamori explores the notion of a God who "enfolds our broken reality...who embraces us completely" but that precisely in this— because the *one* Lord both wishes to love sinners and yet must also sentence them to death—atonement means God's "experiencing unspeakable suffering, going through agonies, and offering himself as sacrifice" (pp. 20–22; cf. pp. 27f.).

[19] See the impressive collection of essays, *Stricken by God? Nonviolent Identification and the Victory of Christ*, eds. B. Jersak and M. Hardin (Grand Rapids: Eerdmans, 2007). Interest in "the character of God" (p. 433) is frequently brought into view but left underdeveloped. Compare: acknowledgement of the perplexing co-inherence of divine holiness, patience, vengeance, wrath, and mercy (cf. pp. 30ff., 62), the ideal of mercy 'infecting' justice (p. 229), or the notion of God's "abyssal compassion" (p. 408).

[20] No less a theologian than Schleiermacher once observed that, while one has good reason to be sceptical of any claim to possess perfect facility with the full compass of theological knowledge and method, persistent confinement to the sphere of one's respective discipline would, in effect, entail the loss of theological science as a whole. His conclusion: "[I]f one is to deal with any one of the theological disciplines in a truly theological sense and spirit, one must master the basic features of them all"—cf. *Brief Outline of Theology as a Field of Study*, ed. T.N. Tice (Lewiston: E. Mellen Press, 1990), §§14–16.

Beyond this broad organization of the material, two studies particularly focused upon systematic issues merit further comment. Recently, Tony Lane has argued the necessary material relationship between divine love and wrath. It is a strong essay, particularly attentive to reception of the theme of wrath within the complex web of human sensibility and experience. At its heart lies the thesis that wrath's misinterpretation is best remedied through a proper coordination of all the attributes of God's life—and especially God's love and wrath—in a singular harmony, even if this harmony "finally defies a logical systematization."[21] While the theological decisions offered in the course of his analysis are largely judicious and illuminating, this last admission is less satisfying. We will argue, by contrast, that it is both imprudent and anticlimactic to leave this crucial premise undeveloped. By no means does this require logically resolving the "problem" of the *simplex multiplicitas*, which is God's life. Rather theology is in all its parts "a mystery discerning enterprise," an attempt to clarify the profundity of the self-revelation of the triune God.[22]

A second essay of note is Stefan Volkmann's 2004 doctoral thesis, *Der Zorn Gottes: Studien zur Rede vom Zorn Gottes in der evangelischen Theologie*. Though it is a work rare in situating the notion of wrath within a doctrine of God, at the same time, Volkmann elaborates a strikingly different conception of the latter than we seek. His purpose is principally to refine the biblical metaphor of "divine wrath" into a more scientific, and so more nearly adequate, model for theology. All human speech is metaphorical and so intelligible on the basis of its syntactical structure, semantic content, and pragmatic context. Volkmann argues, however, that the metaphorical status of statements concerning divine wrath by no means compromises their veracity. Rather it is precisely through the "creative capacity" of such metaphors that one finds coherently joined together "two semantic units which we regard as belonging to two different semantic fields," in this case divine and human anger.[23] It is precisely when analyzed as a metaphor that the meaning of God's wrath becomes intelligible.

---

[21] Tony Lane, "The Wrath of God as an Aspect of the Love of God," in *Nothing Greater, Nothing Better: Theological Essays on the Love of God*, ed. K.J. Vanhoozer (Grand Rapids: Eerdmans, 2001), p. 167.

[22] Thomas G. Weinandy, *Does God Suffer?* (Notre Dame: University of Notre Dame, 1999), p. 32. Weinandy borrows this theme from Gabriel Marcel and Jacques Maritain (cf. pp. 27–39).

[23] Stefan Volkmann, *Der Zorn Gottes: Studien zur Rede vom Zorn Gottes in der evangelischen Theologie* (Marburg: Elwert, 2004), p. 260; cf. p. 70. The definition of a metaphor, as "that figure of speech whereby we speak about one thing in terms which are seen to be suggestive of another," is taken from J.M. Soskice (p. 52 n. 43). For a parallel example, one taken from the realm of physics, he suggests "Licht ist eine Welle" (p. 43f.). See also Volkmann's reference article, "Zorn Gottes: Theologiegeschichtlich und dogmatisch," *Religion in Geschichte und Gegenwart: Handwörterbuch für*

Such considerations, on the one hand, are not exhaustive of the task as he envisions it. Subsequent space, even the bulk of Volkmann's exposition, is given to the study of distinctly Christian understandings of God through secondary analysis of German-language theology (specifically that of Luther, Schleiermacher, Ritschl, Barth, and Elert). As prolegomena, however, a theory of metaphors is fundamental to his analysis. This conceptual environment, it is claimed, provides a scientific basis for discussion of wrath by means of neutral, negative, and positive analogies. Most notably, perhaps, the material content of the thesis—including the operative concept of "anger"—is thereby made dependent for its serviceability upon analytic categories borrowed from modern psychology.

In brief compass, such is the topography of theological scholarship focused upon the wrath of God. Our organization of this material is neither an attempt at drawing hard and fast lines—since the actual connections between literary, historical, practical, and systematic concerns are, in practice if not in theory, considerably more complicated. Neither is it an introduction to those resources, which have most powerfully shaped our own constructive proposal. This summary is simply an expedient, a means of introducing and contextualizing our claim that, despite the respective strengths of available studies, a systematic framework for situating wrath coherently and compellingly among the others of the perfections of God's life has gone largely undeveloped.

II. Renewed Interest in the Divine Perfections

The last few years, by contrast, have seen a renaissance of interest in the broader topic of the divine perfections. In many respects, this renewal is indebted to Karl Barth's own exceptional handling of the doctrine, and especially to his now famous belief that a fulsome and responsible statement that "God is" constitutes both the most difficult and most extensive task of dogmatics, one which "consists in defining the subject of all the statements that are here necessary and possible."[24] While a genetic account of the development of this doctrine in late modern theology is not our task,[25] by way of anticipation, we can point to some of the most important features

---

Theologie und Religionswissenschaft, vol. 8, ed. H-D. Betz, 4th ed. (Tübingen: Mohr Siebeck, 1998), pp. 1905–1906.

[24] Karl Barth, *Church Dogmatics* II/1, eds. G.W. Bromiley, T.F. Torrance (Edinburgh: T&T Clark, 1957), p. 257.

[25] Among the most important resources, cf. Friedrich Schleiermacher, *The Christian Faith*, eds. H.R. Mackintosh, J.S. Stewart (Edinburgh: T&T Clark, 1928); Hermann Cremer, *Die Christliche Lehre von den Eigenschaften Gottes*, ed. H. Burkhardt (Giessen: Brunnen Verlag, 2005); Isaak A. Dorner, *Divine Immutability: A Critical Reconsideration*,

characteristic of this renewal and thereby enumerate some of the most important resources available for a project such as ours.

Among the most provocative arguments are those which favor the positive and descriptive nature of the task. The former proposal, for example, suggests that for the theologian the perfection of God "is not a mystery of darkness or irrationality, but rather of Light."[26] The latter adds to this a decisive shift away from analytic and deductive modes of inquiry, claiming that such methods are wholly inadequate to the "singular and antecedent identity" of God, an identity which is "possessed of its own incomparable uniqueness and of a majesty which can only be characterized as it sets before us the free acts of God's aliveness."[27] In a similar fashion, the task is dramatically reconfigured where divine attributes are understood as irreducibly a matter of God's trinitarian life. Thus, for example, explicitly christological resources will necessitate the affirmation that God "does not empty himself into the world" in revealing himself to creatures, while pneumatological resources protect the fact that God is only "known by us when and insofar as he himself wills."[28] A great deal depends, furthermore, upon a robust account of the asymmetrical relationship between divine and human moral action. More specifically, while the doctrine is primarily concerned "to investigate whether descriptions which the church puts forward agree with God's self-disclosure attested in scripture," it is no less responsible for an account of that "very particular form of [creaturely] life that ought to take shape in correspondence."[29] Finally, there is a heightened awareness of the irreducible

---

ed. R.R. Williams (Minneapolis: Fortress Press, 1994), and *A System of Christian Doctrine*, ed. A. Cave, J.S. Banks (Edinburgh: T&T Clark, 1880).

[26] Katherine Sonderegger, "The Absolute Infinity of God," *The Reality of Faith in Theology: Studies on Karl Barth Princeton-Kampen Consultation, 2005*, eds. B. McCormack and G.W. Neven (New York: Peter Lang, 2007), p. 48.

[27] John B. Webster, "The Immensity and Ubiquity of God," *Denkwürdiges Geheimnis: Beiträge zur Gotteslehre, Festschrift für Eberhard Jüngel zum 70. Geburtstag*, eds I.U. Dalferth, J. Fischer and H-P. Grosshans (Tübingen: Mohr Siebeck, 2004), p. 539; among others, cf. esp. his "Life in and of Himself: Reflections on God's Aseity," *Engaging the Doctrine of God: Contemporary Protestant Perspectives*, ed. B.L. McCormack (Grand Rapids: Baker Academic, 2008), pp. 107–124; "The Holiness and Love of God," *Scottish Journal of Theology* 57, n. 3 (2004): pp. 249–268; *Holiness* (London: SCM Press, 2003); "God's Perfect Life," *God's Life in Trinity*, ed. M. Volf, M. Welker (Minneapolis: Augsburg Fortress, 2006), pp. 143–152.

[28] Colin Gunton, *Act and Being: Towards a Theology of the Divine Attributes* (Grand Rapids: Eerdmans, 2002), p. 110; also, "The Being and Attributes of God: Eberhard Jüngel's Dispute with the Classical Philosophical Tradition," *The Possibilities of Theology: Studies in the Theology of Eberhard Jüngel in His Sixtieth Year*, ed. J.B. Webster (Edinburgh: T&T Clark, 1994).

[29] Christopher R.J. Holmes, "The Theological Function of the Doctrine of the Divine Attributes and the Divine Glory, with Special Reference to Karl Barth and His Reading of the Protestant Orthodox," *Scottish Journal of Theology* 61, no. 2 (2008): p. 207; cf.

nature of the task. Within the sphere of theological science—no less than within the life of the community of worshipping Christians—"it is . . . impossible to speak about or to God without some commitment concerning the divine attributes."[30]

An account such as this of fundamental theological decisions—being incomplete, too succinct, and far oversimplified—can function merely as an intimation of the kinds of claims with which we will engage throughout this book. Even at a glance, however, it suggests constructive potential and new found vigor. These observations commend together a positive, descriptive, thoroughly trinitarian task focused upon a twofold object: by nature, the life of God and, by grace, the lives of God and creatures lived out in creation and redemption. Precisely through engagement with resources like these,[31] we aim to achieve a more nearly adequate grasp of the relationship between wrath and the life of God. The present argument is therefore intended to be transparent in its indebtedness, not only to the theology of Karl Barth, but to a number of theologians who, similarly influenced by his magisterial reworking of the doctrine, have already taken significant steps beyond it.

III. Purpose, Plan, and Limitations

For these reasons—the lacuna in systematic scholarship on the topic of wrath, the timeliness in relation to the pressing questions of the day, and the

---

also, *Revisiting the Doctrine of the Divine Attributes: In Dialogue with Karl Barth, Eberhard Jüngel, and Wolf Krötke* (New York: Peter Lang, 2007).

[30] Stephen R. Holmes, "The Attributes of God," *The Oxford Handbook of Systematic Theology*, eds. J.B. Webster, K. Tanner and I.R. Torrance (Oxford: Oxford University Press, 2007), p. 54. Or as Barth writes, it is "impossible to have knowledge of God Himself [the triune God] without having knowledge of a divine perfection" and vice versa—*Church Dogmatics* II/1, p. 323. For similar studies by S.R. Holmes, cf. "Trinitarian Missiology: Towards a Theology of God as Missionary," *International Journal of Systematic Theology* 8, no. 1 (2006): pp. 72–90; "Something Much Too Plain to Say: Towards a Defense of the Doctrine of Divine Simplicity," *Listening to the Past: The Place of Tradition in Theology* (Grand Rapids: Baker Academic, 2002), pp. 50–67.

[31] One may also wish to consult: Eberhard Jüngel, "Theses on the Relation of the Existence, Essence and Attributes of God," *Toronto Journal of Theology* 17, no. 1 (2001): pp. 55–74; Wolf Krötke's full-scale reworking of the doctrine, *Gottes Klarheiten: Eine Neuinterpretation der Lehre von Gottes 'Eigenschaften'* (Tübingen: Mohr Siebeck, 2001); and Ellen T. Charry, "The Soteriological Importance of the Divine Perfections," *God the Holy Trinity: Reflections on Christian Faith and Practice*, ed. T. George (Grand Rapids: Baker Academic, 2006), pp. 129–147. For an overview of the task of the doctrine, see Stephen R. Holmes, "The Attributes of God," and Oswald Bayer, "Eigenschaften Gottes: Christentum," *Religion in Geschichte und Gegenwart: Handwörterbuch für Theologie und Religionswissenschaft*. 8 Vols, ed. H-D. Betz, 4th ed., vol. 2 (Tübingen: Mohr Siebeck, 1998), pp. 1139–1142.

need to continue refinement of this creative approach to the divine perfections—a more robust analysis of God's wrath contributes significantly to the ongoing project of Christian systematic theology. Unfolding in five subsequent chapters, our argument is constructed in two inextricably linked parts. Key to its success is a clear mending together of two activities often thought exclusive, namely systematic theological reflection and a disciplined reading of the texts of scripture. We will take these in turn, signaling where appropriate their interdependence.

Part one, to begin with, develops the task of the doctrine of the divine perfections as it relates especially to the theme of God's wrath. The object is to make explicit the inner logic of biblical language concerning the divine character—its deep contours, its presuppositions, its coherence. Three important limitations attend this otherwise unwieldy project. First, it is neither possible nor necessary to attempt a complete proposal for the form and content of the doctrine of God. Rather our focus will be on those points requisite for a clear, disciplined reading of the biblical material of part two. The whole essay, furthermore, has been devised from the ground up. While the proposal itself moves within a distinct intellectual environment, in the final analysis, I have selected both the topics which need to be treated and the interlocutors who, in my own judgment, were most challenging, stimulating, and illuminating. Second, therefore, the argument works from and toward the intellectual and doxological space characteristic of—though not exclusive to—the Reformed tradition.[32] Third, the argument unfolds in conversation

---

[32] Brian Gerrish suggests that Reformed confessional unity is conceivable in terms of the five habits of mind characteristic of Reformed theologians. Reformed thinking is: 1) *deferential*, reaching first for the writings of elders, not simply to know about them but rather to know what they themselves knew; 2) *critical*, such that continual interaction with traditional thinkers includes both their criticism and our own; 3) *open* to the insights of every scientific pursuit, precisely because the possibility of repeating mistakes is arguably more tolerable than the alternative, which is the ignorance bred by isolation of the gospel from secular thought; 4) *practical* in orientation, seeing knowledge of God as affecting both oneself and society; and 5) *evangelical*, insofar as every *verbi divini minister* is solely characterized by the all-encompassing word of the gospel—cf. "Tradition in the Modern World: The Reformed Habit of Mind," *Toward the Future of Reformed Theology: Tasks, Topics, Traditions*, eds. D. Willis, M. Welker, M. Gockel (Grand Rapids: Eerdmans, 1999), pp. 12ff. Eberhard Busch has argued somewhat differently that, while the purpose among the Reformed "is not to *have* a confession, but to *confess* in the challenges of daily life," nonetheless there are certain deep-lying decisions which characterize biblical reasoning in the Reformed tradition—cf. "Reformed Strength in its Denominational Weakness," *Reformed Theology: Identity and Ecumenicity*, eds. W.M. Alston, M. Welker (Grand Rapids: Eerdmans, 2003), p. 27. He proposes three such interlocking features: "an unwillingness to reduce divine truth to only *one* concept" (p. 30); an understanding of law as a gift of God, both that we might rely on his grace and justice and "in order to guard us against the danger of conforming ourselves to the rules of a world estranged from God" (p. 31);

with primarily *modern* figures and ideas, and thus gives disproportionately little attention to certain other monumental, premodern theologies. While these latter works would undoubtedly have enriched this project, our focus is nevertheless appropriate, for only with Schleiermacher, Ritschl, and their contemporary heirs is the longstanding Christian affirmation of wrath's place within the doctrine of God met with such thoroughgoing skepticism and fiery hostility. In light of these limitations, this project could have been undertaken in a very different manner. The constructive contribution of part one lies in the proposal that wrath, as one instance of the variety proper to the life of God, may be efficiently and effectively located among the perfections of God as a *redemptive mode* of divine perfection and, more specifically, as a redemptive mode of his righteousness.

Part two, a close exposition of a few representative passages of scripture, is a necessary complement to part one. The relationship between wrath and righteousness is developed in three interrelated studies, each one turned toward a different aspect or orientation proper to this movement of God's life. Scripture, we will argue, points to wrath as proper to God's character, not in the same manner as the righteousness that overflows from eternity in the triune life of God, but nonetheless as the righteous God who is present in opposition to all human opposition. Myriad scripture passages intersect this question, and we will not attempt a summary of every one. As already noted, this has been admirably executed elsewhere. Ours is rather an experiment in the limited task of taking a few key passages of scripture as far as possible—sticking with them, pursuing them. Broadly speaking, such theological exposition moves upwards only slowly and where necessary from its roots in the biblical material. It will be made clear that this approach is adopted not despite the stated understanding of the task of the doctrine of the divine perfections but rather in obedience to its basic character as a repetition of the self-revelation of the triune God.

In tying the two parts of our argument together, we can anticipate one significant criticism, namely that the overall structure sets an abstract concept, i.e. the notion of *a mode of divine perfection*, determinatively over the scriptural exposition. The decision to lead with a development of the task of the doctrine of the divine perfections, however, is simply one of economy. It is a way of analyzing and critiquing in theological perspective *only once* that which will be continually necessary in examination of a number of passages of scripture. In point of fact, the research of part two was present in complete—if rough—draft prior to part one. Our core proposal, therefore, is that an appeal to wrath as a mode of divine perfection

---

and, finally, consideration of the church as the community of individuals called together by Christ, bound to him, and so bound to one another, precisely that we might use our gifts for common benefit (pp. 32–33).

functions as a contracted *description* of the reality of God's life. As with all such theological concepts, this one facilitates clarity of thought and speech without replacing the larger body of personal report, narrative, and imagery to which it renders its service. Whether the resulting, much abbreviated description is both malleable enough to preserve what needs preserving in the biblical witness and robust enough to avoid certain other precarious or unsatisfying accounts of how wrath may be placed among the divine perfections, may be determined only in light of the whole argument.

Part One

In our introductory chapter, we offered a representative summary of theological approaches to the wrath of God, concluding that further clarification of this fundamental and perplexing biblical theme is particularly promising where wrath is taken up within the doctrine of God itself. The purpose of this study, therefore, is to propose with systematic specificity one option for locating wrath among the perfections of the divine life.

As a whole, part one offers a detailed analysis of the task of the doctrine of the divine perfections. In Chapter 2, specifically, we will argue that a doctrine of the divine perfections is serviceable precisely to the extent that it allows its unique subject matter, the triune God, to provide for its development its purpose, limit, and criteria. In chapter 3, we will argue that just as God's dramatic self-revelation warrants a variety of identity descriptions, so also this event suggests in its unfolding a most fitting arrangement for the doctrine of the divine perfections. Part one will conclude with the proposal of a critical distinction between providential and redemptive modes of divine perfection as one cogent way of relating wrath to the perfection of God. In each case, we are concerned with the same subject matter, i.e. the dramatic self-manifestation of the triune God, and in each case the aim remains the same: a cogent proposal for the place of God's wrath in the self-critical confession of the church.

Chapters 2 and 3 are therefore intended to be read together. Our argument is that this preliminary study furnishes an environment of theological views and concepts particularly adequate to an examination of the place of wrath among the perfections of God's life. It is therefore an extended analysis of those issues raised in a critical reading of the scriptural material, which pertains to the matter of God's wrath. Attending to these issues up front, rather than in the course of the theological exposition of scripture which constitutes part two, is prudent if not necessary.

This organization bears at least two distinct benefits. First, it sets the whole work clearly within the intellectual environment of the doctrine of the divine perfections. Second, it is economical. While not the only manner in which the doctrine could be or has been conceived (we are arguing for a particular understanding in terms of its systematic advantages), this arrangement will simplify what might otherwise be, for the author, an impossibly repetitive task and so too, for the reader, a tiresome ordeal. In any case, the intention is not to separate the doctrine of God from theological exposition of scripture. What has been distinguished here has been distinguished for heuristic purposes. A unified reading of the argument, it is hoped, will bear this out.

2

THE SUBJECT MATTER OF THE DOCTRINE OF THE DIVINE PERFECTIONS: CONTENT IMPRESSING FORM

Because this study of wrath's place among the divine perfections is fundamentally shaped by a particular conception of the manner in which God reveals himself, we need not devise a conceptual framework or critical criteria for making sense of the material witness. Rather we are given both, or so we will argue, in and with the content of God's self-manifestation. Karl Barth saw this in his characteristically lucid way and followed through on it by bringing all "scientific" talk of God's identity—scientific insofar as it reasons in a manner appropriate to its particular object—under a majestic description of the God who loves in freedom. Within this dialectical scheme, knowledge of the divine life is given as a gift of grace, rich and multivalent, bottomless in its depth, and continually folding over on itself such that apparent disunity and impossible multiplicity are anchored finally in the resplendent glory of the triune being of the one God, Father, Son, and Holy Spirit. It is this development of divine love and freedom, which, perhaps understandably, often receives the bulk of attention when commentators turn to Barth's doctrine of the divine perfections. Rather than pass over too quickly into an exposition of the inseparable love and freedom in which God has his perfection, however, we will reach further back in hopes of clarifying more precisely the subject matter of the doctrine as a whole.

There are various ways of approaching the divine perfections. Laid alongside each other, they display in some respects remarkable agreement and in others considerable difference. Our task, however, though a delicate and provisional one, is by no means an arbitrary choice between available alternatives. We will not only pursue detailed development of the doctrine as it is employed here but will argue for its relative strengths. What follows is therefore an exercise in both clarification and justification. A central focus of the present chapter will be to argue that the divine perfections, as properties of God's singular being, are cogently developed as one pays specific attention to the subject to whom they belong, the living God. For this reason, the subject himself—above and prior to creation, just as God *is* for creatures and among them, in personal address and even in confrontation, in self-differentiation and simplicity, as well as in the asymmetrical correspondence of the divine processions and missions—the identity of this One, will be treated in every respect the primary subject matter of the doctrine. Theology, which speaks of *divine* perfections, we will argue, is bound to speak of precisely *this* God and to speak of him in the concrete manner in which God gives himself to be known.

To explore the sources and implications of this fundamental orientation, we will carefully unfold three themes that emerge as one attends to the scriptural witness. Taken together, they specify that the subject matter of the doctrine of the divine perfections is (1) the living God, (2) self-named as Father, Son, and Holy Spirit, (3) and made manifest, out of the eternal resources of his life, in the drama of creation and redemption. Because it is impossible in this limited space to draw out every dimension of such "thick" theological themes, our objective will be to propose those which are most important for our study and to analyze them together in their interconnectedness. Though in reality, these three themes belong inextricably together, we will consider them in order and, where appropriate, assess the key systematic decisions to which they give rise and direction.

I. The Living God

If from one particular perspective, the task of the doctrine appears to be the general task of synthesizing and predicating qualities to a subject, we should begin by arguing for the subject matter of the doctrine as it is here understood. Specifically, the perfections of God are neither conceptual developments of the character of a certain substratum—i.e. the specification of one essence in relation to others, an essence which must be individuated in order to bear an independent, identifiable existence—nor are they explorations of qualities divisible from the one who bears them. A theology of the divine perfections is, in this first instance, a scripture-authorized specification of the livingness in which God presents himself to human beings and has himself prior to and above the decision to be God in and for creation.

A positive dogmatic statement on "the life of God" encompasses two movements.[1] Primarily and properly, God's life is the eternal movement of

---

[1] John Webster has argued for the fundamental place of this twofold movement within theological science, most recently under the rubric of "God, and all things in God"—cf. "Principles of Systematic Theology," *International Journal of Systematic Theology*

the perfection which God has from and for himself as Father, Son, and Holy Spirit. Above and prior to the act of creation and redemption, God lives from eternity to eternity in the enactment of his inestimable plentitude and so in the sundry perfections of his freedom and love. Secondarily and derivatively, God is alive in a movement of grace toward creatures. Outgoing and unhindered, God not only sets creaturely life in its place of moral responsibility and possibility but, most marvelously, wills to be incarnate as Jesus Christ to work for the salvation of those set decisively against his truth, beauty, and goodness. In this movement *ad extra*, no less than in his movement *ad intra*, God's life is revealed in irreducible complexity and unswerving direction. If there is a correspondence between the two—and we will argue that this is certainly the case—it is the irreversible order in which God fulfills fellowship with creatures, neither despite the splendor of his perfection nor through its abrogation, but precisely in light of his livingness, his majestic presence, and his eternity. It is to an expansion of this claim that we now turn.

God's Livingness Above and Prior to Creation

God is identified in scripture neither as the world's nameless ground of interconnectedness, nor as a fundamental principle of unrestricted choice, whether characterized as the basis of all human possibility or, alternatively, as the basic threat to human existence. Divine perfections, rather, are at each and every moment and in the most proper sense descriptions of *the living God*. For the canon of Old and New Testament scriptures, it is the living and active God who lies at the heart of its narrated history—a point we will be exploring in detail below. While the work of creation and redemption forms its material core, it is not on the basis of God's *opera ad extra* that God is known in his livingness. God is extolled as the living God because, first and foremost, he is the one who ἔχει ζωὴν ἐν ἑαυτῷ (Jn 5.26). In this, the singularity of God rests: ὁ μόνος ἔχων ἀθανασίαν (1 Tim 6.16). The logic thus moves irreversibly from this proper basis to God's subsequent self-revelation as ὁ ἀρχηγός τῆς ζωῆς (Acts 3.15) or to God's derivative act of creation by breathing נִשְׁמַת חַיִּים into the dust of the earth (Gen 2.7; cf. Jn 20.22). The work of God's hands testifies to the livingness in which he has his being full and complete from himself. The living God is indeed for and among human beings—this is the end which he has chosen for himself. As we will argue, God is such even in his wrath. The very testimony through which God is known *in his life*, however, prevents confession from simply

---

11 n. 1 (2009): p. 56. See also his "Life in and of Himself: Reflections on God's Aseity," *Engaging the Doctrine of God: Contemporary Protestant Perspectives*, ed. B.L. McCormack (Grand Rapids: Baker Academic, 2008), pp. 107–124, and "God's Perfect Life," *God's Life in Trinity*, ed. M. Volf, M. Welker (Minneapolis: Augsburg Fortress, 2006), pp. 143–152.

and hastily collapsing God into his livingness for and among creatures, which is to say, into a consideration of the significance of the divine perfections for the created order.[2]

A detailed example of this tendency is instructive. Affirmation of the eternal priority of God's life has been criticized (wrongly, we argue) as an inherently speculative enterprise. The concern is that such logic invariably isolates the being and activity of God from any meaningful relationship to creation. One alternative, it is argued, is to justify all *theologia* by resolving, if not virtually exhausting, discussion of the divine perfections in their significance for human life. Perfections of God are thus developed as answers to the riddles of human injustice, anxiety, or estrangement. One significant example is Catherine M. LaCugna's influential monograph, *God For Us*. The treatment which the divine perfections are accorded, though brief, thoroughly illustrates the core convictions and conceptual developments at work in the argument as a whole. It also brings to light the attendant ambiguities which, as we will show, neither adequately account for certain aspects of the scriptural witness nor adequately achieve LaCugna's central concern, namely to establish "a theology of God inherently related to every facet of Christian life."[3]

---

[2] In regard to this theme, compare the attentiveness of Isaak Dorner, *A System of Christian Doctrine*, eds. A. Cave and J.S. Banks (Edinburgh: T&T Clark, 1880). God, as absolute Essence, is distinguishable from the cosmos "as the self-related Causality[,] . . . both originator and originated" (I, p. 248). "He is a sea of self-revolving life; an infinite fullness of forces moves, so to speak, and undulates therein" (I, p. 259). In particular, there is highlighted the "especially picturesque" imagery of the first chapter of Ezekiel—'living beings and forcibly revolving and flashing wheels'—which nonetheless represents "the mere forecourt of the divine sphere," and so even in its power must be contrasted with that absolute Life which is "exalted above passivity or diminution and transitoriness, as well as above increase" (I, pp. 259f.). In God alone is found "a fullness, an absolute πλήρωμα of divine energies" (I, pp. 263f.).

[3] Catherine Mowry LaCugna, *God for Us: The Trinity and Christian Life* (San Francisco: Harper SanFrancisco, 1991), p. 250. Subsequent references will appear parenthetically in the text of this subsection. For similar examples of an overemphasis upon God's life in and for the economy, see Jürgen Moltmann, *The Trinity and the Kingdom of God*, trans. M. Kohl (London: SCM Press, 1981): "God is from eternity to eternity 'the crucified God'" (p. 159); "The economic Trinity not only reveals the immanent Trinity; it also has a retroactive effect on it" (p. 160); "The pain of the cross determines the inner life of the triune God from eternity to eternity" (p. 161). See also Robert W. Jenson, *Systematic Theology*, 2 vols. (Oxford: Oxford University Press, 1997): "The biblical God is not eternally himself in that he persistently instantiates a beginning in which he already is all he ever will be; he is eternally himself in that he unrestrictedly anticipates an end in which he will be all he ever could be. It holds also—or, rather, primally—with God: a story is constituted by the outcome of the narrated events" (I, p. 66); "God is what happens between Jesus and his Father in their Spirit . . . God is what happens to Jesus and the world . . . [H]ow God would have described his own being had he been without the world, we cannot even inquire" (I, p. 221). In the case of each theologian, as also with LaCugna, the axiom "the 'economic' Trinity is the 'immanent' Trinity and

Treatment of the divine perfections in *God For Us* is, to begin with, thoroughly informed by an ontology, which "focuses on personhood, relationship, and communion as the modality of *all* existence" (p. 250) or, more tellingly, one able to "support a vision of authentic human community . . . characterized by equality, mutuality, and reciprocity" (p. 266). God himself is therefore understood as existing in a peculiar divine fellowship, "a unity of . . . three centers of divine identity," wherein each person "is irresistibly drawn to the other, taking his/her existence from the other, containing the other in him/herself, while at the same time pouring self out into the other" (pp. 270–1).[4] Most significantly, however, it is argued that because the starting point is "the economy of redemption," *perichōrēsis* must be understood as rooted "not in God's inner life but in the mystery of the one communion of all persons, divine as well as human" (p. 274). This understanding of fellowship between Creator and creature—neither essentially asymmetrical nor irreversible—differs dramatically from that which we propose to follow and so deserves careful consideration. Tersely stated, God and humanity are, according to LaCugna, "eternal partners" locked in perichoretic dance (p. 304).

As each of the divine predicates is constructed, it becomes increasingly clear that LaCugna's proposal is not merely indifferent toward, but actually set in direct opposition to, the consideration of the living God as we have sketched it above. This must be the case, it is claimed, for where *theologia* appeals to the self-sufficiency of God and so to one who has his life *from himself*, theological reflection becomes irrevocably alienated from human life and faith. Each perfection is therefore refined in accordance with a concept of "personhood," which both fulfills and is itself constituted by the mutual fellowship between God and humanity. Most telling in this respect is LaCugna's contention that "the perfection of God is the perfection of love . . . the antithesis of self-sufficiency" (ibid.). Such an ontology, it is claimed, both underwrites a genuinely soteriological doctrine of God and prevents theology from devolving into the isolation of God from creatures. We can observe at this point the incidental likeness, which appears between LaCugna's proposal that "the living God is the God who is alive in relationship" (ibid.) and the position we are developing. The decisive difference is that the former notion of livingness is exhausted by God's fulfillment of and desire for communion with his creatures. As love, God is not sufficient to himself. God requires creatures to be—specifically—the God *of love*.

Both formally and materially, an assertion like this will determine the trajectory of one's doctrine of the divine attributes. Without a meaningful

---

the 'immanent' Trinity is the 'economic' Trinity" is identified as a key inspiration and source. For this *Grundaxiom* in its original context and interpretation, cf. Karl Rahner, *The Trinity*, trans. J. Donceel (New York: Herder & Herder, 1970), p. 21.

[4] A primary influence here is Patricia Wilson-Kastner, *Faith, Feminism and the Christ* (Philadelphia: Fortress, 1983).

way of speaking of God prior to or above creation, and more precisely because "LaCugna is not thinking of God on the basis of revelation but of God incorporated into her relational ontology that views the Trinity as a description of persons (divine and human) in communion,"[5] there is ostensibly never a moment when the world was *not* necessary to God's very being. At the very least, where one conceives Creator and creature in a relationship like this, without an accompanying framework for supporting meaningful assertions about the life which God has from himself, the burden remains on that one to demonstrate how God and creation are not finally either competitors on the same plane of existence or beings utterly co-extensive in nature. To avoid this, one must proffer a more robust argument than an occasional, logically unintegrated and thus immaterial claim that the *oikonomia* is "the concrete realization of the mystery of *theologia* in time, space, history and personality" (pp. 222–223).[6] Statements like this signal a concern to express some difference between God and world. In the absence of a specific account of divine aseity, however, this kind of formulation will consistently terminate in the ambiguous claim to speak of God's life without any criteria for distinguishing it from the dynamism of existence-in-general or the world-process.

By contrast, a consideration of the perfections of God as distinctly divine perfections, is cogent where one attends to and more fully integrates into theological reflection the manner in which the triune God ἔχει ζωὴν ἐν ἑαυτῷ. This is not all that a rightly ordered affirmation of God's self-sufficiency involves or implies, of course. Throughout this chapter, we will find it necessary and informative to return to this theme under new aspects

---

[5] Paul D. Molnar, *Divine Freedom and the Doctrine of the Immanent Trinity: In Dialogue with Karl Barth and Contemporary Theology* (London: T&T Clark, 2002), p. 135.

[6] Cf. also LaCugna, *God For Us*, p. 228. Something of God beyond God's relationship to the world is held in reserve, and is apparent in certain assurances that 'God alone' is the exemplar and fulfillment of the divine perfections: "God alone exists in every moment in perfect communion. . . . God alone is incorruptible love. . . . God alone can thoroughly empty Godself (*kenōsis*) without ceasing to be God. . . . God alone is infinitely related to every last creature. . . . God alone can *begin* to love without any reason" (pp. 301–305). Indicative of the uniqueness of divine action, it is unclear how such language does not in fact suggest an asymmetry between Creator and creature and, specifically, the lordly freedom proper to God's nature. In our judgment, this intention to preserve the so-called 'mystery' of God's life conflicts with the author's skeptical posture regarding theological language. While God's inmost essence is manifest in the *character* of his relation to the world, she writes, without the requisite transeconomic perspective "there is no reason whatsoever to maintain that the *structure* of that external relationship which we perceive in our experience somehow mirrors a similar but more primordial threefold structure in the innermost recesses of the divine being" (pp. 226, 227). See Gordon Kaufman, *Systematic Theology: A Historicist Perspective* (New York: Scribners, 1968), p. 102 n 9.

and from different concerns, not the least relevant of which asks whether redemption itself is conceivable where the God immanent to creation is not, in fact, immanent precisely as the transcendent One. That issue will be taken up in the second section of this chapter. Asking after this relationship here at the outset, however, gives sharp focus to the task of the doctrine in a way which other responses to LaCugna's theology have not. An adequate response, for example, requires something more than Ellen T. Charry's recent suggestion that theologians return to a "contemplative" or "reflective" model of soteriology. It may be that in the desire "to benefit from God's beauty and to satisfy our moral cravings," the perfections of God are indeed given appropriate and renewed emphasis.[7] However, the diagnosis that "the new trinitarianism [LaCugna being included among its chief exponents] tends to lose sight of the soteriological value of the divine perfections" does not penetrate to the root cause.[8] Many within this theological movement, in fact, intend to argue the very same point, namely that the doctrine of God should be determinative of the Christian life and faith. What is reduplicated in Charry's response is a failure to root the divine perfections in a notion of the primacy or prevenient abundance of God's life.

God's Livingness for and among Creatures

A doctrine of the divine perfections will also make clear that this essential *asymmetry*, which is to say, a genuine relationship between Creator and creature determined at every point by the prevenience of God's life—as in the relationship between authority and obedience, gracious Giver and grateful recipient, light and light's reflection, primary and secondary, original and derivative—does not compromise the integrity of the created order or conceptualize a God estranged from creatures. Rather such a doctrine cultivates this unity in its most robust form. From the affirmation of God's self-sufficiency, in other words, one may subsequently and derivatively attend to the fact that, as the אֱלֹהִים חַיִּים (cf. esp. Deut 5.26; Dan 6.26), God lives neither in an inwardly turned repose nor as one morally indifferent toward the world. We have to do rather with the glory of the Lord, God alive in our midst, the One seeking freely and gratuitously to give life to creatures, and so sustain them in their own, particular being as not-God. In this relationship, the triune One is alive such that "at his wrath the earth quakes, and the

---

[7] Ellen T. Charry, "The Soteriological Importance of the Divine Perfections," *God the Holy Trinity: Reflections on Christian Faith and Practice*, ed. T. George (Grand Rapids: Baker Academic, 2006), p. 132.

[8] Ibid., p. 136. It would be more fruitful, in this respect, to develop the specific claim that "the divine being, including the attributes, depends upon and derives its meaning from the actions and/or relations of the divine self-realizations that should be seen to constitute God as such" (pp. 133–34).

nations cannot endure his indignation" (Jer 10.10).[9] Falling into the hands of the living God, therefore, means terror for those who spurn his Son (Heb 10.31), and yet, above and prior to such warnings, there is given the promise that God has elected to be for his people the מְקוֹר מַיִם חַיִּים who quenches thirsty souls (Jer 2.13; Jn 4.14; Ps 42.2; 36.9). The point to hold always in focus is that the announcement that God is σωτὴρ πάντων ἀνθρώπων (1 Tim 4.10) and the giver of life (Ps 119.154; cf. Rom 2.7) directs theological attention not merely to great acts, to the qualities they instantiate, or to their negative or positive effects upon human life—e.g., adoption as υἱοὶ θεοῦ ζῶντος (Rom 9.26; Hos 1.10). In these acts, rather, one's gaze is drawn hopefully toward the subject himself, *the living God*.

Giving conceptual space to this insight is one way in which a theology of the divine perfections works in obedience to the asymmetrical unity in which God both *is* and actively *announces* himself. An exposition of the perfections of the One who creates, reconciles, and redeems is more nearly adequate to the depth of testimony in the Christian scriptures insofar as it seeks to describe this singular Subject in this twofold movement. What is claimed in this doctrine about the being of God is not that he is one thing in himself and another toward creatures but that, in the perfections made manifest here and now, and in a mode appropriate to finite creatures, it is God himself whom human beings are given to know. To begin otherwise from an immanent-economic distinction, by contrast, even where this is intended in a heuristic rather than material sense, will run the risk of making the unity of God's life a conceptual problem from the outset. The potency, surety, and concrete form of God's redemptive work and the perfections manifested therein are clarified not where God and world are made coterminous or mutually dependent but where God is recognized as alive in his self-sufficiency.

The Pliability and Purpose of "Substance" Language

Two clarifications of this claim regarding the living God are essential. First, the livingness which God has uniquely *a se* is not intended here, in formal terms, as a categorical rejection of the language of substance (οὐσία). Certain construals of this latter concept, of course, may adversely affect theological reasoning. They may confine discourse upon the being of God, and so upon all being, within the bounds of a static, nonrelational or hierarchical view of reality.[10] Presuppositions like these create innumerable

---

[9] Unless otherwise indicated, scripture quotations are taken from the *New Revised Standard Version*.

[10] Compare John Macquarrie, *Principles of Systematic Theology* (London: SCM Press, 1977), for whom the image of "a rock persisting through time" best captures the primarily "static idea" of substance (pp. 74–75, 109). Alfred North Whitehead identified the "reversal of the Aristotelian dominance of the category of 'quality' over that of

difficulties for the task of articulating, for example, how divine perfection—God in his very being—includes either the irreducible fellowship of Father, Son, and Holy Spirit or God's presence to and action in creation.

Most radical, however, is the charge that every such treatment constitutes "metaphysical essentialism," the error of which lies in claiming to know "precisely *what* God would be had he not determined himself to be God-for-us in Jesus Christ . . . [and] to know *how* his being would have been constituted in the absence of his relation to us."[11] This fundamental error is made possible, it is argued, whenever one treats "the whatness of a thing as something complete in itself without regard for its actual existence."[12] In and of itself, this is a valid and important concern. Without further specificat-ion, reflection on the possibility that God might not have created could tend toward abstraction. This criticism, however, invites more careful consideration.

Let us consider the premises upon which this specific, multifaceted criti-cism rests. There are at least three of them, and all are made explicit. The use of substance language, it is argued (1) commits one to a static, nonrelational model of reality, (2) compels speculation on alternative states of affairs or "other worlds," and (3) is formally and materially indifferent toward narra-tives of drama or existence. Each of these premises is put forward as a necessary implication of speaking about God as God is apart from the act of electing to be creator and redeemer. Furthermore, all are cast not simply as criticisms of *a* concept of substance but rather as criticisms of *the* concept of substance, as if it were a thin, easily grasped and uniformly applied notion. By contrast, William P. Alston has recently argued that none of the qualities typically attributed to substance language—qualities such as "immutability, timelessness, lack of real relations to the world, impassibility, inertness, being static or rock-like"—follow necessarily from the category itself.[13] Much to the contrary, Alston contends that the function of substance

---

'relatedness'" as a central thesis of his 1927–28 Gifford Lectures, published as *Process and Reality: An Essay in Cosmology*, correct. ed., D.R. Griffin and D.W. Sherburne (London: The Free Press, 1978), p. xiii.

[11] Bruce L. McCormack, "The Actuality of God: Karl Barth in Conversation with Open Theism," *Engaging the Doctrine of God: Contemporary Protestant Perspectives*, ed. *idem* (Grand Rapids: Baker Academic, 2008), pp. 215–216. Compare the attempt to consider what is "inside God"—LaCugna, *God For Us*, p. 225.

[12] Ibid., p. 221.

[13] William P. Alston, "Substance and the Trinity," *The Trinity: An Interdisciplinary Symposium on the Trinity*, ed. S.T. Davis, D. Kendall and G. O'Collins (Oxford: Oxford University Press, 2001), p. 201. Similarly, Edward Farley suggests that in the history of philosophy 'substance' can signify "any specific thing that has properties, a term for what specific things share, a term for primary genres or types of things, and a formal term for being"—*Divine Empathy: A Theology of God* (Minneapolis: Fortress Press, 1996), p. 166.

language in ancient philosophy, and principally in the Aristotelian tradition, was to offer descriptive tools for analysis of finite, created substances, and particularly the substance of living organisms.

The concept of substance, it would appear, is a deceptively pliable one. Its sense and purpose require careful evaluation in each new context. If such terms do in fact commend themselves to a pursuit of the subject matter of theology, the key issue is how they will be made serviceable to the task. At every step, as Donald MacKinnon contends, "their employment must include the enlargement of their sense by reason of *the totally novel use to which they are bent*."[14] The notion of substance—as with all theological descriptions of God's life—gains entrance into theological discourse not on the basis of the denotation it has acquired through general or habitual use but rather as it acquires a veracity and serviceability on the basis of its obedient attention to God's self-revelation. This is a claim of great consequence and will be explored in detail very shortly. It needs to be anticipated here because it suggests, first, that deploying this concept need not relegate theological inquiry to its "backward" reference, to that which is immobile, unchanging, and unrelated. To say that *God is the One he is*, i.e. to make a substantialist claim to divine "thisness," does not necessarily exclude God's livingness but can be offered in interpretation and protection of the promise that in every respect "I will be who I will be" (Ex 3.14), "the same yesterday and today and forever" (Heb 13.8). In a matchlessly mobile manner, in other words, it calls attention to the all-encompassing presence of the transcendent God.

Second, and closely related, it suggests that a concept of substance facilitates a focusing of theological attention upon the *events* of God's self-revelation. If it is indeed key to Aristotle's ontology that "every substance is a subsisting energy—and act—and hence an actuality," then, as Stanley Grenz has argued, the substance of God makes claims about divine action and not "merely" about God's existence.[15] Such considerations suggest that one overreaches in claiming that through the mere use of substance language theological discourse is committed to the sphere of the static and the ahistorical. A more compelling argument recognizes the pliability of

---

[14] D.M. MacKinnon, "'Substance' in Christology: A Cross-Bench View," *Christ, Faith and History: Cambridge Studies in Christology*, eds. S.W. Sykes and J.P. Clayton (Cambridge: Cambridge University Press, 1972), p. 289. Far from being an essay in speculation, he writes, conceptual analysis set in terms of substance—and specifically in terms of the *homoousion*—is a part of analytical philosophy. Dogmatics takes up such notions as a result of being confronted by the person of Christ, and so "with questions that for their clear statement demand the use of just such notions as Aristotle explores in the *Metaphysics*" (pp. 288–289).

[15] Stanley J. Grenz, *The Named God and the Question of Being: A Trinitarian Theo-Ontology* (Louisville: Westminster John Knox Press, 2005), p. 30.

such language and, on that basis, seeks to identify the peculiar manner in which it is or might be employed.

Thus far we have explored three explicit features of this criticism. There is, however, an additional premise lying implicit within the argument. It is assumed that that which is revelatory about an event is the event itself, specifically as an economic happening and not as an actuality, which takes place *in and along with* the divine self-announcement. Were the latter valid, God's self-witness would be conceived as pointing beyond itself—and in fact we are arguing that it does just this—to the eternal reality in which God has his life *a se*. Testimony to God's livingness, we argue, declares not only that God lives now or that God is for his people a fountain of living water, but more radically that God is this precisely as God is livingness *in himself*. If this is a valid interpretation, then, as Thomas Tracy has contended, God is known in the enactment of his life "not simply because His work is there, but because He is active in His work".[16] One strength of this assertion is that it rightly protects against a de-historicizing of the doctrine of God. At the same time, it leaves open the possibility of construing God's self-revelation as a silent, uninterpreted, event.[17] It is equally necessary, then, to clarify the indispensability of attention to the event of God's livingness as the concrete self-declaration of *God* in which God reveals himself as alive above and prior to his creatures. The deployment of a concept of substance therefore sharpens theological description of who God is precisely in his relationship to creation, and so contributes irreplaceably to a critical account of the divine perfections. Its principal function, as Christopher Stead has superbly argued,

> is to claim that God is not limited or prescribed by our experience of him, but exists in his own right . . . To characterize God as a substance

---

[16] Thomas F. Tracy, *God, Action, and Embodiment* (Grand Rapids: Eerdmans, 1984), p. 23.

[17] This is how I interpret Paul Molnar's thetical statement: "while the doctrine of the Trinity begins with an experience of God in the economy, it nonetheless directs us away from our experiences and toward God's Word and Spirit as the source of theological knowledge"—*Divine Freedom and the Doctrine of the Immanent Trinity: In Dialogue with Karl Barth and Contemporary Theology* (London: T&T Clark, 2002), p. 311. For MacKinnon, cf. "Substance in Christology: A Cross-Bench View," a notion of 'substance' rightly employed closes off the possibility of regarding individuals "as 'logical constructions' out of events" without thereby devaluing personal histories (pp. 284–285). Compare, finally, George Hunsinger's suggestion that, particularly with respect to Barth interpretation, "a great deal can depend . . . on whether emphasis is placed on the *history* as personal address or on the history as *personal address*"—*How to Read Karl Barth: The Shape of his Theology* (New York: Oxford University Press, 1991), p. 285 n. 3. While the two are presumably indivisible, he argues that the former recognizes the logical priority of objectivism over personalism in Barth's theology, and the latter is exemplified in Eberhard Jüngel's theology of 'Word-event'.

is to stake a claim against reductionist theories which in effect represent God as dependent on the human experience which he is invoked to explain.[18]

It was to better understand the implications of one such reductionistic theory that we examined LaCugna's proposal of a relational ontology.

It was to avoid this reductionism, furthermore, that we argued God *can be* toward us because he *is* the one he is in the fullness of eternity. To be the holy One, Father Son, and Spirit, God does not require a people in whom covenant fellowship will be realized. To be the righteous One, and so to be worthy of praise, God does not need to create the voices of his creatures. God is the God of love not as human beings are given to know him, and to love him, and so to be loved by him. God is and does all these things, of course, but not in an act *constitutive* of his perfection. From eternity he has his holiness, righteousness, and love—and the manifold abundance of his perfection—from himself. This is the livingness of God and hopefully clear at this point is the sharpness of the demands which it places upon a theological account of divine wrath. The question can be dismissed if, on the one hand, this description and all such language about God is conceived of as referring merely to a particular human experience or if, on the other, God's life is reduced formally to an undifferentiated and so unidentifiable substrate. If one or both of these conclusions, however, are deemed unfitting, such that wrath too must be premised as belonging to the very life of God, the question becomes whether, in fact, God is alive from eternity in his wrath.

Dynamism, the World Process, and Intentional Divine Action

A second clarification follows. Just as the livingness of God cannot be neatly transposed into a formal rejection of all substance language, neither is it commensurate with an abstract commitment to "dynamism" in theology. We attended briefly to this point in relation to the world-process. We argued that it is a tendency of certain constructive proposals, like LaCugna's *God For Us*, to obscure the distinction between God and world by precluding formal reference to the divine aseity. The most immediate consequence for our thesis is that, in this account, the systematic exposition of divine wrath drifts away from its proper emphasis on the subject who bears it. Its limit becomes, instead, an analysis of particular human experience(s) or the observation of patterns of movement or consequence inherent to the system of nature. Even if subsequently attributed to God—protesting that, even so, one intends by this to speak meaningfully about God!—the question of a

[18] Christopher Stead, *Divine Substance* (Oxford: Clarendon Press, 1977), p. 273; cf. p. 268.

formal justification for the assertion remains. To begin alternatively from the self-witness of the living God, however, suggests that divine perfection is intelligible only in its uniqueness.

It is one of the revolutionary features of Barth's doctrine that he hit so elegantly, and yet so relentlessly, upon this point. The self-revelation of God "is a definite happening within general happening," he writes, but one

> so definite that, while it takes part in this happening, it also contradicts it, and can only be seen and comprehended together with it in its contradiction, without the possibility of a synthesis, apart from the synthesis proclaimed and already fulfilled in itself.[19]

From this perspective, the attempt to convey God's uniqueness by means of a notion of *actus purus* is no less accountable to the demand that the term acquire its veracity and serviceability solely on the basis of obedient attention to God's self-revelation. The particular life of God resists analysis within the category of general happening, transcending even the sum total of worldly movement, the event from which all other action is conceived as receiving its origin and telos. The term may be made serviceable, however, under the further specification that God's life is such in its singularity. God's life is *actus purus et singularis*, suggests Barth, and so "an act which utterly surpasses the whole of the actuality that we have come to know as act."[20] Were this qualification not observed, were one instead to continue under the opinion that God's life is "only a higher degree of the movement which we know well enough as our own," it is his claim that one would be confronted by the dispensability of any particular idea of God as well as doubt as to whether the so-called divine life, now indistinguishable from nature or human action, could execute redemption.[21] The livingness of God resists reduction to a general concept of dynamism because it is in all respects the activity of a very particular agent.

Therefore, one further way of specifying this particularity is to observe that the movement itself consists of action *undertaken* rather than undergone. It displays peculiar qualities "with credible frequency" and with a "minimum degree of continuity" such that the pattern of its enactment becomes, in the judgment of Thomas Tracy, evidence of the constancy or, perhaps better, the trustworthiness of the one who is at work.[22] The specific events of this drama, in other words, are more cogently organized around a notion of personal agency than around a notion of general happening.

---

[19] Karl Barth, *Church Dogmatics* II/1, ed. G.W. Bromiley, T.F. Torrance (Edinburgh: T&T Clark, 1957), p. 264.

[20] Ibid., p. 263.

[21] Ibid., pp. 270–271.

[22] Tracy, *God, Action, and Embodiment*, pp. 8, 131.

Following after the livingness of God therefore might be conceived as the pursuit of character trait predicates which, for the theologian,

> constitute a vocabulary of great flexibility and richness that is keyed to the identification of significant intentional action. What we ordinarily refer to as character appears in the complexly interwoven patterns of a person's purposive activity.[23]

Claims about God's character are valid on the basis of the actions presented in evidence, or what Christoph Schwöbel has called "a comprehensive policy of action."[24] As descriptive of divine action, this notion would imply neither that God engages in linear, discursive reasoning, nor that God exists in a state of unfulfilled expectation or need.

Claims to intentional action are, *mutatis mutandis*, as appropriate to God's eternal life and his electing grace as they are to human agency. One recalls here not primarily those divine promises in which there are announced the distinct plans which the Lord has for his people's welfare, for their hopeful future (Jer 29.11). This is plainly one aspect of the matter. Where one limits matters of God's intention to a consideration of that which will come to pass, however, the *future* is logically made the center of God's life in a manner as equally inadequate as the way in which misuse of substance language might isolate God in his eternal, nonrelational, and static *past*. Divine intentional action is rather invoked to specify that, as God undertakes his work, God himself is disclosed in his eternal character.[25] Its soteriological significance is the assurance that, once again, "I will be who I will be" (Ex 3.14), and "the same yesterday and today and forever" (Heb 13.8). Speaking of God's life as in every respect "unrestrictedly intentional action" requires appropriating the concept of intentionality and altering

---

[23] Ibid., p. 19.

[24] As distinguished "from mere behaviour that follows a mechanism of stimulus and response"—cf. Christoph Schwöbel, *God: Action and Revelation* (Kampen: Kok Pharos, 1992), pp. 51–52. While this applies strictly to moral attributes, he suggests apparent contradiction between the so-called metaphysical and moral attributes may be resolved by relating them through mutual qualification, and so in their complementarity—the former as those which make "the existence and intelligibility of the world plausible in the framework of a conception of God," and the latter as they are "based on the model of divine action understood in terms of personal agency" (p. 61).

[25] Tracy argues for "a necessary logical relation between a crucial set of predicates used in characterizing persons and 'stories' that treat human behavior as *intentional action*"—cf. *God, Action, and Embodiment*, p. 4. This principle is itself grounded in the observation that "we generally seek to understand the unfamiliar in terms of the familiar" (p. 108). By contrast, the present study employs the former insight as it thinks *from* the event of God's self-revelation.

it—radicalizing it!—in order to render it serviceable for theological reflection on the divine perfections.

As a whole, the argument up to this point is shaped by the same concern, namely that the livingness of God himself cannot disappear behind rigorous consideration of the divine perfections. We have argued that a doctrine of the divine perfections, and so an exposition of God's wrath, will properly begin from a particular understanding of God *in his livingness*. Its impetus is neither an abstract rejection of substance language, nor, inversely, does the doctrine aim at conceptualizing all reality under a general theory of the forward advancement of the world process, whether in its various characterizations as indeterminacy and chaos, on the one hand, or as regularity, conservation or law, on the other. By contrast, a pattern of judgment is found in scripture through which the livingness of God is made known in ever richer and more variegated modes of perfection. In this exclusive sense, properly in himself and derivatively toward creation, *vita maxime proprie in Deo est.*

II. *The Self-Named God: Father, Son, and Holy Spirit*

Along the same path, we are urged toward a second, equally concrete indication of our subject matter. We tread once again that territory we have already surveyed, this time paying attention specifically to the manner in which descriptions of God's identity are given inextricably in and with the revelation of the divine name. In God's self-revelation, we will argue, there is no noetic gap between God's presence to us and his identity, between our knowing *that* he is and our knowing *how* and *who* he is. The task of the doctrine of the divine perfections is a self-critical refinement of elaborate and variegated confessions of the living God as Father, Son, and Holy Spirit. God may reveal himself and may be known to his people—he invites and permits their address—precisely because he knows himself as the triune Lord. The call to glorify the triune name therefore encompasses both the truth of Christian confession as well as the shape of the Christian life.

God as "Thou": Theology Spoken in the Second Person

The existence and essence of God may be related to one another in a number of plausible ways. Assertion of God's existence, for example, might be rooted in the acknowledgement of a universally intuitable notion in order to explain a progress of human knowledge or to provide a foundation for Christian knowledge distinguishable from God himself in his act of self-revelation. Wolfhart Pannenberg argues, in anticipation of his own exposition of the name of God, that God is present to all human life as "the undefined infinite which is formed by the primal intuition of our awareness of reality, as the horizon within which we comprehend all else by limitation."[26] Open from its origins to this field of the infinite, the human mind is aware of God not as the triune Lord but as "a something" nonthematically present or "merely existing" in the world, yet "a something," which simultaneously transcends the world in its totality. It is therefore subsequent knowledge of the essence of this Infinite, which concretizes primitive awareness. Or as Pannenberg himself concludes, it is "only in terms of the sum total of its manifestations and existence" that this "something" may be fully identified as God.[27] One positive feature of this arrangement—assuming the universality of the experience—is that the need to begin a doctrine of God with proofs for God's existence disappears behind the primary concern to account for *how* the "undefined something" might finally be identified as God.

In exchange, however, there is admitted into theological discourse the possibility of dividing assertions of God's existence from those of God's identity. It is not merely that the argument moves toward ever greater specificity, such that one is only finally able to confess the triune name. Rather, this specific theological argument is most conspicuous as an instance of reasoning about God, which begins from a distinctly subpersonal[28] concept of "the Infinite," arranging descriptions of the divine life around a general notion of potency—such as Pannenberg's "field of power"—rather than around the self-communicating "Thou" who, we will argue, is witnessed to in scripture. In this account, revelation is not an objective disclosure in which God presents himself. The encounter is not with a mysterious "Thou," who speaks and acts with a particular authority to finite creatures. The relationship is not a moral one, shaped decisively as an individual is called, equipped, and sent out in obedient service. God as such is indeed to be sought in his manifestation in the world, but the initial intuition or experience receives its content most fundamentally from this concept of the Infinite. This primary notion shapes the logical space for articulating that

---

[26] Wolfhart Pannenberg, *Systematic Theology* I (Grand Rapids: Eerdmans, 1991), p. 356.

[27] Ibid., p. 358.

[28] See Karl Barth's historical analysis and his thesis that, in every respect, it is the revelation of divine action which "informs us what a person is"—*Church Dogmatics* II/1, p. 284; cf. pp. 268, 284–297. More specifically, the 'sub-personal' might be taken to denote absence of the "inseparable relatedness" definitive of all particular, free persons—cf. Colin E. Gunton, "Trinity, Ontology and Anthropology: Towards a Renewal of the Doctrine of the *Imago Dei*," *Persons, Divine and Human: King's College Essays in Theological Anthropology*, eds. C. Schwöbel and C.E. Gunton (Edinburgh: T&T Clark, 1991), p. 56; cf. p. 59. See also the excellent essay by Kevin Vanhoozer, "Human Being, Individual and Social," *The Cambridge Companion to Christian Doctrine*, ed. C.E. Gunton (Cambridge: Cambridge University Press, 2003), pp. 158–188.

"God is love" and fills the notion of "spirit" operative in Pannenberg's trinitarian theology.[29]

Alternatively, a doctrine of the divine perfections may attend to the fact that the event in which God makes himself present to creation is the singular source and occasion for both knowledge of his existence (that it is God the Three-in-One who encounters creatures) and knowledge of his essence (that he has from himself a life of abundant perfection, whether as holiness, righteousness, eternity, etc.).[30] In this manner, knowledge of God is at every point knowledge of God as he is revealed *in his name*. Of course, this procedure does not rule out the subjective possibility of ever-greater knowledge of God. It does suggest that knowledge grasped *per solam fidem* expands as one is drawn into the intensity of God's richness rather than into a breadth of qualitatively new acts or genuinely new dimensions of his character. A doctrine of the divine perfections reflects the ever-new *depth* of God's life as a means to fellowship with God and as a means to confessing the glory of Father, Son, and Holy Spirit. An argument for this fundamental theme, however, requires beginning further back.

Repeating and Adorning the Triune Name

Neither itself a divine perfection nor a description of God's working in the world, the triune name is rather the irreplaceable specification of God in his presence to creatures as Father, Son, and Holy Spirit. In the life of Jesus Christ, the eternal Son of the Father made incarnate, and in the power of the Holy Spirit, God reveals the reality in which he properly knows himself and, on that basis, derivatively gives himself to be known by creatures. The name is the concrete indication of the Lord's openness and accessibility toward himself and to creatures. But it is this in the irreducible sense that God—precisely as Father, Son, and Holy Spirit—possesses a unique perfection, a distinct manner of working, a love in freedom.

This name is therefore neither the product of creaturely imagination nor of social convention but the gift of God himself in his majestic presence. Just as God is dependent upon nothing else for his livingness, so this name is given to God by God alone. Theological reason therefore follows after this singularity, seeking to repeat what it hears, and so to know, worship, obey, and enjoy God as the triune One. As we will argue below, the doctrine of the perfections may not be reduced to an abstract analysis of the relationship

---

[29] See Pannenberg, *Systematic Theology* I, pp. 396ff.; also, C.E. Gutenson, *Reconsidering the Doctrine of God* (London: T&T Clark, 2005), pp. 80, 167.

[30] Thus Dorner's noteworthy rearrangement of the doctrine of God: " . . . the proof for the divine existence and the proof for the essential and constituent attributes are not two proofs, but are one and indivisible, and can only attain completeness side by side"—cf. *A System of Christian Doctrine* I, p. 190.

between God and humankind. It depends rather for its veracity upon reasoning which moves *from* "the narrative of the relationships among the Father, the Son and the Holy Spirit[,] . . . God naming God"[31] *toward* the reality of his presence to and among creatures.

The *locus classicus* for this claim is John 14–17, and an exposition can be effectively organized under the asymmetrical testimony to God's presence to himself and his presence to creatures. Properly, the Son alone may address God as Father, for he alone is the Father's beloved (15.9; 5:18–23; 1.14). This love neither begins in history, as in the interval between Jesus' birth and death, nor does it arise with God's free decision to create another outside God's own life to be the recipient of his riches, for the Son was in the beginning (1.1; cf. Heb 1.2–4). Still less is the Son's inheritance based upon merit or upon the outpouring of God's gratuitous compassion. The Father loves the Son πρὸ καταβολῆς κόσμου, which is to say that their relationship is grounded in eternity, above and prior to all the work of God's creating and redeeming (17.24; 17.5).

Derivatively, however, it is intimated that the Son is given all glory, power, knowledge, and love for a particular mission. Over this inheritance, the Son of God incarnate in Jesus Christ maintains a bold claim, unprecedented for its truth: Πάντα ὅσα ἔχει ὁ πατὴρ ἐμά ἐστιν (16.15). If God's people are to share in the riches of God's glory, it will be on the basis of the Son's unique access to the Father. He alone has knowledge of the Father (17.25; cf. 1 Cor 2.11). The Son is present to creation, speaking not as one who *hears* the voice of God—not, ostensibly, as the first among many to be illuminated— but as the one who himself *sees* God, having stood παρὰ τῷ πατρὶ (8.38), and speaks with his authority. It is from the presence of Glory, finally, and so glory enjoyed πρὸ τοῦ τὸν κόσμον εἶναι (17.5), that the Son is sent into creation without diminishing his own glory, without compromising his authority, without any danger that this most intimate presence in and to finite creation will detract from the perfection of his name. In this movement, his work is to make known and to glorify not his own name as such but, by the gift of his Spirit (15.26; 14.16, 26; cf. 5.25f.), to make known the name of the Father, which the Son is given from eternity. Precisely as this one, he protects, guards, and upholds the people of God (17.11, 12).

This is only a sketch, of course, a gesture toward the riches of scripture. Much more has been said and could be said in this vein. If this is right in what it asserts, however, then there is ample warrant to reserve a place in our doctrine of the divine perfections for the irreducible simplicity in which God as subject makes himself identifiable above and prior to his *opera ad extra*. The name of Father, Son, and Holy Spirit properly belongs to God in his eternity, and even the truest and most effulgent descriptions of his identity

---

[31] Grenz, *The Named God and the Question of Being*, p. 283.

for and among us are misleading precisely to the extent that they obscure this fundamental point. In formal terms, theological reasoning is governed by the basic distinction between the eternal divine processions—*filiatio* and *spiratio*—and the missions in which Son and Spirit are at work in and for the world. This is particularly clear, we have argued, in the testimony of the fourth Gospel. From the foundational description of he who was in the beginning (1.1) to the disciple's eschatological confession, "My Lord and my God!" (20.28), the relationship between Father and Son is revealed as a mysterious identity-in-distinction: "The Father and I are one" (10.30). Something more radical, farther-reaching, and more ontological in nature is being claimed for the Father and the Son—and, less directly, so too for the Holy Spirit—than can be summarized in categorical judgments concerning the symbolic role which Jesus fills, the ideals he represents, or the effects which he has upon his disciples.[32]

As a theological theme, the holy name of God therefore encompasses the openness, invitation, and accessibility which God has properly in himself and on that basis wills derivatively, which is to say graciously, for his people to share in. This can be expanded and clarified in two directions. The first clarification concerns the relationship between the irreplaceable triune name and the task of glorifying God through effulgent descriptions of his identity and perfection. The triune name is indispensable to theological reflection because of the mutual address of Father to Son and Son to Father, eternally grounded and equal in glory, by which Father, Son, and Holy Spirit are both self-known and self-revealing. While God's identity is indeed rendered by his acts, i.e. in the drama of creation and redemption we will shortly consider, functionalist descriptions of God as well as appeals to the divine perfections themselves—whether those of Redeemer, Holy One, Sustainer, Sophia, Servant, or Lover—are only ever *descriptions* of the One at work, and so do not name God by the name which he gives to himself.[33] A previous observation concerning the livingness of God thus seems appropriate here as well: theological descriptions derived apart from their eternal reference threaten to terminate in talk of creation.

---

[32] Compare D. Moody Smith, *The Theology of the Gospel of John* (Cambridge: Cambridge University Press, 1995), p. 130.

[33] For this reason, absent in the argument of this essay is a critical consideration of 'inclusive' or 'expanded' language proposals for the triune name. Where theology thinks from the self-revelation of God's being in act, as one scholar has sensitively argued, "only a revealer could disclose a new name for the Almighty Lord—not disciples, mystics, or scholars"—Katherine Sonderegger, "On the Holy Name of God," *Theology Today* 58, no. 3 (2001): p. 397. Against "recent attempts to synthesize the descriptivist and direct reference theories of naming," Grenz argues that their shared emphasis upon naming as a passive act is what renders this inapplicable to the triune God who always remains both active agent and passive recipient—cf. *The Named God and the Question of Being*, pp. 288–289.

Nonetheless, the task of the divine perfections occupies an inimitable place in theological reflection. Without such descriptions, as Edward Farley observes, we find ourselves in a preposterous relationship to an "abstract thou, a thou without contents, features, characteristic appearances, and behaviors." He therefore proposes, by contrast, that matters of personal presence and of character description are

> ever enmeshed in the trusted entity . . . To relate to God even in prayer and praise is to relate to one-deemed-as, as merciful, creative, loving, or holy . . . The Eternal Thou is, in other words, ever a designated Thou. *As undesignate, it is simply vacuous.*[34]

We have argued that this is how God indeed reveals himself. He offers his very identity in and with his self-presentation as the one who *is*. More exactly, we will argue below that the triune name is irreducibly necessary to our doctrine insofar as it is approached dramatically. The name is recognizable as belonging to the Eternal One at work, precisely where matters of agential action, concrete contexts and relationships, and the distinct timeline of God's unfolding acts are seen to move from promise to fulfillment.

Presently, this procedure can be contrasted with considerations of God's self-given name which defer to general, linguistic analysis—focusing, for example, on issues of etymology, grammar (e.g., *idem per idem* construction), or the act of naming (*nomina sunt realia*)—in order to secure an account of the divine essence. One sees this in practice, for example, where discussions of the divine attributes are prefaced by an analysis of יהוה, the Lord's name revealed at Sinai. The assumption here is that the grammar is in and of itself transparent to the simplicity, infinity, or immutability constitutive of God's life.[35] We have made a different approach by reversing the relationship

---

[34] Farley, *Divine Empathy*, pp. 91–92. Emphasis supplied. This despite an essentially "existential, interpersonal, and doxological approach" to the attributes of God, wherein "the activity of God, not the distinction of God and the world, is the starting place" and "attributes as analogical expressions of God's being are all absent" (p. 88).

[35] See Grenz's extended consideration of the historical scholarship behind the MT's יהוה, as well as the LXX's more philosophically laden ὁ ὤν, 'the existing One'—cf. *The Named God and the Question of Being*, esp. pp. 133–173. By way of summary, Grenz calls attention to scholarly consensus on 1) the dynamic sense of the Name, i.e. God's efficacious "being present" to and for his people and, more specifically, that this activity is centered on the *history* of Israel, in the sense that 2) it is his being faithfully "the God of Abraham, the God of Isaac, and the God of Jacob" (cf. Ex 3:6, 15), which decisively links past with present (pp. 142–145). In this sense, the saga of "Yahweh's ongoing relationship with Israel . . . discloses further the significance of the divine name, yet always in keeping with the revelation given to Moses at the burning bush. . . . [W]hat comes to the fore in this ongoing drama is the continual presence of the one who was already present with the patriarchs and hence whose very name denotes such a never-ending

between these two; the drama of creation and redemption, or what Otto Weber refers to as "the total witness of scripture,"[36] *confirms* the irreplaceable name of the Lord. In the scriptural witness, there are degrees and depths in which the name of the Lord is disclosed and received. There is both unfolding and consolidation, and this is intimately related to the call not simply to utter the name of the Lord but to glorify it and to adorn it as well.[37]

Creation and the Free Presence of the Majestic One

A second clarification of the proposed concept of divine presence is required here. All theological descriptions of the perfections of God are determined (consciously or unconsciously) by an underlying conception of

---

and hence covenant-remembering presence" (pp. 149–150). This distinction, of course, is not always a tidy one. According to F. Turretin, for whom the crucial point is that the name 'Jehovah' is unique and non-transferable to creatures, etymology and narrative description are perfectly complementary. Jehovah, in other words, is the principle name of God, from which the divine essence may be derived, specifically (1) God's eternity and independence, i.e. his nature αυτοων, (2) his causality and efficiency, just as "the first and most perfect in each genus is the cause of the rest," and (3) his immutability and constancy in truth, declared in the concrete act of "fulfilling the promises given to the patriarchs"—*Institutes of Elenctic Theology, 3 Vols.*, trans. G.M. Giger, ed. J.T. Dennison (Phillipsburg: P&R, 1992), III.iv.5. Richard A. Muller's discussion is equally illuminating. While Calvin evinces a rare caution in such matters, it is argued that the typical practice among the Reformers, and then variously among the Protestant Orthodox, was "to move from the holy name . . . toward the discussion of the existence and essence of God [and thus] not only the identification of God with Being but also the assumption that the highest being is the source and goal of all things"—cf. *Post-Reformation Reformed Dogmatics: The Rise and Development of Reformed Orthodoxy, Ca. 1520 to Ca. 1725: Vol. 3, the Divine Essence and Attributes* (Grand Rapids: Baker Academic, 2003), p. 249. Occasionally among the latter, e.g. Perkins and Trelcatius, the name 'Jehovah Elohim' (Ex 6.2; 3.15) was judged an encapsulation of the orthodox view of the divine essence: one God in three persons (cf. p. 257). Though divine simplicity was likewise indicated in many of these cases through the initiation of discussion of attributes with the divine name(s) rather than the attributes themselves, the name Jehovah ostensibly indicating simplicity and eternity of essence (p. 217).

[36] Otto Weber, *Foundations of Dogmatics, vol. 1*, trans. D.L. Guder (Grand Rapids: Eerdmans, 1981), p. 416. Attending to this history, by contrast, yields three dogmatic insights: (1) Yahweh "makes himself known in his self-distinction from everything which is not-God in the concrete sense . . . and thus gives to the people, to whom he turns, the possibility of calling upon him"; (2) he remains himself in his name; and (3) the name is inseparable from his covenant history such that "God is not 'also' but 'actually' the covenant God" (pp. 417–419).

[37] By contrast, see proposals either for spare treatment of the perfections or for their systematic marginalization within the doctrine of God: Jenson, *Systematic Theology* I, p. 223; Thomas F. Torrance, *The Christian Doctrine of God: One Being Three Persons* (Edinburgh: T&T Clark, 1996), esp. pp. 235ff.; and Macquarrie, *Principles of Christian Theology*, pp. 202–210.

the God–world relation. In other words, the assertion that God is intimately present in and to creation precisely as the transcendent Lord requires for its articulation a peculiar understanding of the creative act itself. Our argument assumes the classical and compelling statement of the origin of the world according to which God called the world forth out of nothing by his Word and knit it together by the power of his Spirit, separating it from the dark and formless chaos. For the entirety of this work, Irenaeus wrote, God needed nothing but "his own hands . . . the Word and Wisdom, the Son and the Spirit, by whom and in whom, freely and spontaneously, he made all things."[38] Accordingly, no logical or ontological basis conceived to lie outside the gratuity of God's own life explains the manner or end for which God is present to the world in his perfection.

The importance of this claim rests in its correspondence to the manner of God's redemptive act, for in this work God remains lordly subject: able freely to love his creation, free to speak into it, free to communicate himself through it, free even to be made incarnate in it—ὁ λόγος σὰρξ ἐγένετο καὶ ἐσκήνωσεν ἐν ἡμῖν (Jn 1.14)—and in this concrete act free to establish fellowship with finite creatures. Because he undertakes this work in his freedom, God is fully present to creation, in every single facet or layer of its particularity, without either overcoming his work in its finitude or acting in mitigation of his own transcendence. The cosmos, in other words, is neither God's antithesis nor his nemesis but rather the work of his hands and the theatre of his glory.

This ontic freedom before creation correspondingly provides to creatures the possibility for a veracious knowledge of God. Precisely because the Word became flesh, in other words, ἐθεασάμεθα τὴν δόξαν αὐτοῦ (Jn 1.14). This is confirmed primarily in the concrete act in which the Son, who knows God face to face, takes our flesh to himself in the power of the Holy Spirit. As a result, "our flesh is therefore present when He [Jesus Christ] knows God as the Son the Father, when God knows Himself."[39] This is confirmed subsequently in that act in which God commandeers the language of the apostles and the prophets—in and of itself a wholly inadequate vessel—and through the inspiration and illumination of his Spirit establishes it as the unique instrument of his self-disclosure.[40] Precisely because the world-reality is created by God, "it is in no position to set up a real opposition to his will to reveal himself to us," and so God is free to take words which already belong to him, give himself to them, and give to them their veracity.[41]

---

[38] Irenaeus, *Against Heresies*, Ante-Nicene Fathers, vol. 1 (Edinburgh: T&T Clark, 1986), 4.20.1.

[39] Barth, *Church Dogmatics* II/1, p. 151.

[40] See Gunton, *Act and Being*, p. 73.

[41] Barth, *Church Dogmatics* II/1, p. 211. So too Dorner's terse and penetrating thesis: "Since God cannot on the one hand desire to appear otherwise than He is, and since

God's freedom before creation, of course, in no way sets aside the distinction between *archetypal* knowledge (God's self-consciousness) and *ectypal* knowledge (that which we draw from God's Word). God remains God in his self-revelation. Human beings thus know him truly, and always in a manner appropriate to finite creatures.[42] This is the veracity of human knowledge of God which, because it binds knowledge to its exclusive source, requires human beings at each point to "keep to the name which he gives himself."[43] Intimacy and majesty are thus for God corresponding, not competitive, modes of perfection. Or in the original idiom of scripture, Christian confession must be said to encompass both the affirmation that ἐν αὐτῷ ζῶμεν καὶ κινούμεθα καὶ ἐσμέν (Acts 17.28), as well as the mystery through which, in this very presence, God remains incontestably ὁ θεὸς ὁ ποιήσας τὸν κόσμον καὶ πάντα τὰ ἐν αὐτῷ, οὗτος οὐρανοῦ καὶ γῆς ὑπάρχων κύριος (Acts 17.24). It is the freedom of God's love demonstrated in the incarnation which secures systematically the fittingness of finite language for confession of the triune God. In this particular sense, noetics are decisively a function of ontics.

The doctrine of *creatio ex nihilo*, of course, is not a formulation directly carried over from the pages of the Old and New Testaments. Bearing an impressive—though not undisputed—pedigree within the Christian tradition, it is a proposal drawn from and deployed in response to the lordship, aseity, and eternality of God and therefore formulated with respect to the strict contingency of all that is not God. As such it performs a tremendous amount of theological work. Negatively speaking, the doctrine rules out two rival conceptions. In the Epicurean and Stoic philosophical systems, which confronted the early church Fathers—Irenaeus foremost among them—we are provided with clear examples of each. On the one hand, the former philosophy, particularly in its Valentinian manifestation, invoked an intricate systemization of intermediaries to protect divine purity and transcendence. Within this near-dualism, as Richard Norris observes, the world was regarded "an unintended product of a temporary disorder within the life of the Pleroma."[44] God is depicted as existing in a state of eternal repose, aloof

---

God does not on the other hand prevent [i.e. anticipate] a dualistic power in His revealing will, there only remains to see in the divine revelations of Himself, revelations of what He is and how He is (not revelations of what and how He is not), and thus to see the revelation of objective attributes"—cf. *A System of Christian Doctrine* I, p. 200.

[42] See, e.g., Herman Bavinck, *Reformed Dogmatics, vol. 2: God and Creation*, trans. J. Vriend, ed. John Bolt (Grand Rapids: Baker Academic, 2004), pp. 107–110; and Francis Turretin: "The object of the knowledge of God is both himself (who most perfectly knows himself in himself) and all things extrinsic to him"—*Institutes of Elenctic Theology*, III.xii.3.

[43] Barth, *Church Dogmatics* II/1, p. 59.

[44] Richard A. Norris, *God and World in Early Christian Theology: A Study in Justin Martyr, Irenaeus, Tertullian and Origen* (London: Adam & Charles Black, 1966), p. 61.

to this transient, finite, and polluted world. The latter philosophy, on the other hand, drives toward the conclusion that God is so immanent to the world as to be indistinguishable from it. It does this by identifying the *logos* as the inner logic permeating the whole of the cosmos. As Ermin Micka concludes in his significant doctoral dissertation, within this account "the world is god and god is the world."[45] The first view thus sets God competitively over against the world; the second elides their distinction. By contrast, we have already referred to St. Irenaeus—the second century "child of the church" and bishop of Lyon—and his conscious effort in *Against Heresies* to expound the incorruptible God as the creative and redemptive Power present in the world without compromising either term. Knowing God in his utter transcendence, in short, is precisely that which implies and grounds an articulation of God's intimate presence to the world.[46]

A robust affirmation of *creatio ex nihilo* likewise undergirds the proposal that, in terms of volition and power, the world cannot in and of itself constitute a limit upon God or compromise the fact that in his presence, God remains uniquely himself. As creation, the world and its inhabitants are precisely that: creatures standing always under the lordship of the holy God and so existing by grace. The Creator, therefore, not only can be but, as Kathryn Tanner has deftly argued, in a genuinely radical way *must* be present to the whole of creation, "directly productive of everything that is, in every aspect of its existence."[47] In this *non-contrastive* relationship,

> created being becomes what it is and this all the more fully, not by way of separation or neutrality from God, but within the intimacy of a relationship to divinity as its total ground. The more one talks of the realization and perfection of created beings, the more one must be willing to talk of God's immediate creative working.[48]

---

[45] Ermin F. Micka, *The Problem of Divine Anger in Arnobius and Lactantius* (Washington D.C.: Catholic University of America Press, 1943), p. 8.

[46] On the insightfulness and importance of Irenaeus' effort, see Thomas G. Weinandy, *Does God Suffer?* (Notre Dame: University of Notre Dame, 1999), pp. 91ff.; Denis Minns, *Irenaeus* (London: Geoffrey Chapman, 1994), p. 33; and Norris, *God and World in Early Christian Theology*, p. 70.

[47] Kathryn Tanner, *God and Creation in Christian Theology: Tyranny Or Empowerment?* (Oxford: Blackwell, 1988), p. 47. Cf. Ingolf U. Dalferth, *Becoming Present: An inquiry into the Christian sense of the presence of God* (Leuven: Peeters, 2006): "There can be nothing beyond the reach of the presence of Father, Son and Spirit, i.e. nothing that is not involved at each present in God's creative, salvific, and perfecting activity" (p. 151).

[48] Tanner, *God and Creation*, p. 85. Tanner is here following her own rule for first-order theological statements: "whatever you say about God and world, do not simply identify or oppose their attributes" (p. 28). Related is Edward Farley's claim that every available notion of immanence applicable to the divine symbolics includes in itself the transcendence of God. God comes forth in redemption, in other words, as "an unfathomable,

Properly speaking, then, a doctrine of the divine perfections will clarify and protect a relationship between divine and creaturely life which, crucially, is one of *direct* rather than of *inverse* proportion. God's presence as Father, Son, and Spirit—his willing, speaking, and acting—is not simply the limit of the creature. It is this too. But it is a limit which actually precedes the creature and calls it forth into the willing, speaking, and acting that conforms to God's own life. Fellowship between God and creatures is possible through the presence of the God whose freedom and transcendence do not nullify but rather establish and uphold that which is not-God.

To summarize, in this section we have argued that knowing and confessing God's name may be articulated in terms of one's response to God's particular act of creation and redemption, for, as John Webster has written, "God's *name* is his enacted identity, God's sheer, irreducible particularity as *this One* who is and acts *thus*."[49] God makes himself accessible by the revelation of that name by which he knows himself, and a doctrine of the divine perfections is one particular response to this act, seeking to glorify Father, Son and Holy Spirit by carefully attesting God's perfection. Creation, far from standing in a competitive relationship to God, is by its very contingency suitable as the theater of the divine glory. In it God may be graciously present in his fullness. Furthermore, we have argued that understanding and repeating this triune name requires attention primarily to the history in which the name is made manifest rather than to grammatical considerations. A doctrine of the divine perfections, which seeks to respond to God's self-revelation by a self-critical account of how it confesses and glorifies God will therefore look to descriptions authorized by the drama of creation and redemption itself. The systematic importance of the singular God alive prior to and in this concrete drama—an assumption implicit in all we have thus far considered—is our third and final specification of the subject matter of the doctrine of the divine perfections.

III. *The Eternal God*

It was the brilliance of Karl Barth's vision and insight to work out a doctrine of the perfections of God under the thesis that one "cannot in fact leave the sphere of His action and working as it is revealed to us in His Word."

---

reconciling love, a voice that summons seemingly invincible historical powers to justice, to a creativity that knows no bounds"—*Divine Empathy*, pp. 142–143. Farley references Hartshorne: "to be maximally *related* to the world is to be 'surrelative' and this is a transcendence" (p. 144), a compelling claim so long as it does not necessitate reversing the relation such that the world is maximally related to—and so co-equal with—God.

[49] John Webster, *Holiness* (London: SCM Press, 2003), p. 36.

This claim, as he expands it, rests upon the twofold premise not only that "God is who He is in His works" but likewise that God

> is the same even in Himself, even before and after and over His works, and without them. They are bound to Him, but He is not bound to them. They are nothing without Him. But He is who He is without them. Yet in Himself He is not another than He is in His works.[50]

A theology of the divine perfections therefore works in a manner appropriate to its object as it reasons responsively *from* God's self-revelation *toward* an account of his identity as Father, Son, and Holy Spirit.

At the same time, it may be argued that the concrete events of creation and redemption are unpredictable in their unfolding and inscrutable in their seeming contrariety. A core instance of this perplexity, the wrath of God would appear to be one more description, which terminates either in an undifferentiated, uniform, and so rather colorless concept of the *essentia Dei* or, alternatively, in an irreconcilable multiplicity, the unity of which lies altogether beyond the horizon of human understanding. The former bespeaks the all-consuming notion of Oneness-as-divine, whereas with the latter, the variation of historical process threatens to become determinative of God's own life. In light of this, the task will be, first, to properly characterize this variation or "operational complexity"[51] and, second, to specify that which is encompassed in the judgment that theology should work responsively after God's identity rather than in anticipation of it. We will argue that the solution to each relies for its cogency upon the undiminishable importance of God in his eternity.

Divine Action and "the Fullness of Time": A Biblical Sketch

An understanding of God in his eternity may begin with straightforward, positive identifications of this unique mode of divine freedom. In the Old and New Testaments, God is repeatedly shown to have his life beyond the determinative or constitutive power of a creaturely succession of times, roles or acts. He is spoken of not only as "the high and lofty one who inhabits eternity [שֹׁכֵן עַד]" (Isa 57.15), but likewise as the triune Lord who is at once τὸ ἄλφα καὶ τὸ ὦ, ὁ πρῶτος καὶ ὁ ἔσχατος, ἡ αρχὴ καὶ τὸ τέλος (Rev 22.13; cf. 1.4, 17; 2.8; 21.6). Neither simply by derivation nor through his relationship to finite reality but rather absolutely in himself, God is first and last, מֵעוֹלָם עַד־עוֹלָם (Ps 90.2).

Still more radical is the message that both the protological and the eschatological converge upon Jesus Christ as the incarnate Word and the

[50] Barth, *Church Dogmatics* II/1, p. 260.
[51] Stead, *Divine Substance*, p. 175.

inexhaustible wisdom of God. It is in the person of the Son, in other words, ὅς ἐστιν πρωτότοκος πάσης κτίσεως, that "all things hold together" (Col 1.17; 2.3). He is God's wisdom installed "ages ago . . . at the first, before the beginning of the earth" [מֵעוֹלָם נִסַּכְתִּי מֵרֹאשׁ מִקַּדְמֵי־אָרֶץ] (Prov 8.3), and in his perfection he is unperishing, μένει εἰς τὸν αἰῶνα (1 Pet 1.24f.; cf. Isa 40.8). God's working through finite, discursive, and irreversible time, therefore, is not an act undertaken primarily and properly from within this succession itself. Neither are such acts the outworking of an essentially reactive and strategic knowledge. whether conceived as calculation in the face of present novelty or as synthetic estimation of an appropriate course of action. It is rather that which προώρισεν ὁ θεὸς πρὸ τῶν αἰώνων (1 Cor 2.7), and so irreducibly the execution of his gracious will, rooted in the eternal resources of his life.

Because God is both before and after as well as in all the events of creation and redemption, we can observe finally that, with the perfection of the eternal God, the life of Jesus Christ neither merely transpires nor is it haphazardly or uncertainly taken up. In every respect, it is rather the lordly enactment of God's freedom, the culmination of a plan realized in τό πλήρωμα τοῦ χρόνου (Gal 4.4; cf. Eph 3.11; Tit 1.2). God is not subject to the co-planarity of mundane distinctions but works over and through history in order to secure fellowship with creatures: "changing the times and seasons" (Dan 2.21), using the evil intentions of others for the purposes of his own good plans (Gen 50.20), and thus ensuring that by his eternal calling and purpose πάντα συνεργεῖ εἰς ἀγαθόν (Rom 8.28). In the alternation and turn of time, and through the baffling complexity in which all things are given their place—and perhaps especially in the fullness of God's wrath—the work of God is both incomprehensible in its wholeness and absolutely certain in its efficacy (Eccl 3.11, 14; cf. Isa 43.10, 13).

Eternity: The Perfect Movement of the Triune God

Apparent even in this brief summary is the substantial difference which obtains between this claim and two alternative understandings of the relationship between God and time.[52] On the one hand, there is the thesis that "God operates in the processes of creativity to insure maximum harmony

---

[52] George Hunsinger argues the weaknesses of both of the following notions: (1) eternity as God's "abiding present" (*nunc stans*), the enduring moment in which all times are known merely "as functions of present consciousness," and (2) eternity as a "flowing present" (*nunc fluens*), an "everlastingness . . . that accompanies the succession of time as it occurs" and so "shapes and directs the temporal process largely by virtue of possessing the plenitude of a larger essence and a greater amplitude for the future"— cf. "*Mysterium Trinitatis*: Karl Barth's Conception of Eternity," *Disruptive Grace: Studies in the Theology of Karl Barth* (Grand Rapids: Eerdmans, 2000), pp. 186–188.

with intensity . . . to see that the puzzle-pieces of reality fit together with the least discord and the most beauty."[53] A specific manner of conceiving the relationship between eternity and a concrete variety of historical, divine action follows. If God is to be protected from implication in any "absolutely coercive act," it will be premised that "God merely influences the particular outcome of each moment" rather than choose it, guide it, or in any respect determine it—either in its course or in its outcome. In the specific case of wrath, it is claimed, divine influence is felt in the contradiction of personal aims and in patterns of guilt and remorse.[54] Conceptualizing the relationship between divine and human action in competitive terms, in other words, necessitates a peculiar manner of conceiving God's relationship to time. A concept of the unbounded potentiality requisite for an organic process of divine self-realization replaces a robust biblical concern for the freedom in which God effects his own ends in his own lordly timing. More concisely, a concept of everlastingness displaces God's eternity.

On the other hand, there is that form of overemphasis which assumes an incommensurability between the God who has exclusively an "eternal present" and the notion of finite time, defined as "the mode of existence by virtue of which things have a past, present and future."[55] The crucial question here does not revolve around the catholic definition of eternity, i.e. "the total, simultaneous and perfect possession of interminable life."[56] In and of itself this is an attempt to articulate the being of God in eminently positive terms. Rather, the ambiguity arises in relation to certain expansions of this claim wherein divine eternity is attributed not only to God as unbegotten

---

[53] Jerry K. Robbins, "God's Wrath: A Process Exposition," *Dialog* 33 (1994): p. 255. For the antecedent, see Whitehead, *Process and Reality*: God is thought to move from his primordial nature—conceived of as "the unlimited conceptual realization of the absolute wealth of potentiality," a state of being in and of itself "deficiently actual"—toward concreteness and consciousness, by means of "the objectification of the world in God" (pp. 343–345). Though the latter emphasis upon God in his 'non-temporal becoming' appears decisive, William J. Hill identifies two divergent lines for interpreting Whitehead's work. The first is that of Charles Hartshorne and John Cobb, which presses toward "the consequent nature as alone actual and concrete, with the primordial nature designating an abstract realm of pure possibilities for God that is real only as embodied in the consequent nature". The second is Lewis S. Ford's "more nuanced" re-interpretation, which "stresses the subjective dimension to the primordial nature, namely, the non-temporal decision wherein God renders himself actual as a subject". In contrast to the first, this second interpretation seeks to "ground the God of a temporal becoming in dependence upon the finite world (the consequent nature) in an ontologically prior non-temporal becoming that is the source of the never-ending creative advance into novelty"—cf. "The Historicity of God," *Theological Studies* 45 (1984): pp. 325–327.

[54] Ibid., pp. 255–256.

[55] Bavinck, *Reformed Dogmatics* II, pp. 162–163.

[56] Boethius, *On the Consolation of Philosophy* 5.6.4. Bavinck provides references to its subsequent use in theology—cf. *Reformed Dogmatics* II, p. 163.

(ἀγεννητος) and incorruptible (ἀφθαρτος), but decisively as his being negates all temporal succession. Where this latter notion presses a formal opposition between eternity and time—purifying or absolutizing genuine difference—time itself becomes increasingly a matter of illusion. This is further suggested where the work of creation and redemption are ascribed to God upon the analogy of "the abundant and exuberant life of the cheerful laborer [i.e. God], for whom time barely exists and days fly by."[57] Here, God lives absolutely. Unclear, however, is whether and how God chooses particular times and specific covenant relationships, enact patience for sinners, and finally take to himself a life history in the person of Jesus Christ. The danger is thus that an abstract and absolute opposition between God and the economy undermines the fittingness in which God undertakes sundry variegated acts for the sake of his creation. In short, an "absolute timelessness" renders God's eternity implausible.

A more compelling theology, by contrast, elucidates the perfect unity in which God has the "unchangeable possession of his unbounded life and . . . the authentic renewal of his grace every morning."[58] To clarify and explore this proposal, we can draw out at length two concrete criteria. An account of God's work in its historical variety is cogent, in the first instance, as it is worked out as *an act of the triune God*. As is apparent in the preceding biblical sketch, the theological question is not that of the so-called vicissitudes of life *per se* which, it is surmised, require a transcendent ground for their unity-in-distinction. It is a question more exactly of the decisiveness with which the event of the incarnation of the eternal Son of God itself defines time as the irreversible succession of past, present, and future in which God brings to fullness a fellowship between himself and creatures. A theology of God's eternity, therefore, requires some clarification of its inner relation to classical trinitarian theology.

Their connection is formally established in the prototypical movement of the trinitarian processions. Because God lives in a unity of substance and through the genuine self-distinction of subsisting relations—the Son being μονογενοῦς παρὰ πατρός (Jn 1.14) and the Spirit ὃ παρὰ τοῦ πατρὸς ἐκπορεύεται (Jn 15.26)—he has from himself a "succession" that bespeaks more than absolute, undifferentiated homogeneity. "[T]he unique time of the triune God," in other words, "[is] the time of God's self-identity,

---

[57] Bavinck, *Reformed Dogmatics* II, p. 163.

[58] Henri Blocher, "Yesterday, Today and Forever: Time, Times, Eternity in Biblical Perspective," *Tyndale Bulletin* 52, no. 2 (2001): p. 198. It is an indication of the overly cautious character of his exposition, however, that this is for Blocher a mere analogy—i.e. a perceiving of the problem through "the window" of trinitarian theology—and not a thesis to be correlated more robustly with the God-world relation. So too, a second analogy is derived from human awareness of time "in memory, in anticipation and projection, [and] in the synthesis of moments that this implies" (cf. pp. 199–201).

self-differentiation, and self-unification."[59] Karl Barth saw with unprecedented clarity that, though eternity is the perfection of this singular movement, it nonetheless can and must be distinguished from creaturely time by the fact that in and with this divine movement,

> there is in Him [God] no opposition, competition or conflict, but peace between origin, movement and goal . . . between potentiality and actuality, whither and whence . . . In Him all these things are *simul*, held together by the omnipotence of his knowing and willing.[60]

Within such limits, God can be conceived both as perfectly united in himself and perfectly becoming one with himself. Eternity is the "beginning, succession and end" as well as the "pure duration" most apposite the divine life.[61] On this basis, eternity can be cogently presented in its significance for a theology of the divine perfections. Primarily and properly, God is eternal as the One who has from himself a perfect union of before and after in the triune persons of Father, Son, and Holy Spirit, and so in himself a fullness to which the variety and plenitude of created time and being itself cannot add but only reflect in its proper measure. Nonetheless, as the eternal One, God is present and active in a series of concrete events, which encompasses not only a variety of action but a variety, which suggests divergence and contradiction.

Reconfiguring the debate in these terms embeds a theology of eternity in a theology of the triune God itself, making it clear that exposition of God's essence and existence, substance and persons, identity and perfections, is in every case a single, indivisible task. This approach does not begin, therefore, by "postulating a metaphysical doubling of the past-present-future structure of time . . . and by identifying it with God's own self . . . God's identification with and God's opposition to the totalized 'almighty time'."[62] This critique

---

[59] Hunsinger, "*Mysterium Trinitatis*," p. 199.

[60] Barth, *Church Dogmatics* II/1, 612.

[61] See respectively, ibid., pp. 608, 612. As with eternity, so too this logic obtains with respect to divine omnipresence: "Even if creation and this relationship of God to creation did not exist, proximity and remoteness in irresolvable unity (and therefore the basis of what is externally manifested and realized in His omnipresence in relation to His creation) would still be a divine perfection" (ibid., p. 462).

[62] Michael Welker, "God's Eternity, God's Temporality, and Trinitarian Theology," *Theology Today* 55, no. 3 (1998): p. 320. According to Welker, the argument that eternity and time find their relationship in "the trinitarian differentiation" must be inductive and explorative. The three modes of being of the triune God are thus correlated with three mutually dependent forms of time: (1) "in the sense of preservation and the guarantee of rhythms and continuity, reciprocity and security of expectations," (2) those which "center on specific events and complexes of events that shape and mark the course of a multitude of other events in particular ways" and follow "the irreversible

is misplaced because the actual roots of this novel proposal—first worked out by Karl Barth—are sunk in the gracious correspondence between God in himself and God in his self-revelation, and so in "the primal Christian conviction that God is truly present to his people in Christ (Immanuel, God with us) and the Spirit."[63] A theology of God's eternity, in other words, is a catholic article of faith. It is not an attempt at proof per se but an instance of *praecedit fides, sequitur intellectus*, which relies for its content solely upon the witness of the Old and New Testament scriptures. As with the doctrine of the Trinity, a theology of God's eternity and its significance for all theological science is the product of theologians following after this singular witness, inquiring

> attentively into what the texts say and how they say it, in search of unifying common judgments which may be rendered in very diverse ways, attempting to redescribe or re-render those judgments so as to do justice to the significance of their various articulations across the range of the canon.[64]

Articulating the possibility of a relationship between eternity and time in terms of the perfect life of the triune God relies upon a close reading of scripture and a clear statement of the biblical reasoning which structures its message.

The gain in such a reconceptualization is not only a compelling alignment of the divine perfections and the theology of the trinity, but additionally a clear intellectual field from within which to argue that God's act of being

---

order of past-present-future," and (3) the form of time which coordinates "the universally metricizable and reversible times" and "the historical, irreversible times" such that through its activity "certain constellations of creatures are again and again torn from certain constancies and historical processes of development in corrective and healing manners . . . Life, which seemed destined to perish, is renewed" (cf. pp. 324–326). Ostensibly this avoids 'speculation'—a concept Welker leaves undefined—by omitting reference to God's life above and prior to creation. The trinitarian modes are interpreted in functionalist terms as *operationes Dei externae*: creating, revealing, and renewing.

[63] Fred Sanders, "The Trinity," *The Oxford Handbook of Systematic Theology*, ed. J.B. Webster, K. Tanner and I.R. Torrance (Oxford: Oxford University Press, 2007), p. 35. See also J.N.D. Kelly, *Early Christian Doctrines*, 5th ed. (New York: HarperCollins, 1978), esp. pp. 262–279.

[64] David S. Yeago, "The New Testament and the Nicene Dogma: A Contribution to the Recovery of Theological Exegesis," *The Theological Interpretation of Scripture: Classic and Contemporary Readings*, ed. S.E. Fowl (Cambridge: Blackwell, 1997), p. 96. So too: "An inquiry which remains at the level of concepts cataloging and tracing the history of the diverse conceptual resources employed in the New Testament texts and theology of the Fathers, will never succeed even in properly raising the question of the relation between the New Testament and later Church teaching" (pp. 93–94).

wholly everything that he is *includes* a concrete variety. This claim to inclusion, in fact, is the second criterion of a more nearly adequate doctrine of eternity. In this mode of his freedom, construed in precisely this way, God is genuinely present to creatures—neither in denial or dissolution of temporal reality, nor in an utter disregard for the changing needs of his people. Under this last constraint—and ostensibly for the sake of the "perfection" in which God absolutely contradicts the past, present, and future of human life—love would thereby show itself as ill adapted to the needs of hopeless creatures mired in sin. In his love, God would be presented as utterly *un*-free. The sufficiency of Christian confession of God's wrath is therefore determined in large part by its correlate, namely the concrete "flexibility and . . . elasticity" included within God's unswervingly gracious act of remaining always himself.[65] The eternal and immutable God

> deals always with man just as he is . . .The one divine will of grace as it were scatters itself in many temporal acts—in a word, *precisely in order to hold fast the unity and immutability of the ethical goal and of himself*, God conditions his action toward free, mutable mankind exactly as the actual condition of man requires . . . [and so] woos their souls and their devotion, that at least atoning and forgiving love may perhaps break the hard heart and kindle love in response.[66]

The many moments distinguishable in God's one work for and among creatures are provided for in the movement of his eternal life as Father, Son, and Spirit. An account of the intensive perfection of God's redemptive presence, therefore, does not imply an ongoing process of re-adaptation on God's part. Rather, "eternally, God is immutably and impassibly adapted to every situation."[67]

---

[65] Isaak A. Dorner, *Divine Immutability: A Critical Reconsideration* (Minneapolis: Fortress Press, 1994), p. 179.

[66] Ibid., p. 185. Compare also: "[S]ince God cannot wish to appear other than he is, and since no dualistic power checks His will to reveal Himself," the revelation of God's attributes is objective and positive—*System of Christian Doctrine* I, p. 186. Compare the influence on Karl Barth's exposition of constancy in *Church Dogmatics* II/1: God "is always the same in every change. The opposite of His constancy . . . is not His holy mutability, but the unholy mutability of men" (p. 496); "God . . . can retract in the most terrible manner by showing Himself as the One He is in His wrath. But He cannot and never does repent of being the One He is" (p. 498); "[E]verything that is said and done in fulfillment of the divine reconciliation and revelation is the execution of the one fixed divine decision, taken once for all. This is so whether in individual cases it means light or shadow, judgment or grace, wrath or patience, Law or Gospel" (p. 505).

[67] Weinandy, *Does God Suffer?*, p. 162. Weinandy is critical, however, of the distinction between ethical immutability and its ostensibly more robust counterpart, ontological immutability: "By making God merely ethically immutable, it is difficult to see what is

The strength of such a descriptive exposition is clear. It does not begin from an intuitive judgment concerning the *essentia* fit to exist in an absolute eternity, an eternity itself thought through as a rejection of the irreversible sequence of finite time. It is rather a dogmatic summary equivalent to the twofold claim that, in the idiom of the scriptures, God is both the Father of Lights with whom there is "no variation or shadow of change" (Jam 1.17), as well as the fact that:

> With the loyal you show yourself loyal; with the blameless you show yourself blameless; with the pure you show yourself pure; and with the crooked you show yourself perverse. For you deliver a humble people, but the haughty eyes you bring down (Ps 18.25–27).[68]

In this precise sense, God is the one "who is eternally new while always one and the same, who is never other than he who he is in the unlimited freedom and inexhaustible newness of his creative and saving acts, and whose unpredictable deeds unceasingly take us by surprise."[69] As one key instance of this variety, God's wrath is not an illegitimate swerving of God from his natural or proper action. Wrath is not the exercise or development of new capacities in the divine life. As with every mode of God's perfection, wrath is rather the constancy of God in the fulfillment of his own ends as they are revealed in his Word and Spirit. As we will argue more fully in part two of this essay, such variation is only ever a movement from eternity to eternity, from perfection to perfection, but in this it is nonetheless the genuine movement of God's life.

Responsive Theologies and the Divine Perfections

The analysis of the variation proper to divine action, and especially the foundation of this variety in God's eternal life, belongs inextricably to the task of the doctrine of the divine perfections. It belongs to this task because it is precisely through his concrete acts of creation and redemption that God elects to reveal his identity. The material distinction between Creator and creature stringently regulates the form in which the perfections may be filled with content. Returning to the quotation from Barth with which this section began, i.e. that God is to be found "in the sphere of His action and working

---

the metaphysical foundation for his immutable goodness and love. These are merely posited because God always acts in a perfectly good manner; but why does he always so act?" It is left unclear, in other words, whether the goodness and love of God are "truly rooted in what God actually *is*" (p. 62).

[68] Cf. Mal 3.6; Heb 13.8; Jer 29.11; and Isa 46.10.

[69] Thomas F. Torrance, *The Christian Doctrine of God* (Edinburgh: T&T Clark, 1996), p. 239.

as it is revealed to us in His Word," we can propose that in light of God's eternity there is no other rule to be followed, no abstract concept of divine perfection to which one might otherwise defer.

Only in the unchanging and ever new acts of God—*ad intra* as well as *ad extra*—is God's identity disclosed. Thus the method for deriving the attributes of God is given along with their material content: theological reason must respond descriptively to God's self-revelation rather than work constructively toward it. Most penetratingly stated,

> [D]ogmatics must give precedence to *definition by description* over *definition by analysis*; its account of the being of God and of God's perfections is to be determined at every point by attention to God's given self-identification—and thus by biblical-historical description of the particular freedom which God exercises in his lordly acts . . . [Our concepts] must be converted, made serviceable by correction, above all through being filled out by descriptive reference to the event and name of the God whom they attempt to indicate.[70]

In critically approaching the content of the perfections of God—or in entering with Barth into the endless and rich task of saying "God is"—we will observe this fundamental continuity between form and content. The divine perfections in their seemingly boundless variety will be treated as descriptive reiterations of the drama of creation and redemption through which is revealed the *essentia Dei*. As qualities which arise in theological reflection by means of "an attentive thinking-after"[71] the livingness of the eternal and triune God, these perfections will be articulated in terms of personal agency, concrete contexts, and the movement of salvation from promise to fulfillment.

---

[70] Webster, "The Immensity and Ubiquity of God," pp. 544–545.

[71] Early in his career, Barth suggested this approach as an "*aufmerksamen Nachdenkens*"—cf. *Der Römerbrief*, 1922 (Zurich: EVZ-Verlag, 1940), p. xiii. Though the term (*Nachdenken*) was not developed as technical shorthand in the *Kirkliche Dogmatik* II/1, and though the various English renderings in fact eclipse Barth's insight, the method itself remains primary throughout. Compare, e.g., p. 297 ("consideration," *CD* II/1, p. 265), p. 615 ("reflection," *CD* II/1, p. 547), p. 733 ("consideration," *CD* II/1, p. 650), and p. 741 ("reflection," *CD* II/1, p. 657). This is an inherently and self-consciously expansive task. As Barth unfolds each new divine perfection, "one suddenly finds oneself staring yet again at some aspect of how God has reconciled the world to himself in Christ. But this is precisely Barth's point. He has not lost the plot but brought it to its climax. God's perfections are those of his enacted identity and must remain transparent to it"—Robert B. Price, "Letters of the Divine Word: The Perfections of God in Karl Barth's *Church Dogmatics*" (unpublished Ph.D. diss.; University of Aberdeen, 2007), p. 267.

So far we have only intimated the relative strength of those "responsive theologies," which reason *from* revelation as a matter of obedient attentiveness. In what remains, we will consider more carefully this fitting mode of derivation by analyzing the counter example, those "anticipatory theologies," which attempt to reason *toward* the content of God's self-revelation. Both modes of inquiry claim to give sufficient place to divine action. The pivotal question is whether, with respect to each, God's self-revelation is irreducibly necessary to understanding the content of the perfections or whether the witness of scripture functions merely to confirm that which may be grasped (more precisely) by other avenues of inquiry.

Anticipatory Modes of Conceptual Development

It is not exclusively by "an attentive thinking after" the self-revelation of God that the doctrine of the divine perfections has been approached. By contrast, notions of God's "being" have been treated in various respects as the primary intuition or critical presupposition for dogmatic reflection on the character of the divine. In the Boyle Lectures of 1704, for example, Samuel Clarke—a prodigy of Newtonian science turned minister and *defensor fidei*—marshaled the resources of celestial mechanics in pursuit of an irrefutable, metaphysical defense of the Christian faith. He aimed to make evident for all "considering persons . . . that the being and attributes of God are not only possible or barely probable in themselves, but also strictly demonstrable to any unprejudiced [mind] from the most incontestable principles of right reason."[72] For the basis upon which the possibility and content of knowledge of God's perfection is derived, Clarke turned not to the event of God's self-revelation but to the mechanical regularity discernible, via physiology and physics, both within and without human beings.

The argument proceeds according to a basic axiom of universal mechanics, i.e. that "there is nothing in the effect which is not in the cause,"[73] in order to develop the basic observation that "something now is" into an elaborate proof for a self-existent being. The idea of this being, it is claimed, forms the *sine qua non* of every other idea, for this "self-existent" is the "most simple being, absolutely eternal and infinite, original and independent" (p. 14). In light of Clarke's belief that "the substance or essence of the self-existent being is itself absolutely incomprehensible," however, the remaining lectures focus on expounding those things which can in fact be known, i.e., "strictly

---

[72] Samuel Clarke, *A Demonstration of the Being and Attributes of God*, ed. E. Vailati (Cambridge: Cambridge University Press, 1998), p. 7. Parenthetic citations in this paragraph are to this work.

[73] See Michael J. Buckley, *At the Origins of Modern Atheism* (New Haven: Yale University Press, 1987), p. 187.

demonstrable" attributes such as omnipresence, simplicity, intelligence, freedom, wisdom, etc. (p. 31). Clarke argued his investigation yielded indisputable conclusions. The evidences for God, he writes, are

> so many and so obvious in the constitution, order, beauty, and harmony of the several parts of the world, in the frame and structure of our own bodies and the wonderful faculties of our souls, in the unavoidable apprehensions of our own minds and the common consent of all other men, in everything within us and everything without us,

one may conclude that "nothing is so certain and undeniable as the necessary existence of God and the consequent deduction of all his attributes (p. 91).

By way of analysis, we can observe first that Clarke's approach is concerned foremost with the *ens perfectissimum*, the necessary presupposition of the world, and therein with God as *the* most fundamental cosmological deduction. Not to be underestimated, his specific effort has been highly praised as "the most complete, forceful, and cogent presentation of the Cosmological Argument we possess".[74] Clarke addressed the arguments of his opponents, notably the Spinozists and the Cartesians of his day accused of promulgating an incipient atheism, and he did so by rigorously reasoning from observations of natural phenomena to their underlying basis.

The sword of his success, however, cuts both ways. It is clear from its first pages that the argument manifests, in both form and material, a general indifference toward those explicitly theological resources we have been at pains to develop. Such a justificatory account of the Christian faith need not in this account, and will only in vain, attend to the event of the self-manifestation of the eternal and triune God as its *positum*. In this respect, according to one incisive critic, Clarke exemplifies a larger trend among late seventeenth and eighteenth century intellectuals to enter into Christian apologetics by treating atheism as if it were a philosophy. Pointedly, that procedure entailed acting "as if there were no presence of Christ within Western Europe" and thus "as if one *did not* have to confront this figure in a decision for or against the reality of god."[75] Notwithstanding the social and intellectual differences which obtain between the early eighteenth and early twenty-first centuries, Michael Buckley's judgment is both sound and telling. The modus operandi consists here in a construction of concepts

---

[74] William L. Rowe, *The Cosmological Argument* (Princeton: Princeton University Press, 1975), p. 8.

[75] Buckley, *At the Origins of Modern Atheism*, p. 64. Emphasis supplied. So too Hermann Cremer's assessment of early Christian Apologists—cf. *Die christliche Lehre von den Eigenschaften Gottes*, ed. H. Burkhardt (Giessen: Brunnen Verlag, 2005), p. 30; as well as Barth's critique of all attempts to treat God's being "as if it were only the common truth in all other statements"—*Church Dogmatics* II/1, p. 259.

assumed to be applicable to God in anticipation[76] of, and so apart from, his self-revelation.

Furthermore, to the extent that these approaches are competitive rather than complementary, there is manifested here a pivotal decision for theological reflection. As the path of inquiry forks at precisely this question, one must choose one of the two paths, along with its attendant consequences. Jean-Luc Marion's analysis is particularly relevant. If theology proceeds, like science, "by the apprehension of concepts . . . for it also, the *ens* will be first, and man's point of view normative," but "if theology wills itself to be *theo*logical, it will submit all of its concepts, without excepting the *ens*, to a 'destruction' by the doctrine of divine names."[77] Marion is critically attuned to the tendency of claims concerning the quality or character of God to terminate in creaturely reality when they are not rooted, in his idiom, in the idol-smashing power of God's love. We have suggested this is true of a theological method like Samuel Clarke's. This is not, however, the only form which inherently *anticipatory* theologies assume.

No less significant than a cosmological argument like this, a concept of God may be similarly developed as the ground for reflection on the moral dimension of human life. Immanuel Kant famously developed a concept of God in accordance with the requirements of practical reason, his stated

---

[76] Rather than utilize the classical distinction between *a priori* and *a posteriori* reasoning, we have distinguished modes of analysis which operate in *anticipation of revelation* from those which *follow descriptively or responsively after it*. A number of benefits follow: (1) the distinction leaves open the question of the doxological background to certain classical, post-Reformation theologies, acknowledging that anticipatory reasoning may indeed presuppose the living God as its end, yet pursue a line of argumentation unequal to its object; (2) it avoids an ambiguity inherent to the former pair, an ambiguity exemplified by the fact that both Samuel Clarke and Karl Barth describe their theologies as *a posteriori* in nature, the first with respect to observation of the world's physical and physiological regularity, the second in the theologically appropriated sense of "a following after" [*Nachdenken*] God's being-in-act; (3) a fresh set of terms helps illumine the mixed or complementary use to which the others are sometimes put. On this final point, see Heinrich Heppe, *Reformed Dogmatics: Set Out and Illustrated from the Sources* (London: Allen & Unwin, 1950): the incommunicable attributes are those properties "predicated of God as it were *a priori*, as He is; i.e. they declare the essence of God as it is in Himself absolutely . . . attributed according to essence, *actus* and force," whereas the communicable attributes, "properties of the second order," are known *a posteriori*, "as He is the *principium agendi* [effective principle]" (p. 63). For definitions of *a priori* and *a posteriori* drawn from the realm of specifically theological reasoning, cf. R.A. Muller, *Dictionary of Latin and Greek Theological Terms Drawn Principally from Protestant Scholastic Theology* (Grand Rapids: Baker, 2001), p. 17.

[77] Jean-Luc Marion, *God without Being: Hors-Texte* (Chicago: University of Chicago Press, 1995), p. 81.

concern being "not so much to know what he is in himself (his nature) but what he is for us as moral beings."[78] Under this conceptuality, God functions:

(1) as the almighty creator of heaven and earth, i.e. morally as *holy* lawgiver; (2) as the preserver of the human race, as its *benevolent* ruler and moral guardian; (3) as the administrator of his own holy laws, i.e. as *just* judge.[79]

Between Kant and his antecedents there is a discernible segue "from the god of mathematics and science—the god who either guarantees things or is guaranteed by them—to the god who is an inevitable corollary if human life is to be ethical."[80]

Two concessions are appropriate. First, in one fashion or another, conceptual place must be given to the holiness, benevolence and justice of God. Second, an attempt to compare the arguments of Kant and Clarke errs where it elides certain key differences, or suggests that these two eminently creative and formidable minds worked from identical circumstances or concerns. That being said, in each of these two approaches the order of knowing clearly proceeds from a concept of "being" universally available to and rigorously developed by human reason—in the one case, cosmological in nature and, in the other, moral—to an assertion of the existence of God and so to an account of those properties which must be attributed to him. Each in its own manner thereby roots the divine attributes most immediately within an explanation of the nature of the created order.

We can pause at this point and clarify the significance of such anticipatory reasoning specifically for a systematic account of God's wrath. It might be suggested that the cosmological approach per se does not typically give rise to rigorous reflection on divine wrath. This is not to say, however, that it might not function as the conceptual basis for explicating a principle of destruction or devolution inherent to created being and motion. Wrath might be construed, in this sense, as a mythological representation of one or more laws of celestial mechanics or, specifically from within the history of religions, as an irreducible element of the (perhaps cyclical) manner in which entities fall into and out of existence. The cosmological perspective inherent to either manner of approach would proceed according to a *ratio* in which the world is decisively a subject matter for unaided reason or speculation.

By contrast, the explicitly moral argument exemplified by Kant easily approximates certain traditions of theological reflection wherein God's

---

[78] Immanuel Kant, "Religion within the Boundaries of Mere Reason," in *Religion and Rational Theology*, eds. A.W. Wood and G. Di Giovanni (New York: Cambridge University Press, 1996), p. 165.

[79] Ibid., pp. 165–166.

[80] Buckley, *At the Origins of Modern Atheism*, pp. 328–329.

wrath is invoked primarily as the security or guarantee of worldly justice and social order and, even in an explicitly affective sense, "as a *corollary* or *function* of divine care".[81] In the appropriate context, we will consider several such proposals, not the least important of which relate to passages from Romans 1 and the book of Amos. We can suggest here, however, that two important considerations will be the material content of the assertion and its methodological justification. In some such conceptualizations, we will find that, consonant with an indifference toward the inherently dramatic manner in which God manifests his identity, wrath is precluded from its ground in intentional divine action and attributed rather to the world-process as such. Cosmological and moral arguments are, we suggest, much more relevant to the specific question of God's wrath than they might first appear.

We have briefly explored two historical examples, those of Clarke and Kant. We do an injustice to the perdurance and attractiveness of *anticipatory* inquiry, however, if we relegate it to history. The perfect being theology, which characterizes some contemporary philosophical theology rests on a similar understanding of how the meaning of the divine perfections is to be derived. Thomas V. Morris, for example, treats as axiomatic the notion that the task of the attributes of God is to develop a cogent account of that being with the "greatest possible array of compossible great-making properties."[82] Similarly, Jay W. Richards takes for granted the fact that "most theists believe that God is superlative or maximally perfect in whatever ways it is possible and desirable to be so."[83] What remains unconsidered in this affirmation— which Richards refers to as *the principle of perfection*—is how and whether questions of "possibility" or "desirability" may be legitimately and pivotally deployed in exposition of God's identity.[84]

A focus upon the criterion of "compossibility," for example, bears important consequences for the doctrine. This is manifest with peculiar clarity in

---

[81] Robert A. Oakes, "The Wrath of God," *International Journal for Philosophy of Religion* 27, no. 3 (1990): p. 130.

[82] Thomas V. Morris, *Our Idea of God: An Introduction to Philosophical Theology* (Downers Grove: InterVarsity, 1991), p. 35.

[83] Jay Wesley Richards, *The Untamed God: A Philosophical Exploration of Divine Perfection, Immutability, and Simplicity* (Downers Grove: InterVarsity Press, 2003), p. 15.

[84] In *The Untamed God*, the precise relationship between biblical normativity and the philosophical resources which Richards attributes to the broad theistic tradition, such as the principle of perfection (PP) and the sovereignty-aseity conviction (SAC) is finally unclear. In contrast to the more common tendency to give place of privilege to one of these, Richards' thesis is that "the great strength of Anglo-American Christian philosophy for theology is the tools it offers [i.e. modal logic and possible worlds semantics] for articulating a doctrine of God that effectively honors [all three] . . . without slighting any of them" (p. 46). Compare, however, concessions that the PP and the SAC themselves require a biblical basis (cf. pp. 35–37). It would seem that even on Richards' terms, it is necessary to speak of these three as existing in an ordered relationship.

the tendency among certain philosophical-theological expositions to exhaust exploration of divine goodness (often considered last among the perfections) in the quasi-theological problem of the existence of evil in a theistic universe. The conceptual energy is directed not at a descriptive and responsive account of that which is announced in scripture concerning the divine identity. Rather the attention is directed, first, at achieving a rigorous and clear statement of a question formulated in terms of a priori absolutes like omnipotence and omniscience and, second, at achieving an analytic resolution of the problem.[85] At heart, the endeavor is a thoroughly understandable one. Far beyond the bounds of analytic philosophy and modern theology one discovers a perennial concern among Christian thinkers to affirm the unified and noncontradictory nature of God's being and act. In this, divine wrath is often a featured theme. Great amounts of ink have been spilled, profound insights grasped at, and intense levels of cognitive dissonance endured in order to articulate all those things which scripture asserts of God, and to do so in a manner worthy of the witness as a whole.

In one respect, then, we share the burden under which some of these anticipatory investigations have labored, at least implicitly. We argue, however, that a theology, which is decidedly responsive to its subject matter is bound to think and speak from an intellectual vantage point determined by the concrete self-revelation of God. It will pay attention to the ongoing narrative of God's work for and among his people. It will reflect both the surety and confidence of God's promises and the humility proper to its position under the eternal lordship of Jesus Christ. Specifically, an account of God's wrath will be attentive to the breadth of the material of scripture, to the foundational, patterned, and directional work of God. It will follow-after rather than anticipate its object, work from rather than towards the conclusions of God's self-witness, and so argue descriptively rather than analytically.

In the cases of Morris and Richards, each thinker suggests that he stands in the tradition of Anselm's pursuit of God as *aliquid quo nihil maius cogitari posit*.[86] The critical question of whether this interpretation is pliable enough to account for an incommensurability between Anselm's second-person theological reflection (in prayer and doxology)[87] and an abstract appeal to *perfect being* is beyond the scope of our particular study. At the

---

[85] For example, see Gerald J. Hughes, *The Nature of God* (London: Routledge, 1995). With respect to divine goodness, "the central issue is whether or not God can be held to be *morally blameworthy* for creating a world such as ours" (p. 153).

[86] Anselm, *Proslogion* II, *A Scholastic Miscellany: Anselm to Ockham*, ed. E.R. Fairweather (London: SCM Press, 1956), p. 73.

[87] For example, in *Proslogion* I, Anselm sets the whole of his inquiry under the plea, "Speak now, O my whole heart, speak now to God: 'I seek thy face; thy face, Lord, do I desire'"—*A Scholastic Miscellany: Anselm to Ockham*, ed. E.R. Fairweather (London: SCM Press, 1956), p. 70; cf. Ps 27.8.

very least, this should be recognized as highly contestable ground. It may be that Anselm is first and foremost concerned with confession of the name of the Lord specifically as it is made manifest in Jesus Christ through the power of the Holy Spirit. In that case, it would be a more astute appraisal of his argument to say that it "refers back to the divine enactment, and it is concerned with the conceivability of *deitas* only as a consequence of being overtaken by the 'supreme and inaccessible light' before which the eye of the mind is 'dazzled by its splendour.'"[88] While these brief observations by no means resolve the debate over Anselm's theology, the simple but significant contrast between competing methodologies is sufficiently clear.

Beyond each of these examples, however, it is arguably John Macquarrie who in his *Principles of Christian Theology* most famously among contemporary theologians places a concept of "being"—creatively developed—at the heart of the doctrine of God. An examination of being, he writes, begins neither from abstract conceptual analysis nor from inquiry into the grounding of cosmic or moral realities. It begins much more fundamentally from the experience of a *nothingness* present in individual existence. In this precise sense, i.e. as *that which first falls under apprehension,* being can be taken up as a theological theme. Of course, there remain distinct limitations to what can be said with regard to it, for being is a *transcendens* and so enduringly mysterious and incomparable. Even so, Macquarrie writes—and this exemplifies his conviction that transcendence and immanence are not inherently competitive concepts—because being itself is the condition of all that exists, it can be characterized as "more beingful than anything that is" and, even more specifically and in the most dynamic sense possible, not merely as one existent among others but as the power which in all things "lets-be" and so that in which the religious individual rightly places her faith.[89] One does not "observe" this question, of course. Rather one is

---

[88] Webster, "The Immensity and Ubiquity of God," pp. 540–541. Quotations are from Anselm, *Monologion* 16, *Anselm of Canterbury*, eds. J. Hopkins and H. Richardson (Toronto: E. Mellen Press, 1974), p. 104. This further confirms Robert Sokolowski's contention that Anselm's argument is peculiarly Christian in character. For this, he points to the God-world relation premised implicitly therein, namely that '(God plus the world) is not greater [*maius*] than God alone'. This affirmation, he argues, is neither a theoretical possibility for historical paganism nor a natural conclusion for general reflection on what is sacred or ultimate. Rather it rests upon a distinctly Christian understanding of God as indissoluble and perfect Subject, while yet commending itself as "something simply 'reasonable'"—cf. *The God of Faith and Reason: Foundations of Christian Theology* (Notre Dame: University of Notre Dame Press, 1982), p. 10.

[89] Macquarrie, *Principles of Christian Theology*, p. 113; cf. p. 197. Parenthetic citations in this paragraph are to this work. Pannenberg observes that in the absence of any ascription of 'whatness' or 'essence' to God, finite manifestations of being are conceptually indistinguishable from the being which 'lets-be'. Apart from a realistic account of

intimately *involved* in it, and so Macquarrie understands his proposal to be existential rather than metaphysical or speculative in nature.

This last claim deserves careful consideration. The distinction between an a priori and an a posteriori argument is argued to turn on "one's experience of the world" (p. 16), the former reasoning in advance of experience and the latter reasoning in light of experience. It is precisely this decision to favor experience, however, whether articulated in existential or empirical categories, which makes vulnerable both modes of reasoning to the charge that they are finally speculative in nature. Thus Macquarrie's claim to avoid metaphysics holds true—and understandably so—only within the bounds of his own epistemological presuppositions. At the same time, a transposition of the question into existential terms does not alter the basic fact that Macquarrie derives his predicate concepts from the (mere) effects of divine action. This is most unambiguously illustrated by his appeal to Psalm 94.9, "He who planted the ear, does he not hear? He who formed the eye, does he not see?" All these—hearing, seeing, existing—may be ascribed to God, Macquarrie writes, because God himself, as the one who precedes them, is also the one who bestows being on whatever itself hears, sees, or exists (pp. 118–19). As with Clarke's Newtonian hypothesis, the movement is unambiguously from effect to cause, the scripture reference—despite its inherently dramatic form—being deployed not as constitutive of but merely as illustrative of a thesis derived, in principle, from a refined experience of being itself.

This approach to the divine perfections, present in variegated form in many early-modern and contemporary theologies, and closely related to reason's pursuit of a supreme being—a pursuit which, according to Marion's painstaking and blunt argument, belongs to "the theiology of onto-theo-logy"[90] rather than to Christianity—assumes that, entirely in anticipation of God's self-revelation, concepts may be rigorously and sufficiently refined so as to be applicable to the divine life. By contrast, we have argued that a doctrine of the divine perfections which responsively follows after the drama of the eternal God in his self-manifestation bears distinct strengths. It provides a cogent answer to the question of reference because it eschews a development of features of being-in-general—even of a supreme being—in favor of confessing those particular perfections which in word and act God declares as his own. A dramatic, and so responsive, approach also provides theological categories equal to the richness and particularity of God's life, developing variegated descriptions of the divine perfections out of the confluence of intentional agency, concrete context and the temporal unfolding of God's eternal, electing grace. Unless God is in fact present

---

universals, all talk of being "is simply the hypostatising of an abstraction"—*Systematic Theology* I, pp. 356–357.

[90] Marion, *God without Being*, p. 72.

to creatures, unless he is known to himself, self-revealing, and so in this gives both himself and the descriptions under which he may be truly known, the specter of equivocation will remain.

* * * * *

The threefold argument of this chapter constitutes a single proposal for understanding the task of the doctrine of the divine perfections. It is not a neutral consideration of the subject matter but is thoroughly textured by a particular attentiveness to the material of scripture and by distinct theological judgments. Far from a compromise of the scientific character of theology, we have argued that this feature is necessary to the task because of the uniqueness of its object. One of our core contentions, in other words, has been to consider directly the compelling mutuality between form and material in this doctrine in order to better establish the conceptual environment in which God's wrath may be considered as one particular aspect of God's identity. An investigation and repetition of the character or identity of God is what it is because of its object: noetics follows ontics. The norms, divisions, variations, unity, moral and absolute dimensions, as well as the relational character of the doctrine are all determined by its subject matter, by the eternal livingness of the triune God made manifest in his gracious self-revelation.

Throughout this chapter, we have returned to three interrelated themes. First of all, we have maintained that the attributes of God are exhausted neither by that which is ultimately significant for human life nor by that which founds the cosmos, providing its cause, end, or principle of perfection. The two claims are thus of one piece, namely that without any loss of greatness or perfection on God's part, the world might not have been, and that God's aseity, positively construed as the fullness of his triune life, is a condition for articulating God's identity in and for the world. Second, we have maintained that this Lord is active in creation by his word and spirit, yet not as one actor among others but rather as the unmatchable Glory of Glories, the everlasting 'I', the 'indissoluble Subject', who makes himself present and available as the 'Thou' of all creaturely life. The one God, Father, Son and Holy Spirit, is thus immanent to the world precisely as the transcendent God, eliciting by faith the particular response of his people. Third and finally, we have maintained that out of the resources of his eternal life—the fullness of the acts of procession in which God lives—God enacts a history of creation and redemption. Because, on this basis, the subject matter at hand is both dramatic and lordly, the divine perfections are best developed as distinct identity descriptions, and best articulated through a disciplined and responsive 'following after' the reality of God's self-presentation.

The subject matter of the divine perfections, construed in this way, makes the execution of part two of this essay particularly compelling. It clarifies the inner logic of unfolding dogmatic reflection on divine wrath as a variegated mode of God's perfection in accordance with sustained, theological exposition of several pertinent scripture passages. Before turning to the task of exposition, however, we will explore in our next chapter two final issues concerning the form of the doctrine itself: an appropriate arrangement for the material of the divine perfections and, in service of this, a proposal for the providential and redemptive modes in which God has his perfections.

3

THE ARRANGEMENT AND INNER LOGIC OF THE DIVINE PERFECTIONS: FORM REFLECTING CONTENT

Toward a clearer, more systematic discernment of wrath's place among the perfections of God, we outlined in chapter 2 a particular proposal for the latter's subject matter. A number of criteria emerged as necessary to the task of the doctrine. We argued that an asymmetrical unity-in-distinction between God's life *in se* and God's life *pro nobis* at every point guides speech concerning God's character. We drew out in detail the perfection in which God chooses to be present to and known by creatures while in every respect remaining himself in his majesty. We offered an account of the eternal resources from which God establishes and secures a history of concrete multiplicity and variance with his people, and on this basis we moved to a corresponding contrast between, on the one hand, an essentially responsive and descriptive posture towards God's self-revelation in Jesus Christ and through the Holy Spirit and, on the other, certain anticipatory or analytic modes of exposition along with their inherent ambiguities. In the course of this increasingly specific statement on the task of the doctrine of the divine perfections, however, we have not yet indicated the manner in which these judgments, once made axiomatic for theological reasoning, are to be concretely reflected in a systematic arrangement of the perfections themselves.

In this chapter, we will argue for the arrangement that best reflects the event of the self-revelation of the triune God. In making this point explicit, we will attend closely to the theology of Karl Barth (1886–1968), his influence being particularly discernable in the claim that a dialectic of love and freedom provides a most compelling reconfiguration for theological inquiry. In this theology, we find a conceptualization accommodating of the richness and variation, which, far from illegitimate, is most apposite God's life. At the same time, ours is not an unmeasured step forward. To follow Barth's core insight is to stand in a tradition of both theological continuity and development. Before turning to Barth, therefore, we will first consider two other arrangements of the doctrine: each compelling, each rigorous, each in its own way attentive to the needs of the community of confessing Christians as well as to the integrity of Christian intellectual history. We will describe and analyze the doctrines developed by Francis Turretin (1623–1687) and Friedrich Schleiermacher (1768–1834). Each of these three remains influential in contemporary theology.[1] Our goal is to listen attentively to the inner logic and concerns which these doctrines manifest, and so to situate our own specific proposal in critical proximity to the grandeur and insights of these towering Christian thinkers.

It would be both artificial and unproductive, however, to run each of our specific concerns through the following theological systems. Attention especially to global differences in approach—should they present themselves— would do little to refine our own thesis and little to honor the integrity of each systematic proposal. It will be more effective in the course of our exposition to allow only those matters of particular significance to guide our engagement. In this endeavor, we will be able better to articulate the systematic limitations, accountability, and specificity of our own proposal. Our analysis will observe two necessary limitations. In the first place, we will set aside the task of evaluating the complex matter of the genetic relationship between these three theologians. In the second place, our specific purposes prevent us from considering a doctrine of the divine perfections in all its parts. Either such undertaking would be both more extensive and more intensive than what is required by our specific concern.

The program for the present chapter is focused specifically on the necessary correspondence between the wealth of descriptions which together bespeak the glory of God—and particularly that of God's wrath—and the most adequate form for their presentation. A turn toward this form–content relationship, as we will observe, dramatically reconfigures questions concerning the principles by which attributes of God are distinguished and organized. We can expand upon both principles. Some rationale will have to be deployed, in the first instance, in order more adequately to relate the simplicity of God's life, on the one hand, to the multiplicity of perfections which belong to that life, on the other. An overemphasis upon either point tends, respectively, to reduce the divine names to human invention or to introduce composition into the divine life. In the second instance, some rule

---

[1] For examples corresponding to the Reformed scholasticism of Turretin, cf. John S. Feinberg, *No One Like Him: The Doctrine of God* (Wheaton: Crossway Books, 2001). For Schleiermacher, cf. Edward Farley, *Divine Empathy: A Theology of God* (Minneapolis: Fortress Press, 1996). For Barth, cf. Otto Weber, *Foundations of Dogmatics*, 2 vols., trans. D.L. Guder (Grand Rapids: Eerdmans, 1981).

will have to be established in order more responsibly to arrange the doctrine itself. This consideration too is of great consequence and is related to a host of thorny questions. Two of the most important inquire whether a trajectory or hierarchy obtains among the attributes and, consequently, whether the attributes press in the direction of successive, self-contained treatment or in the direction of an overlapping treatment attentive to their inner relationships. As we will see, to the extent that the subject matter of the divine perfections is itself understood to determine the doctrine's formal presentation, one particular principle should be adequate both to articulating the simple multiplicity of the attributes and to shaping their internal arrangement.

The precise material content of the wrath of God, however, requires a movement beyond Karl Barth's own formulations in at least one significant respect. Simply stated, wrath belongs among the divine perfections as a mode of God's peculiar righteousness. This manner of conceiving the material refuses, on the one hand, to dispossess God of his wrath by relegating it to the sphere of that which is merely "temporary" or "less appropriate" to God's life. Additionally, it denies that wrath may be adequately accounted for in terms of a facile concept of divine "change" or as merely an instrumental "appearance" adopted by God in order to achieve certain ends. Both judgments, we will argue, are overly impressionistic and so unserviceable. Positively, what this thesis supports is the claim that a theology of God's wrath should have as its content nothing other than God alive in his self-revelation,[2] not only as God is present to finite creation but also as he is present to fallen creation, irrevocably set against his purposes. Respectively, then, we will develop an original account of these *providential* and *redemptive modes* of divine perfection. Barth applies no such formal distinction in the context of the *Church Dogmatics* II/1. Such a proposal, as we will argue, would actually have resolved certain ambiguities in his argument.

In light of the argument of chapter 2, one further qualification is appropriate. The constructive proposal that wrath constitutes *a redemptive mode of God's righteousness* should be deployed in every case as a modest instance of conceptual shorthand within a principally descriptive account of the movement of the perfection of God's life. Were this systematic proposal divided from a theological exposition of scripture, in other words, it would be manifestly less adequate. Conceptual development, though a necessary task, should nonetheless remain subordinate to its *positum*. In the present case, insofar as neither righteousness nor wrath can be grasped except in constant relation to the testimony of the prophets and apostles, these

---

[2] As argued in chapter 2, it is precisely by the acts of "God in his self-revelation" that human beings are given to know in finite measure the life which God properly has from himself, in the love and freedom of the One God, eternally Father, Son, and Holy Spirit.

utterances cannot be dispensed with or adequately accounted for as mere "poetical or . . . childlike non-reflective forms."[3]

In part two, we will place the accent upon a more nearly adequate account of wrath's content, paying attention to the drama of God in his self-manifestation and self-interpretation. Arranging the material in this manner is an expedient—a way of articulating only once that which applies to each of chapters 4 through 6. This structure offers the added bonus of making prominent that proposal, which is in many ways the central, systematic contribution of our investigation. In light of this plan, and especially in reference to its distinct limits and possibilities, we can turn to the complex question of a systematic arrangement for the divine perfections.

I. Efficiency and the Way of Intensification: Francis Turretin on the Reformed Scholastic Arrangement of the Attributes

We examine first the work of Francis Turretin, arguably the high-water mark in post-Reformation Reformed dogmatics. In his *Institutes of Elenctic Theology*, the divine attributes are treated within the *locus tertius*, and so under the heading of the one and triune God.[4] The exposition unfolds in accordance with the threefold division of traditional scholastic argumentation. With respect to the question of God, and out of a peculiar concern to identify and refute certain pernicious theological errors, Turretin treats, respectively:

> *that* he is [*quod sit*] (with respect to existence) against the atheist . . .
> *what* he is [*quid sit*] (with respect to his nature and attributes) against the heathen . . . and *who* he is [*quis sit*] (with respect to the persons) against the Jews and heretics (III.i.2).

The discursive presentation of the material, it is important to note, intimates neither a lack of interconnection within this *locus* nor, more broadly, within the *Institutes* as a whole.[5] Rather the structure is calculated to provide an

---

[3] Emil Brunner, *The Christian Doctrine of God*, trans. O. Wyon (Philadelphia: Westminster Press, 1950), p. 247.

[4] Francis Turretin, *Institutes of Elenctic Theology*, 3 vols., ed. J.T. Dennison (Phillipsburg: P&R, 1992), I, pp. 169–310. Subsequent references to this work appear parenthetically in the text of this section and follow the traditional topic-question-paragraph format.

[5] It may be that Reeling-Brouwer's recent argument applies here as well, namely that a methodology which moves from general to particular, as does the Ramist program of Amandus Polanus, is best understood as "a way of *intensification* within the one and simple reality" and therefore that the propositions which it contains "must be conceived *next to* each other, to the extent that the human mind is able to do that"—cf. Rinse H.

economical, clear and compelling way into the subject matter. Proofs of God's existence are followed in orderly fashion, first, by a consideration of the divine attributes and, finally, by a discussion of the triune persons of the Godhead.

The exposition covers a remarkable amount of material, and therefore we will limit our analysis accordingly. We will argue that, while this particular arrangement of the attributes is less persuasive, first, as it deploys general logical principles of distinction and, second, in its inattention to the concrete life of Jesus Christ and the work of the Holy Spirit—i.e., specifically christological and pneumatological resources—a number of theological commitments embodied herein nonetheless point beyond themselves to an arrangement by which they might more adequately be preserved. Not least promising for our purposes is the manner in which Turretin unfolds various descriptions of God's life *out of* the concept of God's goodness.

The Ambiguity of Virtual Distinctions between Attributes

In the very definition of the divine attributes—as "the essential properties by which he makes himself known to us who are weak and those by which he is distinguished from creatures" (III.v.1)—there is ensconced the conundrum that attends the task of predicating qualities of God. The pressing question for theology is no longer whether God exists nor whether any other gods share in or stand competitively over against the monarchy of the true Lord.[6] Neither is it a question of whether Turretin, and so Reformed scholastic theology in general, has in view at this point the God of Abraham, Isaac, and Jacob. These issues have been addressed, and the conclusion has been drawn that the one and only God is none other than the Lord of the covenant of the Old and New Testaments. In turning to the question of God's essence and attributes [*quid sit*], the peculiar concern is rather how to articulate a distinction which, one the one hand, legitimizes a multiplicity of attributes as belonging to the material content of the doctrine while, on the other, protecting within theological discourse the fact of God's undivided essence.

Reeling-Brouwer, "The Conversation between Karl Barth and Amandus Polanus on the Question of the Reality of Human Speaking of the Simplicity and the Multiplicity in God," *The Reality of Faith in Theology: Studies on Karl Barth Princeton-Kampen Consultation, 2005*, ed. B. McCormack and G.W. Neven (New York: Peter Lang, 2007), pp. 68, 73.

[6] It is notable that the divine unity, though indeed applicable to the essential oneness of God, is actually interpreted by Turretin in the exclusivist sense of *singularitas*, not *simplicitas*. The unity of God is therefore the uniqueness in which God rules and, if blatant contradiction is to be avoided, must rule, as the only "infinite, eternal, omnipotent and most perfect being" (III.iii.6). A concept of unity thus serves as a logical bridge, specifying the existence of the God just evidenced and anticipating discussion of the name the One Lord, Jehovah.

In satisfaction of both criteria, it is argued that the divine attributes may be distinguished from each other and from the essence of God "virtually and eminently" [*virtualiter et eminenter*] (III.v.5). The explanation of this somewhat abstruse distinction proceeds as follows. Though in and of himself God is simple and thus insusceptible to every distinction between attributes, nonetheless, two interrelated points of evidence require admitting a multiplicity of attributes into dogmatic reflection. Intellectually, the sundry irreducible formal conceptions require it. The theologian cannot simply elide, for example, God's justice and mercy, for as formal notions their content is irreducibly divergent (III.v.9, 11). Objectively or effectively, moreover, divine power functions as "the principle of diverse actions" and so operates in or toward a variety of objects, producing in them distinct effects (III.v.6, 9).[7] We will return to the question of the cogency of this explanation below.

More immediately, however, the benefits of adopting this conceptualization need to be adduced. In the first place, the application of a *distinctio eminenter* not only formalizes an internal unity of essence in an external multiplicity of attributes but, crucially, it addresses the criticism that such a premise trades upon a blatant category mistake or false distinction. Each attribute is real in its object and in its concrete effect. In the second place and closely related, a virtual distinction specifies the genuine difference between theological iterations of God's character and God as he is in himself. Every description of God, because it arises out of the confrontation between "the weakness of the human intellect [*imbecillitatem intellectus humani*] and the eminence and perfection of the divine nature," will inevitably be marked by a distinct inadequacy (III.v.12). This weakness, however, is a function of the finitude or feebleness of the human intellect and not, for example, a consequence of its moral corruption. Knowledge of God is necessarily inadequate—since discursive reasoning can only conceive the divine being in a partitive manner, i.e., "not according to its total relation, but now under this perfection, then under another" (III.v.3)—but it is not on that account necessarily a function of error or untruth.

Within his interpretive scheme, it is clear that this option is more appropriate than the available alternatives. Of the two which Turretin mentions, a *distinctio realis*—or a distinction between thing and thing—is unserviceable because it either eventuates a concept of divine essence by aggregation, and so articulates divine perfection in terms of something non-essential to

---

[7] This distinction is more commonly termed a *distinctio formalis a parte rei*, a nonessential differentiation arising on the basis of the thing as it is in itself and not, for example, from the limitations of the subject's reasoning or reflection. For a schema of the distinctions at work in classical Protestant theology, see Richard A. Muller, *Dictionary of Latin and Greek Theological Terms Drawn Principally from Protestant Scholastic Theology* (Grand Rapids: Baker, 2001), pp. 93f.

God, or it predicates of God a gross potency or mutability (III.v.7).[8] By contrast, a *distinctio formalis* preserves a certain concept of divine simplicity by accrediting a multiplicity of attributes strictly to finite, human modes of conceptualization (III.v.9), but in this it tends decisively to collapse all such propositions concerning the attributes of God into the inquiring human subject and so, correspondingly, to invest in the self-contradictory claim that God exists but, strictly speaking, in this existence bears no identifiable attributes.[9]

Beyond this relative suitability, however, the proposal is nonetheless burdened by a peculiar disconnect. Crucial to the success of the argument is some justification for the confidence with which a *fundamentum* in God may be postulated as the guarantee that the divine attributes constitute a genuine multiplicity. "[I]n the most simple divine essence," Turretin asserts, "there is ground for forming [*ratio fundandi*] diverse formal conceptions concerning the divine perfections" (III.v.8; cf. III.v.6, 9). Because no actual content and so no further justification is offered for the assertion, however, the lack of interconnection between theological form and material eventuates an unsettling ambiguity. The program does turn theological attention to concrete objects and events in order to articulate the divine perfections as a unity-in-distinction. The logical movement, however, is that of inference, an act of reasoning from economic effects toward the transcendent God who, it is premised, must be their cause. A virtual distinction deployed within the doctrine of God, therefore, though intended to secure an intrinsic basis for an extrinsic multiplicity of attributes, itself provides no further proof or clarification of the commensurability of the Oneness of God's life *in se* and the richness and variety of his life *pro nobis*.

We argued in chapter 2 that this ambiguity is inherent to any theology of the attributes, which accepts general concepts *per se* for its criteria and starting point. A *distinctio eminenter*, because it belongs to the spectrum of standard, logical distinctions is in and of itself an instance of anticipatory theology, a theology which speaks about God by first speaking about that which is not God. It is not a concept generated and governed by the subject matter of theology but derives in the first instance from an analysis of finite reality, and so is generally applicable, for example, to acts of knowing and

---

[8] The second appears closest the Socinian identification of the Holy Spirit, not with the third person of the Trinity, but with divine virtue (cf. III.v.5).

[9] Thus Maccovius and Heidanus understand divine attributes as distinguishable only "according to our conception," and Suárez, "only in our perceptions"—cf. Richard A. Muller, *Post-Reformation Reformed Dogmatics: The Rise and Development of Reformed Orthodoxy, ca. 1520 to ca. 1725: Vol. 3, The Divine Essence and Attributes* (Grand Rapids: Baker Academic, 2003), p. 290, and Heinrich Heppe, *Reformed Dogmatics: Set out and Illustrated from the Sources* (London: Allen & Unwin, 1950), pp. 58–60.

willing, which are distinguishable in their objects and effects but thought to be indivisibly united in the human soul. Critical engagement with this aspect of Turretin's theology requires questioning the terms of the argument itself. In this way, one may explore whether the irreducible descriptions and diverse effects proper to God's action—in short, the content of the attributes themselves—are not better accounted for by a re-conceptualization of the concrete manner in which God discloses his identity.

A Fluidity in Negative and Positive Predication

Subsequent to the principle by which attributes may be distinguished from one another, Turretin specifies the arrangement through which they are best presented. Among the arrangements employed within the Reformed tradition, Turretin writes that "none occurs more frequently" than that which follows the *incommunicabilia et communicabilia*, and he too will follow this form (III.vi.1).[10] Broadly speaking, the division prescribes treating, first, those attributes, which are "so proper to God that nothing similar or analogous, or any trace or image can be found in creatures" (III.vi.3). Included here are properties such as eternity, omnipotence, and immutability. In contrast to these attributes, a second set arises directly in relation to the outworking of God's will to create and redeem, and so on the basis of that act in which "God produces in creatures (especially in rational creatures) effects analogous to his own properties" (III.vi.2). Encompassed by this latter category are the communicable properties, such as knowledge, righteousness, or goodness, each being present in creatures in a distinctly finite mode. This last qualification, we should stress, is absolutely vital: attributes may be considered communicable in the sense of imparting a "resemblance" of God's proper perfection but, in the "formal" sense of an impartation of the *essentia Dei*, "all the properties of God are equally incommunicable" (III.vi.2).[11]

---

[10] While the claim is made in Heppe's *Reformed Dogmatics* that the attributes are "most usually" distinguished as such (pp. 60–62), an observation validated by Turretin's own judgment, Muller argues that the alternative proposals—e.g., classification according to the ways of knowing, absolute and relative, or sufficiency and efficiency—were more commonly employed than is often supposed; cf. *Post-Reformation Reformed Dogmatics* III, pp. 216–226.

[11] Every such communication is (1) a creaturely impossibility and so (2) a miracle of divine grace. Karl Barth illustrates the nonessential nature of the distinction through reference to the "completely unfathomable and inaccessible" nature of divine grace and the manner in which God has "implanted His eternity utterly in our hearts"—*Church Dogmatics* II/1, ed. G.W. Bromiley, T.F. Torrance (Edinburgh: T&T Clark, 1957), p. 345. The distinction constitutes a nonessential, heuristic mode of inquiry which more appropriately describes actuality than possibility—cf. Stephen R. Holmes, "The Attributes of God," *The Oxford Handbook of Systematic Theology*, ed. J.B. Webster,

Where created analogies are made pivotal to a doctrine of the divine attributes and where, furthermore, the doctrine itself is internally consistent, one may reasonably assume the method of derivation to correspond directly to this principle of arrangement. This is exactly the case in the present example. In order to clarify the twofold structure of incommunicable and communicable attributes, Turretin draws upon the classical *via triplex* (III.vi.3). Credited in its mature form to the enigmatic Pseudo-Dionysius (ca. 500), the *via triplex* assumes a derivation of each divine attribute on the basis of its creaturely *analogon*. Because God is Creator and so first cause of all creation, because "everything is, in a sense, projected out from him, and this order possesses certain images and semblances of his divine paradigms," that which is found in creation will reflect the nature of the one who created it (*via causalitatis*; αἰτίας): either as its own deficiencies are extirpated (*via negationis*; ἀφαιρέσεως) or as its goodness is maximally transcended (*via eminentiae*; ὑπέροχης).[12] For an arrangement of the divine attributes, this prescribes that the incommunicable attributes will be comprised of all of the negative propositions [*negativa*] concerning God's being, which are possible on the basis of scripture, while the communicable attributes will be constituted by every such positive description [*affirmativa*] of the divine life. This is the theory.

In practice, Turretin's exposition of the incommunicable attributes manifests a strikingly fluid application of the axiom. Unmistakably positive assertions are laid without further comment or explanation alongside the negative propositions directly prescribed by Turretin's methodological commitments. Infinity, for example, is defined both negatively as the manner in which God is "free from all limit in imperfection" and positively as being an implication of the eminence in which God has "every perfection which can be and be possessed" (III.viii.6). God's immensity, on the one hand, is

---

K. Tanner and I.R. Torrance (Oxford: Oxford University Press, 2007), p. 59; Weber, *Foundations of Dogmatics* I, p. 424.

[12] Pseudo-Dionysius, *The Divine Names* 7.3, *Pseudo-Dionysius: The Complete Works*, trans. C. Luibhéid, ed. P. Rorem (New York: Paulist Press, 1987), p. 108. Friedrich Schleiermacher consolidated this method. He argued that the ways of eminence and negation, which may be transposed into one another, together purify for theological serviceability a set of concepts which only the way of causality may posit as attributes of God—cf. *The Christian Faith*, eds. H.R. Mackintosh and J.S. Stewart (Edinburgh: T&T Clark, 1928), pp. 197f. Determining the usefulness of the method, therefore, will require an account of that presupposed knowledge which "confers the ability to correctly manipulate the exclusion, position and elevation"—cf. Isaak Dorner, *A System of Christian Doctrine* I, eds. A. Cave and J.S. Banks (Edinburgh: T&T Clark, 1880), p. 203. The *via triplex* has been subjected to vigorous criticism. See, e.g., Colin E. Gunton, *Act and Being: Towards a Theology of the Divine Attributes* (Grand Rapids: Eerdmans, 2002), p. 15; Brunner, *The Christian Doctrine of God*, p. 245; Otto Weber, *Foundations of Dogmatics* I, p. 412f.

summarized as his uncircumscribed [*aperigraptos*] nature and, on the other, it is articulated as the unique presence by which God's essence "penetrates all things and is wholly by itself intimately present with each and everything" (III.ix.1, 4). Eternity, moreover, while initially specified as God's freedom "from every difference of time" and so as an abstract act of duration without beginning, ending, or succession, is finally expanded in accordance with the testimony of scripture to include the endurance, constancy, and invariable nature of God. In this respect, Turretin cites approvingly the definition from scholastic theology, namely that eternity constitutes "the interminable possession of life—complete, perfect, and at once" (cf. III.x.1, 3, 6).

This mixed treatment is significant for a number of reasons. In the first place, it denies that a hierarchy may be impressed upon the attributes themselves. Insofar as the so-called incommunicable attributes are given a measure of positive content, the fact that they are treated first does not prove that, in unilateral fashion, they provide the necessary and proper environment from which to understand all subsequent identity descriptions—e.g. the knowledge, righteousness, or goodness of God—as being "truly" divine. This cannot be the case because, in some measure, it is in closest reference to God's concrete means and ends, his being in and for the world, that the divine majesty is itself defined.[13] In the second place, this mixed treatment prevents exposition of the incommunicable attributes from being enveloped by the ineffability of God. In the total absence of any resemblance or analogy for these divine perfections in finite creation, in other words, one would be required to exchange the positive act of Christian confession for a reverent silence. It is exceedingly clear from his own exposition, however, that Turretin does not find himself under either constraint.

This fluidity is significant, finally, because it suggests an attempt to account for scripture's positive testimony to the inextricable nature of God's majesty and his will to be in and for another, and to do so by stretching beyond the possibilities which the arrangement itself offers. Differently stated, the many attributes describe in God the fullness of life, which, expressly because it is above and prior to creatures, shows itself to be the concrete presence of God in and for the world. The more general evaluation thus holds true of Turretin's theology: in utilization of the *via triplex*, what the Reformed Scholastics valued "were no longer patterns of purely rational deduction of attributes but rather categories of analysis or organization into which

---

[13] For understanding the relationship between incommunicable and communicable attributes, this is a more significant factor than Turretin's own direct attempt to soften the element of superordination in his doctrine by claiming for the so-called communicable attributes a correspondingly unique validity, namely that their communication uniquely "commends the goodness and glory of God" (III.vi.6).

biblically revealed attributes were gathered for purposes of exposition."[14] If, in fact, description is in this manner to be prized over deduction, one can ask legitimately whether another arrangement does not better support the mutual interrelatedness of all the attributes, and so better represent God as he is utterly himself in fellowship with the world.

Before turning to the other half of this arrangement, i.e., to the communicable attributes, we can note that this fluidity is not uniformly manifested. The exceptions in Turretin's text—perhaps the exceptions which prove the rule—are those of simplicity, the first attribute treated in the series, and immutability, the last. Simplicity is defined as the quality by which God is "free from [and insusceptible of] all composition and division" (III.vii.3; cf. vii.5). With respect to its multifaceted contrast with finite reality and, crucially, in light of its non-constitutive invocation of scripture—an evaluation which will require further substantiation below—this line of argumentation is purely negative in character. This is less transparently the case, however, with respect to divine immutability, through which all change as well as every possibility of change is denied to God. Logically prior to the eternal decree of election, God is at liberty to act in any manner and toward any end. In light of the decree, however, God remains unmoved from outside himself. Though not as unambiguously as with the discussion of simplicity, Turretin nonetheless gives little evidence here of standing under any requirement of positive exposition. The details of this particular exposition, however, are better examined below as an example of the manner in which scripture informs his argument. We will therefore return in more focused manner to the specific case of immutability once we have considered his treatment of the communicable attributes.

The Unfolding of Divine Goodness

We have argued thus far that a certain fluidity conditions Turretin's deployment of the distinction between the incommunicable (or negative) attributes and their communicable (or positive) counterparts. Only provisionally and improperly therefore could it be claimed that the latter alone offer positive descriptions of the divine life. That being said, there is indeed a self-conscious shift at this point in the argument: the *viae eminentiae et causalitas* are brought to center stage and made the rule of thought. One striking piece of evidence for this turn is the freedom with which Turretin now allows an analogy from faculty psychology to structure his argument. Among the positive or communicable attributes of God, he writes, there are "three principle ones by which his immortal and perfectly happy life is active: intellect, will and power" (III.xii.1). The communicable attributes are therefore to be arranged, respectively, according to: (1) God's directing

---

[14] Muller, *Post-Reformation Reformed Dogmatics* III, p. 213.

activity [*dirigens*], which manifests the attributes of knowledge and middle knowledge, (2) God's enjoining activity [*imperans*], which includes the divine will, along with its attendant distinctions, its cause and its primary rule, and (3) God's executing activity [*exequens*], which encompasses the attributes of power, sovereignty, and justice, as well as divine goodness and the grace, love, and mercy, which belong to it. In terms of distribution, the treatment of the attributes, which Turretin provides is relatively thin, lacking not only a development of the concept of wrath but also any devoted or extended treatment of qualities such as the jealousy, glory, holiness, or spirituality of God. This is perhaps an inevitable feature of a work guided in scope and emphasis more by the perceived errors of the day than by positive and systematic resources.

Nonetheless, one feature of his exposition is particularly relevant to our project. Without offering any rationale, Turretin mines the concept of "the goodness of God" for its various layers. Three irreducible concepts are argued to arise out of this single attribute. We can briefly summarize the progression. First, goodness is that quality by which God is conceived

> not only absolutely and in himself as supremely good and perfect . . . and the only good because he is such originally, perfectly and immutably; but also relatively and extrinsically as beneficent towards creatures . . . because it is of the reason of good to communicate itself (III.xx.2).

This initial development of goodness, reflective of a concern both for God *in se* as well as God *pro nobis*, is all the more striking in its movement from nonrelational to explicitly relational language. It remains unclear in this account whether God's goodness is likewise identical with his active, eternal self-communication such that, for example, goodness may be articulated in terms of God's self-presence above and prior to creation as Father, Son and Holy Spirit.

A second distinct attribute arises at this point. The perfection in which God communicates gifts to his creatures is his goodness; but goodness which includes a bond of union between God and creatures crosses over into the conceptual sphere of divine love: "From goodness flows love by which he [God] communicates himself to the creature and (as it were) wills to unite himself with and do good to it" (III.xx.4). Grace, moreover, arises necessarily as a third distinct attribute of God, for the gifts which God gives—whether as divine favor or as the charismata of the Holy Spirit—are given not merely without regard to merit but, even more gratuitously, "notwithstanding its demerit" (III.xx.7). Finally, Turretin writes that "mercy attends upon the grace of God . . . indicating a prompt and disposed will to succor the miserable" (III.xx.10).

As the goodness of God works itself out in diverse manners [*diversimode*], Turretin argues fittingly for love, grace, and mercy as "qualities contained under" God's goodness (III.xx.1). The argument at this point is less concerned with drawing out distinctions *within* a single attribute—as with the distinctions laboriously drawn, for example, between universal and particular justice (cf. III.xix.2)—and more concerned with acknowledgment and analysis of that which, so long as this does not imply an element of "passive potency . . . by which the attributes might either be elicited from the essence or added to it" (III.v.7), could fittingly be described as "modes" of divine goodness. Goodness is God's self-communication; love, that by which he unites himself with another; grace, the determination to give gifts without reference to either merit or demerit; and mercy, the virtue by which God seeks healing for the miserable.

This is a relatively minor passage within the *locus tertius*, of course. Nonetheless, it constitutes a notable instance in which theological judgment requires for articulation of the divine perfections the concrete manner in which God, unchanging in himself, is perfectly related both to finite creation and even to sinful creatures. As our own proposal focuses upon wrath's place among the perfections of God's life, we can suggest that, while wrath occupies negligible space in the *Institutes of Elenctic Theology*, a matter perhaps not unrelated to the polemical nature of his work and so primarily reflective of the more pressing needs of his contemporary milieu, e.g., to argue for the vindictive justice of God or against a supposed "middle" knowledge, there is at least one clear suggestion that Turretin himself would approve of our claim. This is his fleeting suggestion of a parallel between, on the one hand, the wrath and severity, which "pertain" to God's justice and, on the other, the love, grace, and mercy "occupied with the communication of good" (III.xx.1). With respect to the systematic arrangement, therefore, the relationship between righteousness and wrath appears identical to that of goodness and its modes.

Christological and Pneumatological Resources

Throughout the exposition, we have made scattered reference to how Turretin employs scriptural material in his argument. We have finally and more precisely to explore this dimension of his work. It is not a simple matter to unravel, however, and thus a number of qualifications are appropriate. It is clear, for example, that an analysis of his argument cannot penetrate to the question of the text's doxological background, and so cannot venture conclusions regarding either Turretin's piety or the God he intends to praise, serve, and defend. Moreover, a certain degree of care must be shown for the fact that, as we have already noted, the material content of his text is thoroughly conditioned by the purpose for which it was composed. Turretin's negative argument—his polemic—assumes those tenets of the faith, which at the time were uniformly held, while giving disproportionate attention to certain other matters precisely on account of present controversy and widespread dispute.

Even more significant is the fact that, because Turretin writes under the assumption that "a propositional and conceptual exploration of the notion of divinity is neutrally and universally understandable and transmittable," the resources from which he feels free to draw are marked by a pronounced inclusivity.[15] As even a cursory survey of his writing reveals, he is as fluent in his citations of Hesiod, Cicero, and Plutarch, as in his knowledge of Tertullian, Gregory of Nazianzus, Clement of Alexandria, and John of Damascus. Analytic reason is thus applied to theological inquiry with little discernable anxiety over the possibility that alien material or contradictory presuppositions might thereby intrude.

One of the few scholars to examine the place of scripture in Turretin's theology, Sebastian Rehnman has argued that the Genevan employed analytic reason not to undermine or replace scripture, as certain misplaced criticisms would suggest, but rather to unfold its "metaphysically under-determined" claims and so reveal that which all along was contained implicitly within the biblical texts.[16] So too Richard Muller argues for this order. Broadly speaking, he writes, rational argument was utilized in

---

[15] Rehnman, "Theistic Metaphysics and Biblical Exegesis," p. 170. Rinse H. Reeling-Brouwer reaches a similar conclusion in relation to the *Syntagma Theologiae Christianae* composed by Turretin's near-contemporary, Amandus Polanus (1561–1610). In the early modern intellectual atmosphere, where both the experience and assumption of the unity of knowledge dominated, any disjunction between the results of logical rea-soning and Scriptural study was "unthinkable"—cf. "The Conversation between Karl Barth and Amandus Polanus," p. 101. In this respect, however, late seventeenth-century Geneva stood on the threshold of dramatic change. One potent illustration is the his-tory and fate of the *Helvetic Formula Consensus*. Championed by Francis Turretin, the confession was adopted in 1678 as an authoritative repudiation of certain heterodoxies promulgated by the school of Saumur (i.e., hypothetical universalism, the mediate imputation of sin, and the uninspired nature of the vowel points in the Masoretic text). Nevertheless, its success was short lived, its abrogation effected in 1706 in a movement led by the elder Turretin's own son, Jean-Alphonse, who saw in his own system of the-ology a return to the humanistic spirit of the Reformers. See the summary of Turretin's life and career prepared by James T. Dennison, ed., *Institutes of Elenctic Theology* III (Phillipsburg: P&R, 1992), p. 646; also Martin I. Klauber, *Between Reformed Scholas-ticism and Pan-Protestantism: Jean-Alphonse Turretin (1671–1737) and Enlightened Orthodoxy at the Academy of Geneva* (Selinsgrove, PA: Susquehanna Univ. Press, 1994), p. 21; and Timothy R. Phillips "The Dissolution of Francis Turretin's Vision of *Theologia*: Geneva at the End of the Seventeenth Century" in *The Identity of Geneva: The Christian Commonwealth, 1564–1864*, eds. J.B. Roney and M.I. Klauber (Westport, CT: Greenwood Press, 1998), esp. pp. 81–86.

[16] Ibid., p. 179. Therefore, while it is "not from his independent use of reason that he has come to the knowledge of God in Christ, but through the work of God in history" (p. 169), because reason and natural theology provide us with certain presuppositions concerning "the existence of a just, wise, and good God, and the immortality of the soul," etc., "philosophical or metaphysical inquiry into our idea of God is vitally necessary" (p. 170; cf. I.xiii.5; I.viii.1; I.ix.18; and I.xiii.3).

scholastic theology not merely to "manifest the reasonableness of the Christian doctrine of God" but also to "declare clearly . . . the insufficiency of reason to provide a complete view of the divine essence and perfections."[17] Reason, therefore, is understood to be a tool useful for theology precisely to the extent that it keeps to its inherent limitations.

Having focused our exposition in this way, we can proceed to consider more directly the manner in which scripture references function in Turretin's argument—though with variable success—to avoid an abstract or speculative development of the divine attributes. As signaled above, we will return to the concrete example of the strictly negative account Turretin offers of divine immutability. In his polemic, Turretin has as in view the errors of a theology, which, in practice, fails to distinguish between the actions of the sovereign Lord and the threat of a purely capricious God who can "now will what he before nilled" and vice versa (III.xi.2). In contrast to this voluntarist distortion—and this is the operative move—he reads in scripture that the will and very being of God toward creatures are characterized in every respect by a determinacy. To speak of immutability, therefore, is not to speak of a perpetual indifference, but of the God in whom there is "no variableness [οὐκ παραλλαγή], neither shadow of turning" (Jam 1:17). Unlike human beings, God does not lie but does that which he says (Num 23:19), which is to do all his good pleasure [כָּל־חֶפְצִי] (Isa 46:10). This scriptural material is both provocative and organic, which is to say that such passages, even when introduced by mere citation and left undeveloped, gesture toward the irreducible necessity of locating critical discussion of the attributes of God within the concreteness of covenant life. Even a minimalist invocation of the material of scripture suggests that development of serviceable theological concepts does not of necessity render scripture dispensable.

Rehnman is even more uncompromising in his defense of this method. Whereas a classically, rationally derived notion of immutability would be cast in essentially static and nonrelational terms, Rehnman avers, the immutability conceived of in Turretin's theology receives its specificity directly from the divine decree, naming God not only as "the being that imparts motion in all other beings" but therein as the One who is "constantly involved with the creation".[18] Though Turretin undoubtedly thinks from within this general trajectory, in our estimation, Rehnman's own strong judgments depend too heavily upon supposition. His defense of Turretin's argument begs the question insofar as he too (merely) assumes the content of the specific history of creation and redemption in which fellowship between God and creation is realized. Like Turretin's own argument,

---

[17] Muller, *Post-Reformation Reformed Dogmatics* III, p. 202.
[18] Rehnman, "Theistic Metaphysics and Biblical Exegesis," p. 182.

Rehnman gestures toward a concern for concrete direction, but he does so apart from any further specification of what that direction might be.

Some scholars have maintained that Turretin's arguments, like all those of his time, were constructed upon a body of texts, which "had been established as 'proof-texts' by a lengthy exegetico-theological tradition reaching back into the patristic period."[19] Precisely this judgment, however, if intended as a sufficient defense of the arguments as they appear in Turretin's text, would render these arguments unavailable to contemporary theology and so unconvincing as positive biblical-dogmatic work, the former to the extent that readers no longer share in his common consciousness, the latter insofar as Turretin presupposes his own conclusions. In the present case, distinguishing the immutability of the eternal God of the Old and New Testaments from that of a purely static or eminently nonrelational essence would require incorporating more fully the christological and pneumatological resources which Turretin seems to have presupposed all along. As it stands, this distinctly Christian theological correction of the abstract concept is only imprecisely and partially executed, and the argument as a whole remains prone to a separation of core theological concepts from the broader descriptions they are fit merely to reflect and not to replace.

Our focus has been upon the success with which, in at least one concrete context, Turretin presents the material of scripture as constitutive for the doctrine of the divine attributes. It is thus a critical engagement not from outside, and certainly not from above the tradition in which Turretin stands, but from within it as a debtor and coworker. Taking up Turretin's work in this manner—querying it, criticizing it, learning from it—is not an attempt to transform Turretin himself into a contemporary thinker or to hold him accountable to alien criteria. Much to the contrary, the assumption here is that theology thinks and speaks by centuries rather than decades. Turretin does not belong to the past or to mere historical inquiry—whether as a now superceded relic or as perfectly honed exemplar—but to the very present work of the community of scholars.

By way of summary, we can observe that engaging this theology means wrestling with it as one rigorous attempt to clarify the positive claims of the gospel. This theology of the attributes of God seeks to work from concrete objects and effects in order to identify most adequately the One who is at work, while at the same time accepting that a general spectrum of logical distinctions provides a theologically serviceable principle for relating the attributes to God himself. It thus manifests a distinct tension in its material and formal aspects. While this theology, moreover, recognizes that a certain excellence belongs not only to the *incommunicabilia* but likewise to the

---

[19] Muller, *Post-Reformation Reformed Dogmatics* III, p. 201; cf. p. 134. Also Rehnman, "Theistic Metaphysics and Biblical Exegesis," p. 169.

communicabilia, it not only leaves implicit how these two broad sets of identity descriptions are related to one another but, perhaps more significantly, formalizes this ambiguity by means of the arrangement itself. It is a theology, finally, which bursts the bounds of its own material and methodological distinctions, blurring the distinction between negative and positive descriptions of God's life, yet it lacks transparency as to how the christological and pneumatological resources of scripture and Christian confession are irreducibly necessary to and constitutive of the task of identifying God. For these reasons, this theological arrangement compels further research.

II. Beyond the Subjectivity of Morals and Doctrine: Friedrich Schleiermacher on the Attributes Which Relate to the Immediate Self-Consciousness

Alternatively, an arrangement of the doctrine of the divine perfections, and particularly the location of wrath among those perfections, is glimpsed in the proposal that because theology must be nonspeculative, it must look not only to the resources of the human religious self-consciousness but, more particularly, to love as being both in itself and above all the other attributes that belong to such a dogmatic exposition, identical with the divine essence. We have argued that certain features of the arrangement employed in the post-Reformation theology of Francis Turretin invite correction: the deployment of general logical distinctions, the formal separation of the material of the incommunicable and communicable attributes, and the lack of explicit utilization of christological and pneumatological resources. By contrast, when we turn to the theology of Karl Barth, we will focus on the preeminence of love, even as it is held in dialectical tension with God's freedom. It is instructive to consider in the interim the proposal of Friedrich Schleiermacher (1768–1834). His guiding thesis, that "all attributes which we ascribe to God are to be taken as denoting not something special in God, but only something special in the manner in which the feeling of absolute dependence is to be related to Him," is one of the more famous theses in the history of Christian doctrine.[20] Because of the highly nuanced and technical manner in which it is worked out, it is likewise an obstacle to straightforward interpretation of certain grand claims concerning divine love offered in the final chapters of the *Glaubenslehre.*

Schleiermacher finds warrant within a dogmatic system for a total of eight attributes. A complete overview of his rigorously constructed doctrine, of

---

[20] Friedrich Schleiermacher, *The Christian Faith*, eds. H.R. Mackintosh, J.S. Stewart (Edinburgh: T&T Clark, 1928), §50, p. 194. Subsequent references will appear parenthetically in the text of this section.

course, is not possible. The *Glaubenslehre* moves from start to finish with unparalleled internal coherence. It is to be read as a whole, and so its best insights are not easily grasped apart from a careful and expansive reading of it in its many parts. At the same time, our chief aim is not simply to present a study of the Berliner's theology of the divine attributes. This has been done already by more able interpreters.[21] Our aim is rather to learn from him another potential principle by which the attributes of God may be derived and organized. Our focus is therefore on the interrelatedness of three points concerning his doctrine of God: his antispeculative intentions, his critical reckoning of simplicity and multiplicity, and, finally, the structuring work which the doctrine of God's love performs.

The Antispeculative Program of the *Glaubenslehre*

It is Schleiermacher's contention that the theology of the *Glaubenslehre* bears a decisive advantage over certain of its predecessors in the Reformed tradition. This advantage is its self-conscious attempt to purge Christian dogmatics of the tendency to harvest its content from an analysis of either human understanding or willing. At the same time, this point is partially obscured by the fact that the attributes of part one are gathered under the heading of those "presupposed" by the consciousness of redemption. Schleiermacher's program appears to be, at least on this basis, a clear instance of anticipatory theology. The reality is rather more complicated, however, and the latter judgment, we will argue, misleading.

His intention is rather to present the content of the immediate self-consciousness, or "the feeling of absolute dependence" [*das schlechthinniges Abhängigkeitsgefühl*], as the sole source for dogmatic propositions. "Feeling" therefore functions as a technical concept within the theology of the *Glauben-slehre*, distinct from any general, psychological use.[22] Unlike understanding

---

[21] Above all, see Gerhard Ebeling, "Schleiermacher's Doctrine of the Divine Attributes," in *Schleiermacher as Contemporary*, ed. R.W. Funk (New York: Herder and Herder, 1970), pp. 125–162. Though perhaps the more comprehensive essay, the study by Robert R. Williams, *Schleiermacher the Theologian: The Construction of the Doctrine of God* (Philadelphia: Fortress Press, 1978) proposes a heavy interpretive apparatus.

[22] The feeling of absolute dependence is not itself a descriptive account of concrete human existence but rather a conclusion drawn from a complex analysis of observations concerning relative freedom and relative dependence: (1) because there is no relation in the cosmos in which one can be included without thereby being implicated in a mutual influence and counterinfluence, the feeling of absolute freedom is not a concrete reality; (2) human beings do experience spontaneous activity, simply not as a *pure* freedom; this is due to the fact that a human being, being non-self-originating, is always *given* into a community, which presents her with concrete limits and boundaries; (3) spontaneous activity is experienced as having its source outside the human subject; (4) were this source the world itself, freedom would not in fact exist, even in relative form; (5)

and willing—one could include here doctrinal and ethical formulation—"feeling" lies beyond any admixture of activity and passivity.[23] Unmediated by self-contemplation, it is qualitatively different: "a global consciousness of self in correlation with the world," which mediates every moment of existence and determines concrete transitions between acts of knowing and acts of doing.[24] It is this claim which directly informs Schleiermacher's proposal for a method of deriving and arranging the attributes that avoids recourse to analogy. To avoid anything alien "creeping" into the system of doctrine—since "utterances regarding the constitution of the world may belong to natural science, and conceptions of divine modes of action may be purely metaphysical"—propositions regarding the attributes of God and the constitution of the world will have to be developed strictly from those propositions that are "expressions of religious emotion" (§30.2, p. 126).

The success of Schleiermacher's effort, however, remains an open question. In a highly sympathetic and attentive essay, Bruce McCormack has recently argued that a contradiction runs to the heart of Schleiermacher's antispeculative proposal. The contradiction is generated by the fact that while, as we will see, the attributes of part two are related to "real human existence in time," those of part one, the attributes belonging to a consciousness of the relationship between God and world, are

> *ideal* in nature, being the consequence of a transcendental move that takes as its starting point the religious consciousness in its pure form, abstracted not only from the specifically Christian religious consciousness but from *every* actual moment of religious experience.[25]

Schleiermacher himself once addressed the issue of continuity and so the apparent disjunction in the material—if not formal—aspect of his dogmatics. In his *Letters to Lücke* he claimed that a reversal of the two parts was, on the one hand, inadvisable because of the consequent anticlimax borne out by an arrangement that *begins* with the most concrete and important material. On the other hand, Schleiermacher argued that such a reversal was

---

finally, human beings are dependent for freedom upon some source outside the economy. Thus the logic of his claim: "the self-consciousness which accompanies all our activity . . . is itself precisely a consciousness of absolute dependence" (§4.3, p. 16).

[23] An analysis of human experience in general reveals that life is "an alternation between an abiding-in-self (*Insichbleiben*) and a passing-beyond-self (*Aussichheraustreten*)" (§3.3, p. 8). Only feeling, or piety, belongs to the pure activity of the former.

[24] Williams, *Schleiermacher the Theologian*, p. 23.

[25] Bruce L. McCormack, "Not a Possible God but the God Who Is: Observations on Friedrich Schleiermacher's Doctrine of God," in *The Reality of Faith in Theology: Studies on Karl Barth Princeton-Kampen Consultation, 2005*, eds. B. McCormack and G.W. Neven (New York: Peter Lang, 2007), p. 122.

also imprudent because of his admitted inability to think through certain traditional tenets of Christian faith on the basis of the Christian consciousness alone, the doctrine of creation and the received understanding of miracles being prime examples.[26] In response, McCormack has astutely argued that such a reversal is not only impossible (without altering the material conclusions of the whole dogmatics), but that this irreversibility is itself proof that an element of speculation—a lack of concreteness in one's starting point—conditions the work. Rectifying the incongruity would require, on McCormack's account, rescinding the authority originally conceded to "the ancient concept of the ineffability of God."[27] The success of Schleiermacher's antispeculative program therefore rightly begins with constructive evaluation of this uniformity of procedure. A thoroughgoing account, however, lies beyond the bounds of this project.

Regardless of success or failure, Schleiermacher's intention is clear. To inquire speculatively into possible analogies between Creator and creatures is to commit oneself to a vicious cycle and so the frustration of a process of "endless approximation,"

> for owing to the intermixture of receptivity and passivity in some degree to be found (even if unrecognized) in every available term, we inevitably co-posit something which must then be gotten rid of again by the use of some other term (§55.1, p. 219f.).

Schleiermacher is little interested in this process and so little convinced by the sufficiency of an anticipatory refinement of general, theological concepts. He is concerned rather with the deployment of resources inherent to the concrete experience of the many modifications of absolute causality, and especially those arising most determinately in the experience of redemption.[28] Owing to the identity between God and oneself in this experience, or better, the "coexistence of God in the self-consciousness" (§30.1, p. 126), one need not extrapolate from observations about the created order.[29] As pretheoretical awareness of its object, "feeling" requires no content to be added to it. Crucially, therefore, one need not pursue the speculative route of analogy within a presentation of the attributes of God, for the religious

---

[26] Compare Friedrich D.E. Schleiermacher, *On the Glaubenslehre: Two Letters to Dr. Lücke*, trans. J. Duke and F. Fiorenza (Atlanta: Scholars Press: 1981), pp. 59–61.

[27] McCormack, "Not a Possible God but the God Who Is," pp. 119, 115; cf. also, *The Christian Faith* §50.3, p. 258.

[28] Ebeling, "Schleiermacher's Doctrine of the Divine Attributes," p. 145.

[29] Cf. McCormack, "Not a Possible God but the God Who Is," pp. 114f.; and Schleiermacher, *The Christian Faith*, §32, p. 131.

self-consciousness bears its meaning *immediately*.[30] Its content is impressed upon the person from without so that "feeling" functions as the objective ground and criterion of every dogmatic statement.

A dogmatic presentation of the divine attributes, in other words, is not controlled by critical observations of the world or the acting subject. Over against a theology which works primarily from the content of human knowing or doing, a further strength of Schleiermacher's program lies in the fact that, because feeling bears immediate correspondence to reality and so obviates the need to construct some analogy between world and God, certain skeptical stances toward Christian dogmatics are undercut. Precisely because feeling is "that through which the existence and causality of the codeterminant is *pregiven*, that is, given prior to and thus independent of the productive spontaneity of the self, the codeterminant of receptivity cannot be a product or projection or an inference of the self."[31] Thus, for example, the inapplicability of Ludwig Feuerbach's (1804–1872) otherwise penetrating thesis: "to deny all the qualities of a being is equivalent to denying the being himself" because

> that which has no predicates or qualities, has no effect upon me; that which has no effect upon me, has no existence for me."[32]

Because not only the fact of God's existence but the divine predicates themselves arise with an immediate necessity, and because God exists in specificity—i.e., in a concrete history of the experience of sin and redemption—Schleiermacher's program lies outside the projection critique.

Within the confines of Schleiermacher's theology, which Claude Welch has summarized not unfairly as the attempt to locate religion in "the innermost realm of human existence,"[33] God gives himself to be known objectively, not through the speculative tendencies of general inquiry, but rather as an intui-

---

[30] Cf. Ebeling, "Schleiermacher's Doctrine of the Divine Attributes," p. 145; and McCormack, "Not a Possible God but the God Who Is," p. 112. Colin E. Gunton criticizes the "notion of a directly intuited relation to the divine," which he attributes to Pseudo-Dionysius, for its inattentiveness to the narrative of God's self-revelation, its near modalist character, and its reliance upon abstract concepts of divine perfection— cf. *Act and Being: Towards a Theology of the Divine Attributes* (Grand Rapids, MI: Eerdmans, 2002), pp. 15, 65.

[31] Williams, *Schleiermacher the Theologian*, p. 37.

[32] Ludwig Feuerbach, *The Essence of Christianity*, trans. M. Evans (London: Trübner & Co., 1843), p. 14. Also: "Qualities are the fire, the vital breath, the oxygen, the salt of existence. An existence in general, an existence without qualities, is an insipidity, an absurdity" (p. 15).

[33] Claude Welch, *Protestant Thought in the Nineteenth Century, Volume 1: 1799–1870* (New Haven, CT: Yale University Press, 1972), p. 66.

tion of piety. Having outlined the importance of this fundamental reorientation for the doctrine of the divine attributes, we can advance to the corresponding thesis that, more specifically, it determines the manner in which the attributes themselves may be understood as "manifold" (§50.1, p. 195).

The Principle of Distinction

Whatever one's final judgment concerning the success of Schleiermacher's antispeculative project, it was his own belief that he had thus avoided falling into certain theological errors, which he had inherited from the tradition. By placing the *positum* of dogmatic reflection outside the antithesis of activity and passivity, and so outside the purview of speculative theology, Schleiermacher articulates a basis for the affirmation of a genuine and irreducible multiplicity of attributes in the immediate self-consciousness, while avoiding the division of essence from attributes, which would implicate God in the sphere of contradiction. As we will see, this dogmatic decision yields a distinct classification for the attributes. We have first, however, to explore the status of the multiplicity itself.

All attributes, Schleiermacher writes, "must somehow go back to the divine causality" yet without violating the rule that "they are only meant to explain the feeling of absolute dependence" (§50.3, p. 198). Attributes are indeed traceable to God, in other words, but not as descriptions of the divine essence. Rather they are modifications, or modes, of the divine causality upon the religious self-consciousness (§82 ps, p. 341). This assertion is bound on one end by Schleiermacher's rigorous commitment to the aforementioned ineffability of God, the necessary acknowledgement of the pure and unutterable nature of the divine essence, "which the Scriptures . . . recognize so clearly on every page that we need not quote passages" (§50.3, p. 190). Ineffability is a conceptual summary of the fact that because, according to piety, absolute causality cannot be presented as composite and so nonuniform, neither can one attribute among the others specify anything unique in God. To avoid bringing God into the sphere of contradiction, distinctions between divine attributes, whether articulated in substantial or operational terms, must be denied in relation to God himself (cf. §50.2, pp. 195f.; §55.2, p. 224). Formally, divine ineffability is rooted in the distinction between the purity of absolute causality considered in and of itself and its various appearances in concrete moments of human existence. Key is the critical status of the feeling of absolute dependence outlined above, namely that its pure form is undifferentiated, having no existence "in a single moment as such" (§4.3, p. 16). It appears *in realiter* only in concrete, distinguishable moments of life, and thus it is by this historical progression of life and consciousness alone that the distribution and order of the attributes of God are established.

Schleiermacher's justification of a multiplicity of attributes is bound on the other end by a commitment to the realistic or concrete content of the religious self-consciousness. As an expression of piety, and crucially unlike the speculative theology, which Schleiermacher sought to overcome, his dogmatics actually strains away from a numerical simplicity and the accompanying limitation of speechlessness. This is a particularly clear and helpful feature of Gerhard Ebeling's analysis. Piety, he writes, both "arises from the underlying unity of the feeling of absolute dependence and develops into a wealth of linguistic expression."[34] There is thus inherent within Schleiermacher's dogmatics a crucial limit to its simplifying or unifying task. It is a "fundamental feature" of his approach that the idea of identity is barred from a position of speculative dominance. Rather the concept of identity is turned "to the service of ultimate distinctions of fundamental theology, such as that between God and world, between sin and grace."[35]

In accordance with his antispeculative designs, the attribute of divine simplicity is strictly confined within an appendix to dogmatics, for this concept neither "issue[s] from the relationship between the feeling of absolute dependence and the sensibly stimulated self-consciousness" nor does it constitute a statement about it (§56.1, p. 229).[36] It cannot do so, in fact, because the experience of redemption is itself multiform. Since, in other words, "the consciousness of God is variously realised in accordance with the various elements of life,"[37] one rightly expects a dogmatics to be comprised not of one undifferentiated affirmation but of as many attributes of God as are required to articulate the various modifications of the religious self-consciousness.

If simplicity has any religious value, therefore, Schleiermacher ventures that it rests in a negative and "pictorial" capacity to preserve "the unseparated and inseparable mutual inherence of all divine attributes and activities"

---

[34] Ebeling, "Schleiermacher's Doctrine of the Divine Attributes," p. 138. That the feeling of absolute dependence, despite being undifferentiated in itself, "expresses itself and takes shape in diversity of language is due to the fact that the feeling of absolute dependence is not a separate factor in the life process, not something that lays claim to a specific element alone: on the contrary, it always takes concrete form only in the totality of one of life's elements, i.e. in such a way that it enters into relation to the sensually stimulated self-consciousness" (p. 147).

[35] Ibid., p. 159. Schleiermacher actually writes that it is distinctions between God and world, good and evil, and spiritual and sensible which form "the original presuppositions of the religious self-consciousness" (§28.1, p. 118).

[36] Certain others of the traditional attributes seem to suggest themselves directly in relation to those attributes which belong to dogmatics. These he takes up, either by way of significant revision or by way of rejection, in postscript form. See his treatments of 'unchangeability' (§52 ps, p. 206), 'immensity' (§53 ps, p. 210), 'independence' (§54 ps, p. 218), and 'mercy' (§85 ps, pp. 353f.).

[37] Ibid., p. 147; cf. Schleiermacher, *The Christian Faith* §50.2, p. 190.

(§56.1, p. 231; also §50.3, p. 196). This minimalist affirmation of simplicity, of course, does not violate the distribution necessary to a thorough account of the attributes of the living God. Even with respect to the four attributes of part one, their mutually informative or conditioning nature does not finally resolve into a simplified and untextured whole but remains, like the experience of redemption itself, an irreducible multiplicity. Speculation is therefore more aggressively courted as one strives for an abstract identity—a oneness—within dogmatics.

Though Schleiermacher argues in this manner for a genuine, irreducible distribution of the divine attributes, the limitation is clear. As an account of the various modes of the divine causality, the task of the doctrine and its related arrangement cannot be "a complete knowledge of God" but rather "that completeness alone which guards against letting any of the different moments of the religious self-consciousness pass without asking what are the divine attributes corresponding to them" (§50.3, pp. 196f.; §84.4, p. 352). In this respect, H.R. Mackintosh, the Scottish theologian and editor of the English language edition of *The Christian Faith*, once concluded that while "the undivided unity of God may appear as if it were differentiated in various attributes, just as white light passed through a prism seems to be broken up in distinct colors," in the scheme of Schleiermacher's dogmatics, deity itself cannot be so divided.[38]

This judgment, we argue, is fair so long as it does not lead to the asseveration that Schleiermacher has transposed theology into anthropology. It would be more accurate to say that, in attempting to divest theology of the need to move by logical or moral analogy from the world to God, he has presented God as objectively and exclusively present in the immediate self-consciousness of the human being and therefore formalized God's dependence upon this mediation. He has undertaken substantial measures, in other words, to circumvent the speculative tendencies he perceives in his own tradition. The content of dogmatics indeed follows the unfolding and modification of the religious self-consciousness, but it does so by holding God and world in a relationship of distinction, attending to such modifications as are brought about and available solely on the basis of the living presence of the absolutely inward God. His reticence initially to speak of God *in se*, and the lack of a formal framework, which would justify such a move, is clearly mitigated in the more concrete material of part two, and specifically in Schleiermacher's comments on divine love. In love, we are presented with an all-determinative and genuine identification of the divine

---

[38] H.R. Mackintosh, *Types of Modern Theology: Schleiermacher to Barth* (New York: Charles Scribner's Sons, 1937), p. 75. So too the claim that *throughout* his systematic work, "no direct objective knowledge is given concerning 'That' upon 'Which' we are absolutely dependent"—cf. Jay Wesley Richards, "Schleiermacher's Divine Attributes: Their Coherence and Reference," *Encounter* 57n2 (1996), p. 153.

essence. To understand this, however, consideration needs to be given to the actual arrangement and distribution of the doctrine itself.

An Experiential-Genetic Arrangement

Not unlike that of John Calvin's *Institutes of the Christian Religion*, the doctrine of God presented in *The Christian Faith* is only completed with the whole of the dogmatic system (§31.2, p. 128).[39] In relatively economic fashion, the architectonic builds in two major parts, the second part once again subdivided into two. The divine attributes are said to arise relative to the distinct moments within the feeling of absolute dependence and so are presented formally as concrete modifications of the universal religious self-consciousness. The attributes of the first part—eternity, omnipresence, omnipotence, and omniscience—constitute those which arise as expressions of the general relationship between God and world. There is, therefore, a complementarity manifest among them.

On the one hand, God is unconditioned. This arises in the first instance as divine *eternity*, "the absolute timeless causality of God, which conditions not only all that is temporal, but time itself as well" (§52, p. 203) and in the second as *omnipresence*, "the absolute spaceless causality of God, which conditions not only all that is spatial but space itself as well" (§53, p. 206). On the other hand, Schleiermacher develops God's immanent relationship to the world. *Omnipotence* articulates divine causality not only as the foundation of "the entire system of nature" but also as "completely presented in the totality of finite being" (§54, p. 211). Concurrently, *omniscience* distinguishes the codeterminant of the feeling of absolute dependence, namely God, from every "lifeless and blind necessity" as being in and of itself "absolute spirituality" (§55.1, p. 219).

Robert Williams has argued that these four attributes, in this twofold or "bipolar" movement, provide the basic structure for Schleiermacher's doctrine of God: absolute inwardness "is the limiting principle or *terminus a quo*" of God's self-disclosure while, correspondingly, absolute vitality "is the *terminus ad quem* towards which God's self-disclosure proceeds."[40] The divine causality, which gives rise to the religious self-consciousness, in other words, is equal in compass to the finite precisely to the extent that it is also opposite in kind (§51.1, pp. 201f.). From the outset, Schleiermacher

---

[39] Regarding the relationship between the two, see Brian A. Gerrish's provocative essay, "Theology within the Limits of Piety Alone: Schleiermacher and Calvin's Notion of God," in *The Old Protestantism and the New: Essays on the Reformation Heritage* (Edinburgh: T&T Clark, 1982). The argument favors continuity.

[40] Williams, *Schleiermacher the Theologian*, p. 88. The suggestion that Schleiermacher's doctrine of God is "organized around the principle of coincidence of opposites in God" is a central feature of Williams' constructive argument (p. 70).

argues that God is present in the religious self-consciousness as the one who is both perfectly related to and perfectly transcendent over the finite economy, and his articulation of this point requires a dynamic of mutually conditioning attributes. Each attribute must be considered in its own integrity in order to gain better purchase on the whole and specifically on the character of Absolute Causality.

The four attributes of part one, however, are by no means exhaustive of the doctrine of God. With respect to various criticisms of his arrangement as a whole, Schleiermacher famously commented that, though ingredient to the *Glaubenslehre*, the first part constitutes a mere "portal and entrance hall" to the whole. The propositions found there, including those which pertain to the attributes of God, "could be no more than outlines that would be filled in with their true content from the ensuing discussion."[41] Thus their function is limited to that of ancillary rules for positing others of the attributes—should they happen to arise in the system—as being divine. The attributes of part two, by contrast, are distinguishable from those of part one as determinations of the religious self-consciousness in the experience of redemption. The operative categories are no longer general and ideal but, in this latter sphere, particular and concrete. Each attribute is distilled by combining the content of one's self-consciousness—as poles of the antithesis between sin and grace—with the divine causality that corresponds to the feeling of absolute dependence (§79.1, p. 325).

More precisely, the problem of sin is presented as a disordering of the sensuous self-consciousness and the God-consciousness. This disorder is not permanent; rather it is a condition subject to distinct movements of increase and decrease. Because these two oscillate in inverse proportion—which is to say, competitively—life is experienced as a thoroughgoing antithesis in which moments of increasing freedom for the God-consciousness are set over against moments of arrested development. Redemption, as a turning toward God [*Hinwendung zu Gott*], is therefore equal to the dominance of the consciousness of grace over that sin. This may be contrasted with an original turning away from God [*Abwendung von Gott*], which is constitutive of sin itself and so dependent upon both the illicit dominance of the sensuous self-consciousness and the impotence of the undeveloped God-consciousness.

---

[41] Schleiermacher, *On the Glaubenslehre*, p. 57. Compare the following statements from *The Christian Faith*: these four attributes must be thought of as "always . . . inhering in the other" (§56.1, p. 232); though the first part "abstracts entirely" from the specific content of particular Christian experience, not only can there be "no relation to Christ which does not contain also a relation to God," but more importantly the God-consciousness "does not constitute by itself alone an actual moment in religious experience" (§32.1, pp. 131f.); "the whole realm of Christian piety" is contained in the presuppositions together with the determinations of the antithesis of sin and grace (§29.2, p. 124).

Consonant with Schleiermacher's earlier thesis, this experience generates its own distinct set of divine attributes. As in the first part, here too there are four and, in keeping with the irreversibility of religious experience itself, those related to the consciousness of sin are treated first. In short, *holiness* is defined as the moral demand any deviation from which is "apprehended as a hindrance of life, and therefore as sin" (§83.1, p. 341), while *justice* is summarized as "the connexion . . . between evil and sin" and so the punishment of wickedness in relation to the whole world order (§84.1, p. 346). As with all divine attributes, these denote not the disposition or character of God, nor the divine essence itself, but rather an irreducible mode of divine causality. In the present case, this causality encompasses the peculiar work in which "sin and evil are on the one hand ordained by God, and on the other are to be done away by redemption."[42] Strictly speaking, therefore, holiness and justice point toward and prepare for redemption, and so are dependent upon redemption as their goal, but may not themselves be equated with either its actualization or its enjoyment.

This is a crucial feature of Schleiermacher's theology. Precisely because he re-conceives the content of the immediate religious self-consciousness as the subject matter of the doctrine of God's attributes, the formal distinctions determinative of the systematic arrangement likewise follow this inseparable but antithetical conjoining. One of the most significant implications is that a strict material division must be observed among the attributes of

---

[42] Schleiermacher, *The Christian Faith*, §82 ps, p. 341. Thus the minority thesis among orthodox theologians: "from the beginning everything had been set in relation to his appearing" (§80.2, p. 328; cf. Gal 4:4). In an antispeculative system, neither sin nor grace can be conceived of as existing without the other, for both are present (with inverse proportion) in each moment of concrete human existence, no human being (except for the Redeemer), experiencing either total god-forgetfulness or complete redemption (cf. §11.2–3, pp. 54–56; §63.2, p. 263). Statements about human life outside this boundary would require a protology and eschatology, and so a methodology, significantly other than that which Schleiermacher develops: " . . . strictly considered, nothing which belongs exclusively to a period preceding the Christian development of that antithesis, and also nothing which belongs to a period which will only begin when the incapacity has been completely overcome and has disappeared, can be brought within the compass of Christian doctrine in the proper sense" (§29.3, p. 125). This limit is manifest in his doctrine of sin, one of the great landmarks of modern theology, calculated at every point to eliminate the traditional notion that a fall into sin effected a fundamental change in human nature (§72.6, pp. 303f.); though compare assertions that sin "is ordained by God as that which makes redemption necessary" (§81.3, p. 335; cf. Gal 3:22) and that, conversely, "redemption shows forth as the gain bound up with sin" (§81.4, p. 338). So too with eschatology (§29.3, p. 125). Concerning propositions of the second and third kind, i.e., attributes of God and characteristics of the world, Schleiermacher believed that "our doctrine of faith will eventually learn to manage without them" and so be content only with propositions concerning human states of mind—cf. Schleiermacher, *On the Glaubenslehre*, p. 70.

part two. While, on the one hand, holiness and justice are emptied of a perduring, gospel content, so too, on the other, divine love and wisdom—topics we will shortly consider—will be unseated from their constitutive role in God's judgment upon sin. As already implied, therefore, the cogency of the proposal depends decisively upon that which is assumed to be the subject matter of the doctrine. Where the latter is argued to be the self-revelation of the eternal life of the triune God, this formal and material antithesis is uncompelling.

More to the point, in light of our very particular concern for divine wrath, we can observe that this is the decisive context for understanding why, according to Schleiermacher, wrath occupies no legitimate place in a dogmatic, and so scientific, presentation of the divine attributes. As we saw in the theology of Turretin, here too wrath is inconsequent to the overall arrangement of the attributes. Unlike the former example, however, this is for Schleiermacher a matter of theological critique. To better understand this critique, we can consider first a sermon on the topic—a sermon aimed at obviating the topic from Christian preaching—and subsequently turn to the more systematically interesting rationale for this radical judgment.

Schleiermacher's practical reflections can easily be summarized. In a sermon on the wrath of God from 1830, he announces that apart from faith one may come to the realization that even her happiest experience cannot be interpreted as a sign of God's good pleasure. In this sense, she will be pervaded with a premonition of God's wrath. However, while this experience can always be a saving preparation for rescuing her from her condition "we may by no means flatter ourselves into thinking we are able to bring about the same effect, or even to extinguish the enmity against God."[43] Within these boundaries, and so to the extent that redemption has not already entered into one's experience, wrath will remain a feature of the religious self-consciousness. In no sense, however, does it belong to the attributes of God. This is not merely because its poetic nature would suggest in God some element of passivity. Nor is it due to the fact that such an invocation outside of a personal self-realization could only precipitate further rebellion, whether in the active sense of an intensified fight or the passive (and absurd) sense of a flight from God. In either case, such an experience of wrath could only "weaken the purely spiritual power of a godly sorrow by mixing it with external expectations" and so cast one from freedom back into servitude.[44] While Schleiermacher shares both of these

---

[43] Friedrich Schleiermacher, *Servant of the Word: Selected Sermons of Friedrich Schleiermacher*, trans. D. DeVries (Philadelphia: Fortress Press, 1987), p. 164. The scripture reading and so initial impetus is the notion of Christianity as "the ministry that preaches reconciliation" (2 Cor 5:17f.).

[44] Ibid., p. 160.

judgments, more important in the present context is a third, deeply ingrained commitment.

Schleiermacher develops the attributes in exclusive, partitive, and genetic terms. We observed above that, contrary to the tradition out of which he was thinking and writing, Schleiermacher understood his own theology to strain away from an abstract simplicity toward a genuine and irreducible multiplicity of attributes. Now we can observe that it is strict to the point of proscribing any overlap between the attributes themselves. They are related by means of the antithesis of religious experience and not in the unity of the perfection of God's life. The wrath of God, therefore, is superfluous because it covers no conceptual space not already covered by others of the attributes. Every divine reward, because necessarily unmerited—interestingly he cites Rom 4:4, 16, and Mt 20:14f.—belongs to grace rather than to justice (§84.1, pp. 346f.), and because retributive justice in the remaining sense pertains exclusively to the punishment of wickedness—decisively, neither as reformative nor vengeful but strictly as preventative in nature (§84.3, pp. 350f.)—wrath has left to it neither irreducible scope nor sphere of action. Any inclusion of wrath within a dogmatics could, in this respect, only be the product of an illegitimate importation of poetic language or a conceptual redundancy. The attributes related to a consciousness of sin are for these reasons strictly limited to two.

As the actualization and enjoyment of redemption itself, however, love and wisdom are treated subsequently in part two as propositions relating to the dominance of grace in the religious self-consciousness. In outline of the content of these attributes, Schleiermacher draws out a psychological analogy between God and human beings. *Love*, he writes, is the disposition of Absolute Causality in its "impulse to unite oneself with neighbor and to will to be in neighbor," while *wisdom* is the form of action, or as Schleiermacher refers to it, "the art of realizing divine love properly" (§165.1, pp. 726f.). He thus defines love (together with wisdom) in such a way that it constitutes a markedly different kind of attribute, one which—in contrast to those which refer merely to the effects of the divine causality—expresses the very intentionality and reciprocity of Absolute Causality itself. In this specific sense, love is identical with the divine name.

That none of the others of the attributes are truly redemptocentric is particularly clear with respect to the so-called metaphysical attributes of part one.

Indeed, an omnipotence the aim and motive force of which I do not know, and an omnipresence, of which I do not know what it emits from itself and what it attracts to itself, are merely vague and barely living ideas. It is quite different when omnipotence makes itself manifest in the consciousness of the new spiritual creation, omnipresence in the activity of the divine spirit, and omniscience in the consciousness of the divine grace and favor.[45]

Nowhere more than here, at the climax of Schleiermacher's exposition, is it apparent that the whole of his dogmatics is to be read together. The eight attributes admitted as legitimate developments of the religious self-consciousness may be considered only abstractly and improperly in isolation from this love. Much could be said about this innovative reconceptualization of the doctrine. In the remaining section, we will limit ourselves to those points that are particularly relevant to a more nearly adequate proposal for the arrangement of the doctrine itself.

The Superlative Status of Divine Love

In the closing paragraphs of the *Glaubenslehre*, Schleiermacher writes that love alone may be derived *directly* from the sense of the concrete, redemptive activity of God, that it alone speaks to God's essential motive to be united with the other, and thus that all other attributes receive their concrete determination from love itself. In his own words, and not without some awareness for the ironic climax at which he has arrived, he writes:

> It turns out that we have the sense of divine love directly in the consciousness of redemption, and as this is the basis on which all the rest of our God-consciousness is built up, it of course represents to us the essence of God (§167.2, p. 732).

Attributes which receive their life from the antithesis, in other words, cannot exist in and of themselves for God. In order to understand them as attributes at all, they must "merge for us into the divine love" so that they are all related genetically to this singular telos (§167.2, p. 731). His theology therefore bears out a crucial material order of love over against the others of the attributes, particularly over that of divine omnipotence.

We suggest that this insight—though itself partially obscured by the form of presentation, i.e., that it moves broadly from the abstract to the concrete, or from the general to the particular, by a process of seeming "intensification"—is theologically more significant than that treatment considered above in the tradition of Reformed scholastics. Theology speaks scientifically of God neither by refining a set of concepts purified of their illicit, finite content nor by amplifying select material in order to achieve a compelling, other worldly, infinite reference. Rather a dogmatics gains purchase on the God who confronts the world by expositing divine love, or absolute vitality, as being at every point identical with God's freedom, or absolute inwardness. In this

---

[45] Schleiermacher, *On the Glaubenslehre*, p. 57.

manner, love "expresses God's absoluteness in relation to the world, that is, it is this specific sense in which God is absolute."[46] It is tempting at this point to judge this specific feature a genuine doctrinal genetic development, but such a complicated thesis falls well outside the bounds of our own constructive proposal.[47] At the level of conceptual analysis, however, it is clear that Schleiermacher is able on his own terms to state in a salubrious manner how love is properly *God's* love.

Of course, what makes interpretation particularly complicated is that this telos, unlike the content of the attributes of part one, is not itself an abstraction, but rather completely manifested in and produced by Jesus Christ.[48] McCormack's critique of the continuity of procedure in Schleiermacher's dogmatics is most relevant at precisely this point. It would obscure the real dynamic and structure of the *Glaubenslehre* to convey this difference between love and the others of the attributes as fundamentally an issue of the extensiveness of one's knowledge of God. Such a thesis is mitigated by the idealist orientation of the attributes said to arise from the relationship between God and world. In retrospect, then, i.e., in reading "from the end," his dogmatics as a whole falls short of providing the kind of conceptual space necessary to the accommodation of a multiplicity of attributes, conceptual space such as that which Barth provides in his innovative development of the doctrine.

Schleiermacher takes important steps in the direction of a nonspeculative doctrine of God. In doing so, he articulates an irreducible multiplicity of attributes, which though they relate to the religious self-consciousness, lie nonetheless outside the purview of what it is possible to know about God on the basis of human knowing or doing alone. It is also instructive that, in an innovative manner, he seeks to correct the traditional privilege assigned to divine freedom. Rather it is God's love—and not, for example, the representation of God's omnipotence, itself intended to be filled and governed by love—which is articulated as the identity of the divine essence. Whereas omnipotence, as we saw, adequately presents consciousness of the manner in which God encompasses the whole system of nature, i.e., as the magnitude

---

[46] Williams, *Schleiermacher the Theologian*, p. 127. Williams judges this dialectical arrangement of attributes which separate and attributes which relate God and world to be Schleiermacher's "original contribution" (p. 85).

[47] At the very least, this would involve: (1) establishing strict criteria for what constitutes doctrinal continuity and development, (2) proposing a 'theological cartography' demonstrative of present theological boundaries, (3) differentiating a priori theological judgments from a posteriori historical data, (4) analyzing the relative influences of both the present *Zeitgeist* and more distant theological "ancestors." See Jaroslav Pelikan, *Development of Christian Doctrine: Some Historical Prolegomena* (New Haven, CT: Yale University Press, 1969).

[48] Schleiermacher, *On the Glaubenslehre*, p. 55.

of the divine causality comprehending "all times and spaces" (§54, p. 211), what it lacks is sufficient expression of both the end toward which this causality is directed and the manner in which it effects its end.[49] Love is this end. Not love in general, but that divine love which is set forth in dogmatics as a strictly theological assertion of the Redeemer and the consciousness he supplies to sinful humanity. In creation and in preservation *in general*, and so apart from the concreteness of redemption, "the divine love must always remain a matter of doubt" (cf. §166.1, p. 728).

It is not unappreciatively or without warrant, therefore, if this study turns to a formal arrangement of the attributes more amenable to our subject matter as outlined above. There are a number of incompatibilities between the two. The theology of the *Glaubenslehre*, for example, displays a general indifference toward the form of scripture as a witness to God's self-revelation in that the elements of agential action, concrete context, and temporal unfolding are made fully immanent realities. Rather than follow descriptively after the self-manifestation of God, in other words, Schleiermacher shows a preference for generating critical, foundational concepts from which the whole of a theology may be unfolded. The arrangement of the attributes, as McCormack has skillfully argued, displays an ambiguity concerning the realist or idealist nature of Christian faith and so leaves open the question of how and whether the attributes of God belong to God as a mutually implicating and mutually limiting harmony of perfection. An improvement upon the doctrine would be to carry through his realist program more uniformly than he himself did.

III. An Overflowing Depth: Karl Barth on God's Love in Freedom

We have argued that a doctrine of the divine perfections has as its occasion the reality of God's singular life. Under this thesis, theological considerations of the identity of Father, Son, and Holy Spirit have no other object than God himself as revealed in the drama of creation and redemption. Through the biblical themes of the livingness of God, the triune name, and the eternal God, we described in detail the subject matter of theological reflection. The present chapter has been concerned with the coordinate task of considering the best arrangement for those attributes, one which reflects "the duality in revelation itself" such that in both form and material the doctrine conveys

---

[49] Ostensibly, a causality perfectly uniform in nature would also lack the requisite specification not simply for ordering grace over sin in the context of a dogmatics as a whole but, more acutely, it would lack even the minimal specification required for distinguishing between the two.

simply "the condescension of the One who is free in his deity."[50] We thus begin by considering the thesis that theological descriptions of God's life are in every instance fundamentally shaped by the dialectic of divine love and freedom. It is by this twofold schema that Karl Barth thoroughly revised the received doctrine, and here, more than at any other point, we will follow Barth's own exposition and allow him to be our guide.

The Love–Freedom Dialectic

The argument of *Church Dogmatics* §§30–31 is structured around a dialectic of love and freedom. As each of the divine perfections is considered, attention is paid by turns to the overflow of God's love as "His unique being with and in and for another," namely his grace and holiness, mercy, and righteousness, as well as his patience and wisdom, and to the freedom, which constitutes the "divine excellence" or depth of God's life, which includes his unity and omnipresence, constancy, and omnipotence and, consummately, divine eternity and glory.[51] As a complex dialectical arrangement of mutual amplification and nuance, this structure is significant for at least two reasons.

First, it generates descriptions of God's character unprecedented for their richness and wholeness. Following after the living God, as we have already observed, is both a self-consciously expansive undertaking and one which manifests a peculiar mobility "in the intricate sets of echoes, backward and forward references, recapitulations and variations by which that movement is carried."[52] A critique of uneconomical repetition, therefore, should not be allowed to eclipse the genuine strengths of this descriptive account. It is in this manner, whether now in expansion upon the freedom of God or then through concerted attention to divine love, that Barth secures the living God in his self-revelation as both his subject matter and formal principle.

Second, when employed strictly as a heuristic device, dialectic holds God's love and freedom in a peculiar identity-in-distinction. Other proposed relationships are less successful in preserving these perfections. In point of fact, the substance of Barth's proposal was first intimated by Hermann Cremer (1834–1903). Cremer sought to base an account of the divine perfections specifically upon God's dealings with creatures, i.e., upon God's being *for us* as the Lord of all things, the source of life, our sole and eternal security, and so upon the self-revelation of a divine love which, because it "*alles Denken übersteigt*" [exceeds all thought], cannot be developed according to the strictures of reason—as an abstract exploration of that which is merely

---

[50] Weber, *Foundations of Dogmatics* I, p. 403.

[51] Barth, *Church Dogmatics* II/1, pp. 275, 302. Every parenthetical reference in this section is to this text.

[52] John Webster, *Barth*, 2nd ed. (London: Continuum, 2004), p. 87.

possible—but begins more radically from the fact of redemption as "*thatsächliche Wirklichkeit*" [an actual reality].[53]

In Cremer's exposition, indeed, the dyad of love and freedom is placed in the foreground. Upon closer examination, however, it is clear that divine freedom is treated merely as a necessary component of all authentic love. While it exercises significant material influence on the doctrine, freedom is not constitutive of its form. In one representative passage, Cremer writes:

> One has only to distinguish between the love known to us apart from God's revelation as a natural tendency, an affect or natural power, one which we undertake more or less as an obligation and by which we first will the other for ourselves before we will ourselves for him, and that love whose essence we first know when we have known God, the love which wills itself entirely and only for the other and through which it is possible to love not merely where and when the natural inclination is felt but even where and when it is opposed.[54]

Because the development of God's freedom is limited to freedom's role in opening one up in love for the other, the relationship between the two is one of irreversible order rather than dialectic: freedom is a crucial qualification of divine love. Genuine love is identifiable by the freedom it manifests, such that the act of freely loving another is love's highest sense.

Laid side by side, Barth's constructive proposal differs in a number of noteworthy ways from one such as Cremer's, not the least important difference being that Barth conceives divine love and freedom as related dialectically.

> On the one hand it is a question of the moment of God's aseity, absoluteness or freedom: of God in the exaltation proper to Him in Himself, as against all that is not Himself. And on the other hand it is a question of the moment of the love of God, of the activity of His personal being (p. 341).

He thereby preserves in matters of arrangement a broad consensus within the tradition, while simultaneously advancing beyond the tradition to a statement on the unity-in-distinction among divine perfections, which is unprecedented for its clarity and dynamism. It is a delicate matter to speak so forcefully and effulgently of two qualities, which, in general use, are thought of as existing in contrariety, contradiction, or competition. He therefore

---

[53] Hermann Cremer, *Die christliche Lehre von den Eigenschaften Gottes*, ed. H. Burkhardt (Giessen: Brunnen Verlag, 2005), p. 32. The unity of God's life is perceptible in his opposition to sin and death, an act in which God transcends "*das Gesetz der Folgerichtigkeit*" [the law of consistency] (cf. pp. 42, 122).

[54] Ibid., p. 38.

attempts repeatedly to forestall such a misreading. Dialectic gives expression, he writes, to the "complete reciprocity" between God's love and freedom. Each of these perfections "not only augments but absolutely fulfills the other" without obviating it or rendering it superfluous (p. 343).[55] Again, he begins, God is not "less" in his freedom than in his love: "The truth is that He is it differently . . . He is it in this sequence" (p. 350).

Despite such effort, the success of Barth's particular dialectic is a matter of some scholarly disagreement—it being claimed variously that the arrangement compromises the dialectic by subordinating love to freedom or freedom to love. A more judicious evaluation, by contrast, recognizes in this theology an eminently effective

> device not only for following after the sequence of revelation, but also for constantly turning our thoughts back to God himself, resisting the abstractions to which our inadequate human concepts tend—even those concepts rightly used in describing God.[56]

To the degree that one is able to hold together this material, there being "no love of God in itself and as such, just as there is no freedom of God in itself and as such" (p. 352), and so follow through on this formal presentation, love and freedom will be made irreducibly the environment within which every other divine perfection may most adequately "be understood and expounded as that which alone it can be—a repetition and development of the doctrine of the being of God" (p. 340). Dialectic is therefore an organizational expedient, warranted by the subject matter itself and deployed in order more adequately to confess God's being-for-another as in every respect and in every instance God's own unique act. Unpacking this dense affirmation is the goal of the doctrine as a whole and so the purpose of the twofold exposition which follows.

God's Life as an Act of Fellowship

Barth begins §28.2 of the *Church Dogmatics* with the claim that, fundamentally, the revelation of God's being-in-act is this: "that God is He who, without having to do so, seeks and creates fellowship between himself

---

[55] Barth notes the parallel between this ontological statement and its noetic counterpart: God's self-revelation is constituted by the unity in distinction of God's self-disclosure and concealment (p. 343). In a similar way, the divine perfections of both love and freedom are simultaneous instances of the unveiling and veiling of God himself. In consideration of none of them is one free of either the hiddenness or the veracity of God's self-revelation.

[56] Robert B. Price, "Letters of the Divine Word: The Perfections of God in Karl Barth's Church Dogmatics" (unpublished Ph.D. dissertation; University of Aberdeen, 2007), p. 71. See the meticulous analysis of primary and secondary texts, pp. 70–72, esp. n. 52.

and us" (p. 273), which is to say that God "wills to be ours, and He wills that we should be His" (p. 274). Easily missed is the fact that Barth himself does not begin his exposition by invoking "love" as the principle character of divine action, nor will he do so until he has given a representative picture of this divine act as a whole. Rather, Barth first specifies that the fellowship that God seeks arises and is realized as an overflow [*Überströmen*] of God's essence.

The greater context, we can observe, shows that this particular notion of an "overflow" does not contradict the catholic theological axiom that, with respect to the relationship between God and creation, "nothing is coeternal with God."[57] Barth sustains a clear distinction between, on the one hand, the overflow of fellowship between Father, Son, and Holy Spirit articulable in terms of the shared being of "one substance in three persons" and, on the other, the overflow of fellowship from the triune God to God's creatures, which rests upon the strictly moral character of God's gracious covenanting.[58] The potency of a term like "overflow" in this latter context is that it preserves both the propriety and freedom of this act. Barth attempts thereby to convey initially regarding the triune God that, as Father, Son, and Spirit, and so

in Himself without us, and therefore without this [fellowship], He has that which He seeks and creates between Himself and us" (p. 273).

Fellowship is not "demanded or presupposed by any necessity, constraint, or obligation," whether with respect to creatures or with respect to anything outside God himself; rather fellowship is "rooted in Himself alone" (ibid.).[59]

---

[57] Jaroslav Pelikan, *The Christian Tradition, vol. 1: The Emergence of the Catholic Tradition, 100–600* (Chicago: University of Chicago Press, 1971), p. 36; cf. also pp. 85f.

[58] Cf. "[S]cripture . . . knows . . . a twofold communication of God—one within and the other outside the divine being [from the will of God]"—Bavinck, *Reformed Dogmatics* II, p. 420.

[59] As we will see, in the *Church Dogmatics* Barth conceptualizes the aseity of God's love by means of the term *Überströmen*: "He [God] does not suffer any want, and yet He turns to us in the *overflow* of the perfection of His essence and therefore of His loving, and shares with us, in and with His love, its blessedness . . . His loving in the turning of the One who loves to a loved different than Himself is an *overflowing* of the love with which God is blessed in Himself" (II/1, p. 283). Likewise, this is referred to as "an overwhelming, *overflowing*, free love," superlative precisely because the triune God "is love in Himself without and before loving us, and without being forced to love us" (I/2, p. 377). Thus Barth's critique that Hermann Cremer *over*emphasizes the divine loving, and so denies "the movement that is proper to it in itself" (II/1, p. 282). In claiming that *ewig* [eternally] it is God's being both to will himself and to be *ganz für uns und nur für uns* [wholly and exclusively for us], Cremer threatens to rob God of his deity—cf. *Die christliche Lehre von den Eigenschaften Gottes*, p. 39.

A second specification pertains to the variety inherent to this act of fellowship. Fellowship has its basis, pattern, and fulfillment in the overflow of God's blessing. Nevertheless, because God's love is his own and so unfettered by human opposition, he remains Lord even before and over sinful humanity. The outward act of God's creating fellowship with his people is everywhere unconditioned and uncompromised—with respect to God's act—even in the event of creaturely rebellion. Precisely because God places himself in this relation to us "as He is Himself and affirms Himself, in distinction and opposition to everything that He is not," this conduct

> establishes and embraces necessarily, too, God's anger and struggle against sin, God's separation from sinners, God's judgment hanging over them and consummated on them. There is death and hell and eternal damnation in the scope of this relationship of His. But His attitude and action is always that He seeks and creates fellowship between Himself and us (p. 274).

Barth thus discerns in the relationship between God in his divine perfection and the (sinful) economy a broad, textured, moral relationship, the substance of which must be received, heard, and obeyed rather than deduced from the habitual use of concepts like wrath or, of course, love.

This decision is highly significant for a theology of God's wrath. By his unqualified attention to the singularity of divine fellowship, Barth provides a basis for attending without prejudice to the many modes of divine perfection without inviting the suggestion of an internal cleavage. As we will see, there is need for greater clarification of the formal implications of this point. From this perspective, however, a theological affirmation of God's wrath—a fierce opposition to sin—does not in and of itself contradict or challenge the fact that God's life is defined by a realization of loving fellowship. Wrath is not an exception to God's will for fellowship. Neither is it anything less than the love in which fellowship is given between God and creatures. Rather this goodness "not only conveys certain benefits but God himself,"[60] and for that reason it takes the form of a variegated relationship of gift and command. However initially perplexing—and it is our task in part two below to do justice to precisely this complexity—because *creating and fulfilling fellowship* is the work of the eternal God, and so despite the truth that in it there is "no lack of contrariety," God remains himself through all its diversity. Once again, had Barth begun by *anticipating* the content of this subsection, and so by presupposing the operative concepts, the task of overcoming abstract notions of loving kindness—and, particularly, such sentimental notions as fellow-feeling, disinterested benevolence or blind romance—would present

---

[60] Bavinck, *Reformed Dogmatics* II, p. 215.

itself with peculiar force. By leading with a discursive description of the event itself and only latterly naming it, however, Barth exemplifies a theological method which moves responsively and descriptively according to the form and content of its subject matter, deploying rigorous conceptual analysis only where it is required.

It is thus God's concrete act of "giving us Himself," in all its particularity, which provides the content for the systematic affirmation that we have here to do with the self-revelation of divine *loving*. This does not, of course, temper the strong note of divine aseity ringing continually in the background of Barth's exposition. Above and prior to his love for creatures, God loves as Father, Son, and Spirit. This is the unified act of "deliberation, decision and intercourse" in which "He wills and completes fellowship in Himself" (p. 275). Considered complete in and of itself, it might be possible on other terms to construe this self-sufficiency as a fundamental compromise of the creaturely order. However, if God has and is fellowship in himself, and if it is through an overflow of this life that he seeks and actually creates fellowship with human beings, then attention to God's self-sufficiency secures rather than dissolves or alienates the creaturely order. Because love is God's very being, in other words, "the charge of hostility to the human realm simply falls."[61] God's life is in every respect one which seeks fellowship between himself and human beings. This pure act, however, belongs to God uniquely and so requires careful clarification.

The Singularity of Divine Love

Critical consideration of *God's* love finds first that the good which God in fact gives to his creatures is the good of his own life and so a participation in the loving fellowship of Father, Son, and Holy Spirit. Carefully understood, it is therefore more precise to say God "is" love than that God "has" love and so imparts it to his people (cf. 1 Jn 4:8, 16).[62] As God loves in his *self-communicating* life his will is a *velle bonum alicui*, which is to say that precisely as God takes his people up into fellowship and faithfully accompanies them in life he gives liberally of every good (cf. Ps 73:23; Rom 8:38f.). In his will for fellowship, God is both "the *Good* and the sum of all good things" (p. 276).

Second, God loves without reference to any aptitude or worthiness on the part of the beloved. In this sense, writes Barth, the love of God may extend even to the creature who in and of herself is hostile toward God, throwing

---

[61] Webster, *Barth*, p. 85.

[62] Barth is quick to point out in these particular verses that divine love does not receive its meaning in an abstract manner but, as the context shows, is dependent for its content upon "the concrete being and act of God" revealed in the sending of Jesus Christ (II/1, pp. 275f.; so too Jn 3:16).

"a bridge over a crevasse" in order to gather up the unrighteous and the lost sheep of Israel (p. 278; cf. Lk. 5:31; Mt 15:24). Of course, this is not a blind love. When God loves, he does so in full knowledge of his object, and therein lies the miracle of his loving. "What He sees when He loves is that which is altogether distinct from Himself, and as such lost in itself, and without Him abandoned to death" (ibid.).

To speak of divine love is, furthermore, to say that God loves as an end in itself. It would be an altogether different thing if God loved creatures in order to glorify himself or to accomplish the salvation of sinners; therefore Barth inverts the order as a more appropriate reflection of the drama of God's self-disclosure: love is the end to which God wills both his glory and the salvation of his people. Divine love thus defies any provisional or functional assignment. Love is not evoked as a means to another end and subsequently discarded. Rather, the effort to specify divine love's origin, explanation, or occasion, Barth suggests, will finally resolve itself in the self-referential truth that "He loves because He loves" and for no other reason (p. 279).

Fourth and finally, Barth clarifies that this love is based solely in God's gracious decision to be God for his creatures—διδοὺς πᾶσι ζωὴν καὶ πνοὴν καὶ τὰ πάντα (Acts 17:25)—yet not in such a way that it is rendered arbitrary or capricious. God's loving, Barth writes, is "necessary, for it is the being, the essence and the nature of God," but for this very reason it is nonetheless "also free from every necessity in respect of its object" (p. 280). God's "overflowing" love has no need of another and

> is conditioned by the fact that although it could satisfy itself, it has no satisfaction in this self-satisfaction, but as love for another it can and will be more than that which could satisfy itself (ibid.).

It is the uniqueness of God's love that Barth is at pains to articulate. He carves out conceptual space for the assertion that, though in fact creation has been given concrete existence, it did not have to be so. And as Robert Sokolowski has so penetratingly argued, if the world did not have to be,

> it is there out of a choice. And if the choice was not motivated by any need of completion in the one who let it be, and not even motivated by the need for 'there' to be more perfection and greatness, then the world is there through an incomparable generosity.[63]

---

[63] Robert Sokolowski, *The God of Faith and Reason: Foundations of Christian Theology* (Notre Dame: University of Notre Dame Press, 1982), p. 34. Against a potential charge of speculation, Sokolowski writes that "the possibility that God could be all that there is is not another action, another possible *volitum* that God could have performed; we are not projecting imaginatively something else, some positive alternative, that God might have accomplished. We project the possibility of the world's not existing, not to

As a whole, Barth's tightly woven, fourfold description seeks to clarify the fact that God's loving—his preferring "our being to our not being, our lovableness to our unlovableness"—is in the final instance "grace and not nature" (p. 281). If this act of fellowship with creatures is indeed neither an act of nature nor one of necessity (at least as nature and necessity are commonly understood), then neither can the truth of divine 'freedom' be assumed in its ostensibly intuitive or 'common' sense. The second pole of this dialectic therefore requires attention.

Aseity: Primary and Secondary Meanings

The life of the triune God, the inward and outward movement of his loving, has its actuality in a peculiar freedom. Though this theme is taken up as the primary focus of *Church Dogmatics* §28.3, it is a theme intimated throughout Barth's consideration of the divine loving, and we have had ample occasion in the foregoing sections to develop precisely this point. The present goal, therefore, is not simply to reiterate this material but, first, to complete the love-freedom dialectic as Barth envisions it. The dialectic supplies us with a critical framework, which is not only licensed by the event of God's self-revelation, but, for that very reason, particularly suited to the development of a descriptive account of the divine perfections. In particular it underscores the fact that God not only calls his people to confess his name but "also requires us to understand and name Him beyond all our insights and ideas as the I who lives and loves in a unique way" (p. 298).

This goal of developing descriptive accounts of the unique fellowship which God manifests among and with his creatures—the work of his freedom in love—will be a constant and critical companion in pursuit of a theological account of divine wrath. To this end we will focus, second, on the relationship between divine freedom, as Barth envisions it *pro nobis* and *in se*, and the variability or richness manifest in the perfection of God's life. In all God is and does, he is uniquely himself, and this encompasses both by right and in actual fact not only the manner in which he has his life and his name exclusively from himself, but also the wonderfully variegated works of drawing near to creation, electing to have fellowship with creatures, reconciling lost sinners, and disposing of sin. In this section, the overall task remains the same: discernment of critical resources both proper to the repetition of God's own self-revelation and instructive for descriptive accounts of God's identity as sovereign Lord.

---

suggest another world, but to determine the sense of the world that does exist" (p. 132). It is theologically meaningful to acknowledge human existence as a necessity of divine *intention* and so a result of the free generosity of the One who in no respect needs creatures but chooses them nonetheless. So too Barth, *Church Dogmatics* II/1, p. 500.

For Barth, an account of the mode of divine lordship is decisively shaped by God's gratuitous decision to create and covenant with a people. Divine freedom indeed denotes that God's living and loving "is absolutely God's own, in no sense dictated to Him from outside and conditioned by no higher necessity than that of His own choosing and deciding, willing and doing" (p. 301). The negative affirmation of "freedom from" is therefore true as far as it goes. God's identity as the One who is perfectly free, however, indicates something more than a capacity to choose unrestrictedly between alternatives or to be utterly unrelated to another outside oneself. In light of God's self revelation, Barth suggests that what needs to be spoken first is the proper sense in which God has his freedom from himself. Freedom is not primarily a measure of power or knowledge one holds over against another, in other words, but primarily and positively it expresses what it means "to be grounded in one's own being, to be determined and moved by oneself" (ibid.).

Significantly—and especially so for our own argument—because God's divinity is *not* exhausted or determined by his relationship to creation, all that God does in and for the economy is a fulfillment of this freedom rather than its abrogation. We have already argued this by means of an exploration of the doctrine of *creatio ex nihilo* and the kind of speech it funds for an account of the transcendent God immanently present to creation. We have argued, in fact, that it is the qualitative ontological distinction between the living God and his creatures that secures for theological discourse the coherence of a claim to redemption. Here we point specifically to Barth's argument, observing in particular his fresh sensitivity to the manner in which this divine freedom means "God must not only be unconditioned but, in the absoluteness in which He sets up this fellowship, He can and will also be conditioned" (p. 303). Where freedom is "followed after" specifically as the unique characteristic of God's life, it articulates not simply creaturely reality as it must be utterly distinguished from the reality of God's life, but also illumines the manner in which God will in all things "begin with Himself" and so "can have and hold communion with this reality . . . in spite of the fact of His utter distinction from it" (p. 304).

This concept of aseity, taken in a rich and textured sense, means first and foremost that, as Father, Son, and Holy Spirit, God "is the One who already has and is in Himself everything which would have to be the object of His creation and causation if He were not He, God" (p. 306). One can affirm on this basis that God has his life not thinly, as if with reference exclusively to another reality outside himself, but he has it from himself richly and primordially as the Son begotten of the Father and as the Spirit who proceeds from the Father and the Son. God's actions *ad extra* and *pro nobis* are not constitutive of this triune life but simply and truly its revelation.

Only in clear recognition of freedom's primary sense is Barth willing to explore the second, derivative manner in which "God is free from all origination, conditioning or determination from without" (p. 307). The focus of his discussion is on the nature of the absoluteness in which God is present to the world. With regard to the particular noetic implications, God is not included in the same "category" with anything that God is not. There is no synthesis possible. Any unity, if it exists, is not "expressed by a higher term embracing God and these other elements" (p. 310). There is no concept of being by which human knowing links naturally to God precisely because there is no divine being which God properly shares either with the cosmos or with his creatures. Thus it is the ontic absoluteness of God, i.e., the manner in which God "stands at an infinite distance from everything else" such that "their being and nature is conditioned" by his, which gives rise to the noetic limitation (p. 311).

The Richness Proper to the Life of Father, Son, and Spirit

Barth argues the forgoing point carefully and patiently because, as he has already hinted, God's genuine presence, his communion and fellowship with creatures, does not constitute an abrogation of freedom, an act of compromise along with the attendant costs of a choice conducted between alternative goods. Fellowship is rather the full manifestation of divine freedom. Barth has been at pains to describe the noncompetitive relationship between Creator and creature in order to attain some purchase on the *variety* proper to God's life. We have drawn this out in some detail in relation to his re-conceptualization of the doctrine of eternity. We turn to it now in the context of his own rationale for the arrangement of the perfections.

To begin with, finite creation neither limits God nor is compromised by the drawing near of the Absolute himself. Rather,

> God has the freedom to be present with that which is not God, to communicate Himself and unite Himself with the other and the other with Himself, in a way which utterly surpasses all that can be effected in regard to reciprocal presence, communion and fellowship between other beings (p. 313).

More specifically, God can create out of nothing and transform the being of his creatures and, at the same time, indwell creation and remain present to it without in either case taking away its life and particularity. The revelation of God in Jesus Christ "embraces all these apparently so diverse and contradictory possibilities. They are all His possibilities" (p. 315). God's act of fellowship with creatures, and specifically the complex interrelationship between the judgment and redemption of creatures bound or dead in their sin, thereby displays a unique freedom. The divine loving is not an emptying of God's freedom but its actuality, and freedom is therefore "the peculiar depth" [*der eigentümlichen Tiefe*] of God's life and love (p. 299 rev.). A focus upon God's freedom, in other words, does not turn one away from the reality of divine love, but rather moves one dialectically into its profundity.[64]

One of the more radical implications of Barth's thought and, so he maintains, of revelation itself is that God is not bound to a definite scheme, "to the *quantum* and *quale* of a certain mode of action [*Aktionsweise*] uniformly proceeding from Him" (p. 315; cf. *Kirchliche Dogmatik* II/1, p. 355). One rightly discerns here an intimation of the manner in which, under each of the divine perfections, Barth will attempt to transcend the classical problem of the one and the many. While God remains always himself, with regard to his history and his eschaton, his people's confession and the inspired testimony of God's church, his communion with angels and the world, the gift of faith for his people, in light of his work of creation, preservation, resurrection, and final judgment, Barth asserts that

> God is sufficiently free to differentiate His presence infinitely [*ins Unendliche*], and decisively [*in entscheidender Weise*], not merely with respect to the variations of the creature, but also in Himself . . . according to the demands of His own intention with regard to the creature (ibid.).[65]

God, in other words, is free to secure fellowship in a multitude of ways, free even to indwell the creature. The aforementioned exemplify God's variegated action *ad extra*.

More radically, Barth suggests that the "whole hierarchy" of God's decrees *ad intra*, those decisions grounded in God's being and will, display a concomitant variety, "the variation of which does not destroy but confirms the oneness of God as a divine unity in contradistinction to the unity of a natural force or spiritual principle" (p. 316). All variation, the "apparently overwhelming richness of distinctions within His being," is grounded, consummated, normed, and made law in the incarnate person of the Eternal Son, Jesus Christ (pp. 316–17). A doctrine of the divine perfections reiterates the manner in which "God is," and because its attentiveness is to God's self-revelation, even as it speaks to a variety of modes of divine perfection

---

[64] Cf. also *Church Dogmatics* II/1, pp. 298, 300, 305. On the basis of God's self-revelation, "He is known in His entirety or He is not known at all" (p. 51). Theological exposition, therefore, will neither broaden nor add to one's knowledge but "will only lead us deeper into just this entirety of His being" (p. 52).

[65] With respect to God's unity, while "the concept of a whole which is indivisible or an indivisible which is whole can certainly be an object and a very natural object of human divining and construction," knowledge of God's unity does not result from either one. Rather, "it is the result of the encounter between man and God, brought about by God," an event which "bears all the marks of that which is incomparable (God's uniqueness) and that which is undivided (His simplicity)"—*Church Dogmatics* II/1, pp. 449f.

and action, it speaks only of the one life of God made visible in Jesus Christ. In light of other arrangements we have thus far considered, this suggests one of the most refreshing and useful features of Barth's reworking of the doctrine. In short, this is a manifestation of the descriptive work to which he is committed, assuming that the possibilities of talk of divine perfection are established by the actualities of God's self-presentation. He argues by means of concrete christological insight rather than general formal distinctions.

With respect to the variety manifest in and for the world, however, Barth will not say that God is consequently richer or more abundant in life. God is not more or other than what he is in himself, precisely because as the triune God, Father, Son, and Spirit, there is already otherness in him. We have already considered this in relation to the eternal movement of God's life. We can now expand this and say that the union of the divine and human in Jesus Christ is the once and for all—and so singular—instance of otherness ad extra, "the possibility of all other possibilities," "the quintessence of all possible relationship and fellowship" (p. 317). This is the freedom genuinely apposite to God's life. Before it, every appeal to God as realiter aliter is challenged as an essentially unserviceable, abstract, and alien description of the God who, Barth writes, like the prodigal son goes his own way into the far country:

> It is in full unity with Himself that He is also—and especially and above all—in Christ, that He becomes a creature, man, flesh, that He enters into our being in contradiction, that He takes upon Himself its consequences.[66]

God in himself does not need the world as a source of otherness; before all worlds and from eternity, he has this in the Son. And yet, "because this is so, the creation and preservation of the world, and relationship and fellowship with it, realized as they are in perfect freedom, without compulsion or necessity, do not signify an alien or contradictory expression of God's being, but a natural, the natural expression of it ad extra" (p. 317).

Barth completes his momentous counter proposal for a doctrine of the divine attributes by creatively mining christological resources, and he does so at that very point—namely in relation to the theme of divine freedom—at which the tradition was inclined to resolve the multiplicity of God's life into its simplicity. On the ground of God's self-revelation in Jesus Christ, as it has been described here, he takes up the distinction between incommunicable and communicable attributes of God, which has broadly characterized Reformed theology and develops its material in a more consistent manner.

---

[66] Barth, Church Dogmatics IV/1, p. 186.

Analysis of the perfections of divine freedom—and so, he will go on to argue, an analysis of God's unity and omnipresence, constancy and omnipotence, eternity and glory—focuses on Jesus Christ in precisely the same manner and for precisely the same reasons as the perfections of the divine loving.

Arguably, at this juncture, Barth's exposition lacks transparency to the role that the Holy Spirit plays in the provision of a multiplicity *ad extra*. In response, one might seek a more robust pneumatology and so a theological solution to the systematic thoroughness with which modernity has deposed particularity, that quality which, as one theologian has argued, enables "the things and people of which our world consists, each in their own way, to serve as vehicles of the praise of God."[67] Particularly the scriptural exposition of part two of this essay will be concerned to attend to both concrete resources for theological reflection: the divine acts of hypostatic union and indwelling. Inextricable as these missions are, "it is hard to know whether it is best to go on describing them as two missions or as a single, twofold mission of the Son and the Spirit."[68]

It would be difficult, nonetheless, to underestimate the importance of Barth's own argument, namely that a search for the identity of God undertaken

---

[67] Colin E. Gunton, *The One, the Three and the Many: God, Creation and the Culture of Modernity* (Cambridge: Cambridge University Press, 1993), p. 73. Gunton argues for a twofold activity of the Spirit. On the one hand, the Spirit relates "beings or realms that are opposed or separate" (p. 181), as suggested by Paul's claim to spiritual presence in bodily absence (1 Cor 5:3) and the redemptive work of adoption (Gal 4:5; Rom 8:15). On the other hand, the Spirit also mediates and strengthens the particularity of God's people, the gifts which the Spirit bestows being the most obvious case in point (cf. 1 Cor 12:7, 11, 18), as well as the integrity of Jesus Christ's human nature: "In his life, death, resurrection and ascension is to be discerned the eschatological action of God the Spirit, who thus perfects Jesus' particular humanity in space and time" (p. 205). This work is underdeveloped in Barth's own theology of the divine perfections. There are indications in the *Church Dogmatics*, however, that Barth was aware of the importance of this material. He writes, for example, that the Holy Spirit is "true, eternal God . . . the communion and self-impartation realised and consisting between both from all eternity; the principle of their mutual love proceeding from both and equal in essence; the eternal reality of their separateness, mutuality, and convolution, of their distinctness and interconnection" (III/1, p. 56). The Spirit's holiness means his purpose is the "setting apart, appropriating and distinguishing" of those who receive it (I/1, p. 450).

[68] Fred Sanders, "The Trinity," *The Oxford Handbook of Systematic Theology*, eds. J.B. Webster, K. Tanner and I.R. Torrance (Oxford: Oxford University Press, 2007), p. 48. "The field of the doctrine of the Trinity," he proposes, "can be plotted within the coordinates of two intersecting axes which trace the dynamics of God's self-giving. The defining axis runs from the immanent life of God to the outward acts of God in creation. The other axis connects the two trinitarian persons who are revealed by their personal presence in the missions of the economy, and is therefore the axis running between the Son and the Holy Spirit" (p. 39).

outside the person and event of Jesus Christ produces only a kind of epistemic darkness or confusion, and thus

> without the key to the whole, even though He is undoubtedly present and we objectively meet Him, we will not find Him as God, nor be able to recognize or praise Him as God, for we will meet Him only in the diversity, in the curious details and puzzling contradictions of His presence (p. 319).

This is, for Barth, the perfection of God's life. God is not in himself a "very slender[,] . . . impoverished and spectral being" whose depth and palpability are realized only in relation to the creature. Nor are his perfections lordless principles or a "collection of mighty potencies" which permeate human life and suggest the presence of divinity (pp. 324–5). Rather this wholeness is God's glory, the actuality of his life lived out from its overflowing depths, and thus in his perfections nothing is heard but God himself.[69] It turns on the inextricable interrelationship between God in his freedom and God in his love, most adequately presented in the form of dialectical exposition, and derived solely from attention to the event of the self-presentation of the triune God. In this, Barth indeed provides an architecture flexible enough to accommodate a rich multiplicity of divine perfection, but he does so without indicating more precisely how certain identity descriptions, i.e., those which assume finite or sinful creatures as their object, may be related to the life which God has from all eternity. In what follows, we will propose one such manner of articulating this relationship. We can transition to the fourth and final section of this chapter by means of a critique of one aspect of the arrangement of the divine perfections, along with its material implications, found in *Church Dogmatics* II/1.

The Finite and Sinful Made Present to God: An Overemphasis

In the architecture of Barth's doctrine a mutual amplification is obtained through a conceptually tight cross-consideration of grace and holiness, on

---

[69] In his characteristically overburdened but unambiguous manner, Barth writes that when the New Testament refers to ἡ δόξα τοῦ θεοῦ, "it refers to the legitimate, effective, and actual self-demonstration, self-expression and self-declaration of a being whose self-revelation is subject to no doubt, criticism or reservation" (p. 642). Christopher R.J. Holmes has recently drawn attention to 'glory' as the summary of the divine perfections. Beyond even Wolf Krötke's remarkable thesis, he observes that in Barth's theology glory entails not merely the perfect clarity of divine self-presentation but that "God's clarity, precisely because it is God's, is also luminous; it radiates and goes forth, establishing, maintaining, and perfecting covenant fellowship with the creature"—cf. "The Theological Function of the Doctrine of the Divine Attributes and the Divine Glory, with Special Reference to Karl Barth and His Reading of the Protestant Orthodox," *Scottish Journal of Theology* 61(2) (2008): 216.

the one hand, and mercy and righteousness, on the other. Each of these four attributes are treated specifically as perfections of the divine loving (though in each pairing, he argues, the latter term strikes a distinct note in favor of divine freedom). Precisely as perfections of the divine loving, however, it is not at all clear how grace and mercy, given their material content, might have their basis in the eternal life of the triune One. Such an exposition, we will argue, should reflect not only the fact that God's act of being himself is primarily and properly a matter of God himself but also that, secondarily and derivatively, God is perfect in his relationship to creation—not merely that relationship in which he lives for and among finite creatures, but in a relationship extended precisely to sinful creatures who rebel against every good gift.

With the first of these two concrete attributes, grace is asserted as that perfection of the divine life which seeks and creates fellowship "by its own free inclination and favour, unconditioned by any merit or claim in the beloved but also unhindered by any unworthiness or opposition in the latter" (p. 353). In this respect, grace is an act of condescension, the turning of "a superior to an inferior" [das eines Höheren zu einem Niedrigeren] (p. 354; cf. Kirchliche Dogmatik II/1, p. 398). It thus bridges a twofold inequality between Creator and creature. Not only will every good be received as a gift—since creaturely life per se does not and cannot merit divine favor—but, more to the point, grace has as its object not only the finite but also the sinful creature, the creature "not only not worthy of it but utterly unworthy" (p. 355). At precisely this point, furthermore, one must be cautious of the interpretive license exercised in the English translation. Barth does not intend in his exposition to speak in any systematically precise sense of a "mode of God's being" or "an inner mode of being in God Himself" (p. 353). The original text signals only that the grace of God toward his creatures is indivisibly the work of his own life, a work which might more accurately be rendered "the [distinctive] being and conduct of God" [das Sein und Sichverhalten Gottes] or "the inner being and conduct of God himself" [ein inneres Sein und Sichverhalten Gottes selber] (cf. Kirchliche Dogmatik II/1, p. 397).

However, Barth not only speaks of grace as being commensurate with God's essence and inmost nature but, more radically and problematically, he speaks unqualifiedly of grace as being identical with God himself. Not only outwardly but "in Himself from eternity to eternity" God is gracious (p. 357). At this point Barth anticipates the objection that God's relationship to something other than himself—whether, we can expand, merely contingent and finite or, more momentously, rebellious—has been made constitutive of the divine life. He concedes that from one perspective there is in God's eternal life and being no creature set over against him, and so no "scope" or possibility of "any special turning" or "condescension" (ibid.). By its very nature, however, the gracious work of God frustrates all such reasoning.

One should expect, on this basis, that grace is no less hidden and incomprehensible in relation to God himself than it is in its enactment towards human beings. While there is from eternity "not yet" any such turning or condescension or any overcoming of opposition, nonetheless the inference suggests itself: because grace "is actually revealed and operative as God's being and action in our midst," the key point is that we can attribute to it no other "sphere and source" than the eternal life of God, the whence of the act in which God becomes to us the grace we know in our midst, even if we know it as an act of overcoming opposition and so as grace "in such a very different form" (pp. 357–8).

The perfection of divine mercy is handled in parallel fashion. Here too, mercy is referred primarily and properly to the life which God has above and prior to creation and redemption. "God's very being [*Sein und Wesen*] is mercy . . . His readiness to share in sympathy the distress of another" (p. 369). Mercy is not simply a new capacity of God, a reaction to creaturely suffering, and so an event in which the good pleasure or sympathies of God are influenced *ab extra*. Mercy, according to Barth, is rather a perfection, which "springs from his inmost nature" such that it lies in his will "to take the initiative Himself for the removal of this distress" (ibid.). In this manner, Barth preserves and secures the truth that God requires nothing for his mercy other than his own free life. The life of Father, Son, and Spirit, lived out in its many perfections, and here especially in its *misericordia*, is neither a mathematical nor mechanical relation but "the movement of the heart of God," the compassion to which, as Barth twice iterates, God is eternally "open, ready, inclined (*propensus*)" (p. 370).

Herein lies the transition—and so the intensification—from a concept of mercy as a fitting and self-sufficient actualization of the divine life to the formal assertion that, for the eternal God, mercy abides. Particularly in entering into conversation with Hermann Cremer, and his inadequate claim that mercy is an attitude merely reflective of divine action *ad extra*, Barth offers a bolder and more tenuous judgment. While it is true that "God finds no suffering in Himself," Barth identifies the scriptural theme of divine σπλάγχνα (e.g. Lk. 1:78 and Phil 1:8) as a key criterion for identifying mercy, as every attribute of God, with God's *aeterna et simplex essentia* (p. 371). In order to secure "the sovereign freedom and power of His mercy," he asserts that God can become merciful toward creation "because He pities in eternity" and therefore "because He has only to call to mind His mercy" (p. 372).

In contrast to these, the wrath of God is not offered by Barth as a topic for discussion in its own right—it is not given its distinct place in the arrangement of the attributes—but rather arises as required in the course of an exposition of certain others of the divine perfections. Parallel to God's mercy, for example, wrath may be spoken of as a divine "affection" in the theologically serviceable sense that, contrary to all creaturely affections, "it originates in [God] Himself" (p. 371). More often, the material relationship between wrath and love is highlighted. Barth argues variously that the blessings which overflow from covenant fellowship necessarily embrace God's anger and struggle against sin, that only in this concrete opposition, in fact, "is God known in His being as love and grace" (p. 362; cf. esp. p. 274).[70] So too Barth is attuned to the material relationship between wrath and righteousness. In this respect, the wrath of God will be presented as the "shadow side" of the revelation of God's righteousness (p. 119; cf. also pp. 121, 168). God's condemnation and punishment of sin, correspondingly, may be consolidated under the notion of wrath enacted "for the sake of His righteousness" (p. 394; cf. pp. 402, 410). In every such case, the material connection is made eminently clear while the formal principle of arrangement remains more or less unstated.

At the outset of our consideration of Barth's arrangement of the divine perfections, we highlighted his determination to see to its culmination a systematic account of the divine life strictly as "a repetition and development of the doctrine of the being of God" (p. 340). We found in his proposal a theology superlatively concerned for the inherent relationship between the material and formal aspects of theology. Not only does Barth think through the divine perfections while keeping in view the living God as the subject matter of his theology, but with unprecedented clarity he allows this material to provide the form for its own presentation. The self-revelation of God as the One who loves in freedom determines how Barth speaks and writes. Nonetheless, and perhaps all the more surprising in light of these achievements, the specific instances of grace and mercy—and, by implication, identity descriptions like wrath—require a greater degree of nuance. A more precise account will preserve both points: first, God himself is their irreducible, primary reference and, second, such descriptions are revelatory of God in the perfection of his presence to finite, sinful creatures.

IV. Modes of Divine Perfection

The burden of chapters 2 and 3 has been to provide a cogent account of the subject matter of the divine perfections, the operational complexity of God's life, and the threefold reference necessary to working descriptively and responsively after God's self-revelation. In examining various arrangements of the perfections, we observed that while the proposal provided in the

---

[70] For further examples: God's "wrath is not separate from but in His love" (p. 363); eliminating wrath within "the contingent reality" in which God encounters creatures correspondingly eliminates his grace and love (p. 366); in the cross of Christ God's grace and mercy are attested with "supreme clarity . . . they encounter us as a divine act of wrath, judgment and punishment" (p. 394); "when it is resisted, [God's] love works itself out as death-dealing wrath"—*Church Dogmatics* IV/1, p. 253; cf. also p. 221.

theology of Francis Turretin is strongly concerned with the triune God of the scriptures as its subject matter, it nonetheless allows general logical distinctions and general organizational patterns to determine the arrangement. The cost, we argued, is that the formal presentation conceals both the inner relationship between the material content of the attributes and the dynamism and richness of its object, and tends by conceptual development to move beyond the *positum*—the scriptures of the Old and New Testaments— which we have argued are at every point indispensable.

We observed, by contrast, that the proposal of Friedrich Schleiermacher achieves an eminently high degree of internal consistency by drawing the formal aspects of the doctrine directly from the material and thus allowing the subject matter itself to determine presentation. The arrangement of the doctrine becomes itself part of the argument, adding cogency to explication as one is guided along a path of inquiry organically fitted to its subject matter. The overall success of this approach, however, is nonetheless contingent upon accurately identifying the subject matter. In relation to Schleiermacher's theology, we argued that the profound coinherence of formal and material aspects is problematized by a misidentification of the subject matter itself. His efforts to move theology outside the realm of speculation suggests, in the final analysis, that God is in fact dependent upon the immediate self-consciousness of the individual, and the corresponding form of presentation, as we have argued, only strengthens certain unserviceable material distinctions between attributes.

A more nearly adequate theology of the divine perfections, by contrast, finds in its subject matter both the material content for the perfections themselves and the form of their presentation. It is the self-presentation of the life of God—eternal and triune—which provides for theology a fitting arrangement. Primarily in the theology of Karl Barth, we find a God irreducibly alive in freedom and love, every available description of his life being a manifestation of God's unending richness and continually new wholeness. Such perfection is identical neither with its significance for human life nor with the potencies proper to creation itself. The perfection of God is rather in every instance the Lord himself providentially and redemptively at work. At the same time, it is not made clear in Barth's theology how grace and mercy—and by implication God's wrath—may be ascribed to God without compromising the freedom of the life which God has from himself as Father, Son, and Holy Spirit. We propose in this final section more precisely to locate wrath among the perfections of God's life.

Two Axes for Thinking through the Divine Perfections

The whole sweep of our argument thus far has turned out to intensify the propriety of every biblical description of God's character. God reveals himself, God witnesses to himself in the Old and New Testament scriptures, and in this witness his perfection is announced and demonstrated to be in every respect *his* from eternity. In particular, we have underscored that God's self-testimony does not bespeak the divine effect in the economy but rather primarily God himself as he is graciously, and so derivatively, at work in and for creaturely life. Thus the complicated but crucial matter of God's wrath.

Rather than ameliorate the tension inherent to its systematic interpretation—either by compromising the consistency and verity in which God himself is revealed in his self-revelation or by attributing wrath by sleight of hand to the inner life of God—we have thus far only heightened the theological conceptual problems. But our argument is positive as well. At the heart of our exposition is the proposal that a doctrine of the divine perfections, in both form and content, has not only to attend to the fullness God has from himself, but correspondingly to describe God, first, in his relation to that which is not God and, second, to give an account of God as he is for and among those creatures who in their willing and acting are *set against* him. A systematic account of divine perfection therefore thinks along two axes.

Thinking the divine perfections along the first axis accommodates the fundamental, asymmetrical distinction between Creator and creature, infinite God as he is present to finite creation. God is recognized as One working, speaking, and alive, but he is such in a manner perfectly fitted to that which is *not* himself. By necessity one must think along this axis—giving an account of God perfectly present to finite (but not fallen) creation—because theology includes both protology and eschatology, the former as an exposition of God's act of calling a good creation out of nothing, the latter as the fulfillment of the kingdom of God. Both doctrines make claims to the divine identity, which do not presuppose sin and rebellion. Both doctrines, moreover, attend to divine perfection by speaking decisively of the life of Jesus Christ, who in all things, and distinct from sinful humanity, knows God in the fullness and untainted perfection of his life and work and manifests that perfection in its fullness. This first distinction may be maintained and developed as a *providential mode* of divine perfection.

Thinking the divine perfections along the second axis accommodates the contingency of God's life as it is lived for and among *sinful* human beings. God creates, but creation rebels. A doctrine of the divine perfections that works responsively from the concrete events of God's self-revelation, therefore, should account for the corresponding distinctions in the mode of God's presence. By necessity, one must think along this axis, not simply on account of the distinction between creaturely knowledge of God (*ectypal*) and God's knowledge of himself (*archetypal*) but, more radically, because the mode of his always self-identical love and freedom corresponds to his will for reconciliation and redemption. This second distinction, to which belongs biblical testimony regarding wrath, may be maintained and developed as a *redemptive mode* of divine perfection.

Wrath, a Mode of God's Righteousness

On the basis of the argument of part one, and in service to the argument of part two, we can pause and state most directly the thesis of this investigation as a whole. In short, what we propose is that a biblical-dogmatic interpretation of God's wrath in the Old and New Testaments is more adequate to the extent that it treats wrath not as a perfection of God per se but rather as a *mode* of divine perfection and, more specifically, as a mode of God's singular *righteousness*. Before addressing two judgments constitutive of this thesis— i.e. the choice of terminology and the decision to focus upon wrath's relationship to the righteousness of God—we can indicate the benefits which this proposal bears for interpretation.

It will become increasingly clear in the scriptural exposition of part two that there is widespread uncertainty among theologians as to how wrath is best situated among the divine perfections. Positions which advocate for strong disjunction—offering the rather thin observation that wrath never forms one of the "permanent"[71] or "essential"[72] attributes of God—often provide little by way of supporting argument. Where reasons for this judgment are tendered, furthermore, theologians are often satisfied with striking some sharp note of contrast. It is argued, for example, that unlike the others of the divine perfections, wrath is "contingent upon human sin,"[73] or that the acts of God "are not in general determined by it,"[74] or that its inclusion among others of the attributes "would require God to instantiate a disobedient creation."[75] Alongside these are more moderate positions. It is claimed, for example, that while wrath is not an attribute of God's life, "neither is wrath 'uncharacteristic' of God,"[76] for it functions in a minimalist but very real capacity within theology as "a footnote to the will to fellowship of the covenant God."[77] Over against these alternatives, it will be the argument of part two that wrath belongs fully to God as a mode of his righteousness. As such, it is not precisely an aspect of the freedom and love in which the

---

[71] Weber, *Foundations of Dogmatics* I, p. 437.

[72] Abraham J. Heschel, *The Prophets* (New York: Harper & Row, 1962), p. 291.

[73] Stephen Travis, "Wrath of God (NT)," *The Anchor Bible Dictionary*, ed. D.N. Freedman, vol. 6 (New York: Doubleday, 1992), p. 997.

[74] Wolfhart Pannenberg, *Systematic Theology*, 3 vols. (Grand Rapids: Eerdmans, 1991), I, p. 439.

[75] Jason J. Ripley, "Covenantal Concepts of Justice and Righteousness, and Catholic-Protestant Reconciliation: Theological Implications and Explorations," *Journal of Ecumenical Studies* 38(1) (2001): 105n37.

[76] H.G.L. Peels, *The Vengeance of God: The Meaning of the Root NQM and the Function of the NQM-Texts in the Context of Divine Revelation in the Old Testament* (Leiden: Brill, 1995), p. 289.

[77] Walther Eichrodt, *Theology of the Old Testament*, 2 vols. (Philadelphia: Westminster Press, 1961), I, p. 262.

one God, Father, Son, and Holy Spirit, knows himself from eternity but an identity description of the God who is fully himself in the work of judging and doing away with sin and rebellion and so in the work of redeeming creatures. The wrath of God therefore requires an account of God *differently present* and not an account of the presence of a *different God*.

For the sake of clarity, we can adduce a number of proscriptions. To begin with, a theological description of wrath as a mode of divine righteousness refuses to locate a diversity of identity descriptions in human knowing alone. Second, the concept obviates recourse to an unreflective and inexact subordination of certain biblical identity descriptions to a presumptuous knowledge of God's "most proper" character. It obviates, third, an illegitimate concept of divine change wherein God is conceived as subject to, as identical with or as the benefactor of an unfolding of new divine potentialities. Fourth, divine attributes should not be classified primarily through an assessment of the frequency or endurance of their expression. Fifth and finally, this manner of accounting for God's wrath stringently protects the fact that wrath per se is not manifested in the perfection of the eternal life of Father, Son, and Holy Spirit.

By way of conclusion, we have finally to address two judgments constitutive of this core thesis. First, we can comment on the specific decision to employ the term "mode." For any theological exposition that works primarily through description, and so is governed by its *positum*, we have argued that concepts are admitted into theological work only as they are filled with their proper content. The term "mode" is subject to this same requirement. We are not appealing uncritically to its normative use, e.g., as denoting a particular variety in which some quality or phenomenon is manifested. Rather we are arguing in light of the requirements that emerge from a careful account of the task of a doctrine of divine perfections that this concept adequately accounts for certain biblical identity descriptions.[78]

Second, our decision to focus upon the specific relationship between wrath and God's righteousness is a carefully measured one. One aspect of the beauty of the doctrine of the divine perfections—at least where it is acknowledged as a *theologia viatorum*—is that, in principle, the perfections themselves may be endlessly brought together for mutual amplification and refinement of theological understanding. In each case, however, because the insight that is yielded multiplies in proportion to the directness of the relationship between the two perfections under consideration, a biblical-dogmatic exposition should choose carefully from among the most compelling options. We can suggest briefly that, though love and holiness are each compelling candidates, the former functions most constructively as one pole in the dialectical architecture of the doctrine of the divine perfections as a whole, while the

---

[78] One might also develop a "form" of divine perfection in a theologically serviceable way.

oppositional work proper to the latter is most fruitfully developed as God's jealousy.[79] Such observations, of course, are only preliminary. The decision to focus upon wrath's relationship to righteousness is one best assessed on the basis of God's self-testimony. We now come to the point of undertaking that which we maintained throughout part one to be irreducibly necessary, namely a close theological exposition of scripture.

---

[79] Requisite to this latter judgment is a reconsideration of divine holiness defined, at least in its derivative moment, by God's will for covenant fellowship. Davis E. Willis argues that "God alone is holy in that utterly unique holiness which wills and makes room and time for the derivative, subordinate, and declarative holiness of creatures"—*Notes on the Holiness of God* (Grand Rapids: Eerdmans, 2002), p. 87. According to John Webster, "The Holiness and Love of God," *Scottish Journal of Theology* 57n3 (2004), holiness is both God's "sheer *difference* . . . identical with his triunity" (pp. 256–257) and that by which he "consecrates creatures for fellowship" (p. 259). By his holiness, writes Barth, God both "distinguishes and maintains His own will as against every other will," and at the same time "He condemns, excludes and annihilates all contradiction and resistance to it"—*Church Dogmatics* II/1, p. 359.

Part Two

In the first part, we proposed an outline for the task of the doctrine of the divine perfections. Arguing that the nature of God's wrath is best clarified within an environment that proceeds according to its own critical criteria, and so analyzes wrath within the larger context of biblical testimony to the character of Father, Son, and Holy Spirit, we distinguished in this task two moments. The first was an identification of the subject matter of the doctrine with the life of the triune God. The second was an exploration of a systematic arrangement for this material and, correspondingly, a clarification of those principles or distinctions by which they are most adequately presented. At each step, the co-inherence of material and formal aspects of the divine attributes featured prominently.

The key contribution of this part was to draw out the biblical logic of wrath as a mode of divine perfection. We argued that God's life does not lack depth and texture but is abundantly rich, a plenitude in itself and an ever variegated source of life which nonetheless is constant in the determination to fulfill fellowship not only with creatures but, most marvelously, with human beings who would resist and overturn the truth, beauty, and goodness of the triune God. In light of the essentially asymmetrical relationship between Creator and creatures, a theology of the divine perfections will be judged adequate, at least in part, to the extent that it accounts for these distinct modes of God's perfection. Ever the same through every change, the identity of God includes his wrath, not as the perduring perfection of the eternal movement in which God has his life, but rather *as a mode* of his righteousness. Throughout the variegated witness of scripture, then, we have only ever to do with the One who in the depth of his freedom and out of the overflow of his love, is revealed in Jesus Christ.

In this second part, we turn theological attention to the consistency with which, in the writings of the Old and New Testaments, God's wrath suggests itself precisely in this relationship to his righteousness. Our argument is that to grasp something of the foundation, pattern, and goal of the outworking of God's wrath is to know God as the Just One.[1] Three distinguishable yet inseparable "moments" in the relationship between wrath and righteousness are present in scripture: first, the unyielding and foundational order of

---

[1] Acts 3.14, 7.52, 22.14; 1 Pet 3.18; 1 Jn 2.1, et al.

generosity established under the judgment of the Lord; second, the pattern of self-sacrifice by which righteousness is fulfilled and covenant renewed; and third, the end of God's wrath, with respect to both the eschatological unity of cross and final judgment and the possibility that wrath serves the spiritual education of the people of God. Through close attention to these events in their divine announcement, space is opened up for appreciating with greater precision and rigor the inner logic of God's character as the One who judges, rejects and brings to futureless ruin all opposition to his grace.

This companion part is not an exhaustive account of God's righteousness.[2] Throughout, our task will be the limited one of unfolding a rich picture of divine wrath. Thus we will take up only those aspects of righteousness, which most fully and irreplaceably provide a window into God's unrelenting opposition to sin. The set of passages under consideration—three from the New and three from the Old Testament—were chosen because, as descriptions of divine righteousness, they individually and together provide indispensable insight into the work of God's wrath as the redemptive mode of God's righteousness. We will argue in chapter 4 that an intertextual reading of the vineyard imagery of Matthew 20.1–16 and Isaiah 5.1–7 speaks provocatively to the unyielding and decisive order of generosity established under the judgment of the Lord. In chapter 5, we will turn to Romans 3.21–26, as a classic text on the matter of the acquittal of the guilty, and argue that it offers rich instruction on the work of God in Jesus Christ as it is read critically alongside Exodus 34.6–7. In chapter 6, we will conclude our analysis of wrath against the backdrop of God's righteousness through a theological reading of Revelation 14.14–20 in concert with the book of Amos, particularly the arresting announcement of Amos 3.2. The interplay between the judgment and death of the sinner and the love of God, which constitutes the goal and fulfillment of prophetic exhortation will figure prominently.

---

[2] For systematic reflection on the righteousness of God, see esp. Alister E. McGrath, *Iustitia Dei: A History of the Christian Doctrine of Justification*. 2 vols. (Cambridge: Cambridge University Press, 1986), pp. 51–70; G.C. Berkouwer, *The Work of Christ* (Grand Rapids: Eerdmans, 1965), pp. 254–294; Karl Barth, *Church Dogmatics* (Edinburgh: T&T Clark), esp. II/1, pp. 375–406, and IV/1, pp. 211–283; Herman Bavinck, *Reformed Dogmatics*, 3 vols. (Grand Rapids: Baker Academic, 2004–2006), II, pp. 221–228, and III, pp. 368–377; and John Owen, "A Dissertation on Divine Justice," *The Works of John Owen*, vol. 10 (Edinburgh: Banner of Truth, 1967): pp. 481–624. From an exegetical perspective, see too Stephen Westerholm's discussion, *Perspectives Old and New on Paul: The "Lutheran" Paul and His Critics* (Grand Rapids: Eerdmans, 2004), pp. 261–296, as well as Simon J. Gathercole, "Justified by Faith, Justified by His Blood: The Evidence of Romans 3.21–24.25," *Justification and Variegated Nomism*, Vol. 2: *The Paradoxes of Paul*, ed. D.A. Carson, P.T. O'Brien and M.A. Seifrid (Grand Rapids: Baker Academic, 2004), pp. 147–184.

These are the scripture passages that will be given sustained attention in the pages which follow. Together they exemplify the broad pattern of theological judgment decisive for a scientific understanding of the place of wrath among the divine perfections. Many other passages could have been chosen, and many were studied in the course of research. While the inclusion of such others would undoubtedly have added depth of insight, such an extensive task is not only unwieldy but also unnecessary insofar as their inclusion would not have substantially altered our own conclusions.

Rather than generate on the basis of criteria determined a priori a body of questions suitable to guide our analysis, the passages themselves will provide us with the topics most profitably to be taken up. At each step, the themes of part one will be present either explicitly or implicitly. The theological exposition which follows, therefore, is not a second project, accountable to a separate set of criteria, but it is a continuation of the constructive, biblical-dogmatic essay on divine wrath begun in part one. Whereas an earlier draft of this project was relatively more content to allow the positive task of theological description to fall neatly into its systematic and exegetical moments, and so to treat them in succession, that effort, because it bespeaks an illegitimate division where only a heuristic distinction should be entertained, was eventually abandoned. The present structure is intended to minimize the repetition of material, demonstrate the wholeness of theological exposition, and so to allow the *positum* of scripture to guide the structure of the argument itself. In each of the three chapters which follow, the goal remains constant, namely to offer a proposal for wrath's place among the perfections of the triune life of God.

4

THE LORD'S VINEYARD AND THE RULE OF HIS GENEROSITY: MATTHEW 20.1–16 AND ISAIAH 5.1–7

The purpose of this chapter is a theological investigation of the relationship between God's righteousness and wrath, particularly as they are manifested in the lordly work of God's gathering to himself a people. The self-revelation of God as the righteous One, we will argue, encompasses at least two moments. In the first instance, God is the one who freely provides every good to creatures, calling them into a particular order of life to live *rightly*—which is to say, in a manner which includes rather than excludes generosity—both before him and toward each other. At the same time, this foundational work opens up toward a decisive act, or acts, in which God does what is worthy of himself precisely by judging sin and sinners, extirpating sin in its incongruity, opposition, and rebelliousness.

A systematic account of the righteousness of God attends to a varied and rich history, to the ever new manner in which God has his life eternally from himself. As we have argued at length, properly considered, its subject matter is the living God and, derivatively, God as he lives for and among his creatures. In righteousness, and especially in the mode of his wrath, because God is no less free than he is loving and no less loving than free, redemption may take a surprising route, and the yield of righteousness among God's people, so to speak, may finally be harvested marvelously in another manner. In this concrete set of events, God remains himself in his perfection and so self-identical in the eminent generosity, which properly belongs to him as Father, Son and Holy Spirit.

The burden of this chapter is therefore to think creatively and delicately through the proposal that God's wrath is most effectively described as a redemptive mode of his righteousness. We will not only highlight the distinctive and promising conceptual benefits but, at the same time, clarify and respond to the questions which the proposal raises. We will begin by considering the biblical image of the vineyard of the Lord as a prophetic interpretation of the relationship between the righteous God and his people, attempting to draw out the depth and complexity with which it is made serviceable as a witness to the identity of God. Second, we will ask after the coherence of this single image in its varying uses, paying particular attention to the relationship between righteousness and the generosity, which is proper to it, on the one hand, and God's wrath as a mode of that same righteousness, on the other. Third and finally, we will identify the unity of this gathering work with the encounter between living Righteousness himself, Jesus Christ, and the people of God.

I. The Image of the Vineyard

The scriptural image of God's people as a vineyard is a complex one, encompassing both of the themes intimated above: primarily, the overwhelming goodness of the announcement that what is *right* includes rather than excludes generosity and, correspondingly, the necessity with which the righteous God is the unremitting boundary and unwavering judgment against sin. The exposition of this chapter will be determined principally by two passages focused on this image. Our way into the subject matter is through the parable of the workers in the vineyard found in Matthew 20.1–16. The passages reads:

> [1]For the kingdom of heaven is like a landowner who went out early in the morning to hire laborers for his vineyard. [2]After agreeing with the laborers for the usual daily wage, he sent them into his vineyard. [3]When he went out about nine o'clock, he saw others standing idle in the marketplace; [4]and he said to them, "You also go into the vineyard, and I will pay you whatever is right." So they went. [5]When he went out again about noon and about three o'clock, he did the same. [6]And about five o'clock he went out and found others standing around; and he said to them, "Why are you standing here idle all day?" [7]They said to him, "Because no one has hired us." He said to them, "You also go into the vineyard." [8]When evening came, the owner of the vineyard said to his manager, "Call the laborers and give them their pay, beginning with the last and then going to the first." [9]When those hired about five o'clock came, each of them received the usual daily wage. [10]Now when the first came, they thought they would receive more; but each of them also received the usual daily wage. [11]And when they received it, they grumbled against the landowner, [12]saying, "These last worked only

one hour, and you have made them equal to us who have borne the burden of the day and the scorching heat." [13]But he replied to one of them, "Friend, I am doing you no wrong; did you not agree with me for the usual daily wage? [14]Take what belongs to you and go; I choose to give to this last the same as I give to you. [15]Am I not allowed to do what I choose with what belongs to me? Or are you envious because I am generous?" [16]So the last will be first, and the first will be last.

The parable at hand likens—Ὁμοία γάρ ἐστιν ἡ βασιλεία τῶν οὐρανῶν— God's act of gathering and ordering the lives of his people to "a landowner who went out in the morning to hire laborers" (20.1). In its larger context, the story is a continuation of Jesus' commentary on the nature of the kingdom of heaven and, more specifically, a reply to and judgment upon Peter's questionable concern for his own position and status relative the other disciples (19.27).[1] He—and all hearers—are warned in light of the generosity of God's rule against drawing distinctions of value, position, and contribution within Christ's church. For the purposes of our study, what is most compelling is the parable's basic concern for God's identity and character as he acts toward and for creation by his radical grace. The generosity of God's righteousness, in fact, is the central point of the narrative.[2]

---

[1] Cf. also Mt 13.24, 31, 33, 44, 45, and 47; as well as 18.23; 22.2; 25.1. I am grateful to Katherine Sonderegger for pointing out the pointedly supercessionist interpretation that this passage has elicited, particularly among ancient commentators. Though the larger pericope to which Mt 20.1–16 belongs addresses the life of discipleship (cf. 16.21– 20.34), and not a final reckoning with and judgment of Israel (cf. 21.1–25.46), nevertheless the passage does lend itself either to a contrast between "law people" and "gospel people" or to an identification of "the last" with the disciples who will "be first" precisely as those who judge the twelve tribes of Israel (cf. 19.28). On these, see Ulrich Luz, *Matthew 8–20: A Commentary* (Minneapolis: Fortress Press, 2001), p. 528, and *The Theology of the Gospel of Matthew*, trans. J.B. Robinson (Cambridge: Cambridge University Press, 1995), p. 112. Equally significant, interpretation among ancient exegetes often followed an allegorical route, taking up the landowner's five trips as commentary on salvation history, a history which culminates in the mission to the Gentiles—cf. J.M. Tevel, "The Labourers in the Vineyard: The Exegesis of Matthew 20.1–7 in the Early Church," *Vigiliae Christianae* 46 (1992): esp. pp. 362–369. Seeking a finer point on the polemic, finally, Scot McKnight suggests that the "anti-nonmessianic Judaism" found in Matthew reflects the tradition of the prophets, denouncing every rejection of Jesus Christ as disobedience to God, leading finally to "the withdrawal of the national privilege of the Jewish people (21.43; 23.1–25.46)"—cf. "A Loyal Critic: Matthew's Polemic with Judaism in Theological Perspective," in *Anti-Semitism and Early Christianity: Issues of Polemic and Faith*, eds. C.A. Evans, D.A. Hagner (Minneapolis: Fortress Press, 1993), p. 61. Our own interpretation has followed another route.

[2] This is construed variously as "grace shown to the unworthy"—Donald A. Hagner, *Matthew 14–28* (Dallas: Word Books, 1995), p. 569; as the manner in which "God acts toward us in sheer grace"—Leon Morris, *The Gospel According to Matthew* (Grand

Foreground: Inestimable Righteousness

This parable pivots more precisely on the question of the fairness of a landowner who makes all his workers equal [ἴσους] without regard for distinctions between the quantity or condition of their work. In posing the question this way, it aims at the conversion, *mutatis mutandis*, of one's perceptions of the righteousness which characterizes God's own life.[3] Particularly striking, the narrative does not discourage sympathy for these workers in their malcontent [ἐγόγγυζον[4]]. They have labored longer and under the worst of conditions yet have been paid the same as those who have just arrived and so have enjoyed relative ease. Formally, the legitimacy of the workers' complaint is encapsulated in the everyday notion of a fair wage. Five trips were made to the market to recruit them. The first group was promised "the usual daily wage" [ἐκ δηναρίου τὴν ἡμέρα]. The second, third, and fourth groups were promised "whatever is right" [ὃ ἐὰν ᾖ δίκαιον δώσω ὑμῖν]. No mention was made of the pay which the fifth and final group would receive.

Rapids: Eerdmans, 1992), p. 499; and as "God's way of reigning in grace"—Arland J. Hultgren, *The Parables of Jesus* (Grand Rapids; Eerdmans, 2000), p. 35. Compare Frederick D. Bruner's estimation that this parable lies "close to Paul's gospel of *reckoned* or imputed righteousness"— cf. *Matthew: A Commentary, vol. 2: The Churchbook* (Grand Rapids: Eerdmans, 2004), p. 317. The suggestion of a central focus for the parable is not intended, as with Jülicher's *tertium comparationis*, to reduce interpretation to a single, exclusive viewpoint. As Kline Snodgrass has observed, in the last couple decades, "allegory has resurfaced in a much more positive light" (pp. 20–21) such that parables are often acknowledged as bearing layers of meaning. These layers emerge not as the parable is considered in varying contexts but rather as the multiple perspectives within the parable itself are grasped as basic to comprehending the thrust of the narrative. For his summary of this historical development, see "From Allegorizing to Allegorizing: A History of the Interpretation of the Parables of Jesus," *The Challenge of Jesus' Parables*, ed. R.N. Longenecker (Grand Rapids: Eerdmans, 2000), pp. 3–29.

[3] This crisis over equality is paralleled in Acts 11.15–17. In this instance, Peter's defense of Gentile baptism appeals primarily to God's initiative in giving Gentiles the repentance and life which comes through the Holy Spirit (τὴν ἴσην δωρεὰν ἔδωκεν αὐτοῖς ὁ θεός). God is recognized as Giver, who gives himself, through faith in the Lord Jesus Christ, and who cannot therefore be second-guessed in his gratuitous giving. One important difference is that Acts presents us with a cultic distinction between profanity and uncleanness as the criterion of covenant fellowship (cf. 11.2f.). Aside from these instances, the term ἴσους occurs infrequently in the NT and can indicate: consistent testimony (Mk 14.56, 59), equivalent architectural measurements (Rev 21.16), or the essential identity which exists between Jesus Christ and God (Jn 5.18). For an OT parallel, cf. the LXX translation of Gen 18.25.

[4] Cf. Robert H. Gundry, *Matthew: A Commentary on His Handbook for a Mixed Church Under Persecution* (Grand Rapids: Eerdmans, 1994), p. 398, and Morris, *Gospel According to Matthew*, p. 502 n. 14. Both acknowledge that the response turns on discontent and a credible complaint.

At least two consequences can be noted. First, while the message rests on a comparison between extremes, namely what is due the first and last groups of workers, the promise that the intervening groups will receive whatever is right significantly raises the tension by validating the expectation of equal pay for equal work. Second, we are told that those hired last had been "standing idle all day" [ἑστήκατε ὅλην τὴν ἡμέραν ἀργοί].[5] Nothing about the language itself compels us necessarily to understand this phrase as chastisement or condemnation of idleness. At the same time, however, the distinction most certainly underscores the discrepancy in merit existing between those who began early and those who came only at the close of the day. Both affirmations, set together within the flow of the narrative, make ripe the affirmation of a mundane order of justice, which has as its goal the drawing of accurate, fair distinctions between individuals and their work. As a result, human judgment is operating in anticipation of a false climax, and the character of God in his righteousness has been made the central issue.

With this point in mind, one may briefly consider how presuppositions concerning the content of justice affect interpretation, and so ask finally about the conceptual background to the parable. Justice summarized as "the constant and perpetual wish to render each one what is due (*ius*)," for example, should it be assumed as the measure or criterion of biblical righteousness, would lead one into a very specific interpretation. It is beyond the scope of our study to draw out in any historic detail the applications and sources of this notion as they are found, for example, in the seminal writings of Justinian I (483–565) or the third century Roman *praefectus praetoria*, Ulpian.[6] Sufficient to our argument is the core insight that justice, at least on the classical model, is the practice of rendering good for good, and evil (i.e., punishment) for evil. Any alteration of the terms thus necessitates an alteration of the judgment. A return of evil for good, for example, is not an act of justice but one of malice just as, inversely, a return of good for evil

---

[5] Though in relation to 19.28 Gundry concludes that the latecomers must be Gentiles, cf. ibid., p. 399, it is at best an educated guess.

[6] For a moral-theological analysis, consult Oliver O'Donovan's 2003 Bampton Lectures, published as *The Ways of Judgment* (Grand Rapids: Eerdmans, 2005). He suggests three broad and intersecting uses of the term 'justice' in western Christian discourse: (1) the Roman juristic sense of justice-as-right (*ius*) indicating a state of moral equilibrium between parties which, he writes, would be applicable to the social harmony of the Garden of Eden, (2) the Platonic and Aristotelian understanding of justice-as-virtue, the moral ordering of the individual soul on account of which one is disposed toward rendering to another what is due, either as "special" justice, i.e., as one virtue among many, or as "general" justice, i.e., as "the sum of all virtues," which is also called righteousness, and finally (3) justice-as-judgment, the scriptural demand for justice as an "effective performance . . . which sets wrong right" (pp. 6f.). Further: Nicholas Wolterstorff, "Justice of God," *For Faith and Clarity: Philosophical Contributions to Christian Theology*, ed. J.K. Beilby, (Grand Rapids: Baker Academic, 2006), pp. 190ff.

constitutes every act of mercy. Vital here is that, considered strictly under the classical model, acts of malice or mercy are not in and of themselves *just* acts. It may be emphasized with regard to mercy that relinquishing a right to retribution or compensation for ill unjustly suffered does not, no matter how honorable or virtuous the act should be regarded, constitute an act of justice. Reckoning it as such is simply a category mistake.

We are pursuing this point because, where this understanding of justice is made the critical lens through which scripture is to be read and understood, God's righteousness is rendered "a principle of compensation, of retribution . . . [and so] something explicitly formal, virtually functional."[7] Under this conception, God himself can only be recognized alternately—rather than simultaneously—as perfect in justice and abounding in mercy. The divine perfections tend, in this way, to become the product of moral evaluation of specific, concrete acts, and lost is the coherent and cogent manner in which God's self-revelation speaks to the unity of God's abundantly full life. Close to hand, in fact, is a formalization of the *injustice* of God's generosity. Seductive and intuitive as such a comparison might initially be, therefore, another option presents itself from within the scriptures of the Old and New Testaments as the actual background to this parable. This reading is at once more difficult and more compelling.

Background: Just and Severe Judgment

Most appropriate, in other words, is the original and startling image from the *Song of the Vineyard* in Isaiah 5.1–7. The text reads in full:

> [1]Let me sing for my beloved my love-song concerning his vineyard: My beloved had a vineyard on a very fertile hill. [2]He dug it and cleared it of stones, and planted it with choice vines; he built a watchtower in the midst of it, and hewed out a wine vat in it; he expected it to yield grapes, but it yielded wild grapes. [3]And now, inhabitants of Jerusalem and people of Judah, judge between me and my vineyard. [4]What more was there to do for my vineyard that I have not done in it? When I expected it to yield grapes, why did it yield wild grapes? [5]And now I will tell you what I will do to my vineyard. I will remove its hedge, and it shall be devoured; I will break down its wall, and it shall be

---

[7] Otto Weber, *Foundations of Dogmatics*, 2 vols., trans. D.L. Guder (Grand Rapids: Eerdmans, 1981), I, p. 429. Scott Bader-Saye, "Violence, Reconciliation and the Justice of God," *Cross Currents* 52(4) (2003), judges that it "simply fails as a Christian formulation . . . We worship a God . . . who gives us not what is due to us but rather what is good for us . . . [A]ll justice must be restorative justice" (p. 539). For examples of the critical engagement of Christians with the classical inheritance, see McGrath, *Iustitia Dei* I, p. 54.

trampled down. [6]I will make it a waste; it shall not be pruned or hoed, and it shall be overgrown with briers and thorns; I will also command the clouds that they rain no rain upon it. [7]For the vineyard of the LORD of hosts is the house of Israel, and the people of Judah are his pleasant planting; he expected justice, but saw bloodshed; righteousness, but heard a cry!

This passage constitutes the original instance of vineyard imagery in the tradition of the Hebrew prophets. It offers a picture of inexplicable failure—through the juxtaposition of the matchless care a vineyard has received and its offensive yield—and its consequent destruction. Insight into the force and content of Jesus' own parable, as well as an exposition of the relationship between wrath and righteousness, is aided by careful consideration of this more ancient pronouncement.

Though these two passages may be read alongside one another simply on the basis of their respective places within the canon, there is between them a particularly strong convergence of themes. Indeed, it is this distinct "echo," which is so evocative.[8] The seven verses from Isaiah, not unlike their later Matthean counterparts, unfold in an eminently complex movement of calling, provision, patience, raised expectations, failure, and startling judgment. Whereas both passages center upon the nature of God's judgment and the maintenance of his righteousness, as prophecy, the *Song of the Vineyard* lays bare the truth of the source and purpose of the concrete destruction leveled upon an obstinately unrighteous and corrupted people.[9]

The parable from Isaiah is therefore embedded in the whole sweep of God's providential and redemptive ways. Its reference is not a generally applicable truth of human life but a distinct episode, or set of episodes, in which the righteous God is present to his unrighteous people in the mode of

---

[8] "Echoes" are substantive *allusions* or *recollections* generated on the basis of a single, dominant subtext—in this case, Isaiah 5. The discipline of intertextual reading, as "the study of the semiotic matrix within which a text's acts of signification occur" (p. 15), is detailed in Richard B. Hays' seminal work, *Echoes of Scripture in the Letters of Paul* (New Haven: Yale University Press), 1989. He develops seven criteria by which to assess such claims: availability, volume, recurrence, thematic coherence, historical plausibility, history of interpretation, and satisfaction (pp. 29–32). Compare also Ps 1.3, Jer 12.10, the extended discourse at Jn 15.1–11, and the structural repetition at Mt 21.33–46. The thematic correspondence between "fruits yielded at harvest time" and "works of justice" is well documented; cf. M. Eugene Boring, *The Gospel of Matthew* (Nashville: Abingdon, 1994), p. 414 and Gundry, *Matthew: A Commentary*, p. 425.

[9] A prophetic interpretation of the events as *divine* judgment would be required even in the context of the minority view, namely that the passage is to be read in total as "a retrospective *theology of history*" and so as a commentary on what the Lord had *already* done rather than would do—Otto Kaiser, *Isaiah 1–12: A Commentary* (London: SCM Press, 1983), p. 93.

his wrath. The larger context of the parable is therefore indispensable: in their unrighteousness, the people of God have nurtured insatiable appetites for wealth; they have hoarded property and driven the poor from the land (5.8); they have traded the origin of their life together, their election from among all the nations, for the pursuit of self-indulgence and fleeting pleasures (5.11f.); and they have capitulated to bribery and twisted the law such that it no longer protects the innocent but rather serves as an instrument of suffering (5.23).

The anger of the Lord [אַף יְהוָה] will not attenuate in the face of such persistent rebellion (5.25). God is rather present and unyielding as the guarantee of what is *right*, as is made abundantly clear in the repetition of the hendiadys[10] of justice and righteousness:

> People are bowed down, everyone is brought low, and the eyes of the haughty are humbled. But the Lord of hosts is exalted by justice [בַּמִּשְׁפָּט וַיִּגְבַּה], and the Holy God shows himself holy by righteousness [בִּצְדָקָה נִקְדָּשׁ] (5.15f.).

We will return below to the significance of the parable's distinctly juridical language and themes. Presently, one may note that at least two accounts of the exercise of God's wrath are distinguishable: that which the people have suffered and that which is to come.[11] When Isaiah summarizes the former as a complete act, he carefully binds Judge and judgment. The Lord "stretched out his hand against them and struck them; the mountains quaked and their corpses were like refuse in the streets" (5.25). This is the first instance of potent judgment found in chapter 5.

Nonetheless, in his wrath, God has not yet found his end. The people remain unrepentant, and so it is announced subsequently that God's wrath will fold over on itself and intensify in a second and decisive act. In the envisaged event, the Lord will "raise a signal for a nation far away" and appoint them as an instrument of his justice.

---

[10] "Justice and righteousness" signifies in Isaiah both "the nature of the king's reign as a time of the upright ordering of Judah's life . . . and that the whole situation in which these qualities are to be realized is ascribed to the initiative of God, [such that] Israel is to embody those moral qualities which characterize YHWH himself"— R.W.L. Moberly, "Whose Justice? Which Righteousness? The Interpretation of Isaiah 5.16," *Vetus Testamentum* 51(1) (2001): 62–63. Similarly, Carl Graesser, "Righteousness, Human and Divine," *Currents in Theology and Mission* 10 (1983): "God's action of rescuing the one in need often also involves a punishment or defeat of the oppressor or the enemy" (pp. 138–139).

[11] Brevard S. Childs, *Isaiah* (Louisville: Westminster John Knox Press, 2001), p. 48. Edward J. Young writes that Isa 5.25 "would seem to include all the past judgments of God, judgments which had been sent in order to turn the nation from its sins"—cf. *The Book of Isaiah*, vol. 1 (Grand Rapids: Eerdmans, 1965), pp. 225–256.

Here they come, swiftly, speedily! . . . Their arrows are sharp, all their bows bent, their horses' hoofs seem like flint, and their wheels like the whirlwind. Their roaring is like a lion, like young lions they roar; they growl and seize their prey, they carry it off, and no one can rescue. They will roar over it on that day, like the roaring of the sea. And if one look to the land—only darkness and distress . . . (5.26–30).

Under God's judgment, an irredeemably corrupt people will not merely be *taken* but rather they will be *given* into exile for their sin, and thus denied king, temple and land.

This concrete historical context must be recounted in a theological interpretation of the passage because it is specifically to this history that the *Song of the Vineyard* refers. As a parable it unveils the true nature of these events, attributing the unremitting judgment, which the people of Judah have already suffered, as well as the impending intensification of wrath, exclusively to the righteous God. An analysis of Isaiah 5.1–7, therefore, is inextricably bound to the larger context of the prophecy. Setting aside, at least for now, a more exhaustive analysis of the components of the parable itself, we can specify more fully the theological significance of the link between the image, on the one hand, and the history we have just summarized, on the other.

The chapter as a whole presupposes that it is not events per se, whether national suffering or foreign invasion, which are constitutive of God's self-revelation, but rather that God is known only by these concrete events in their divine self-interpretation. The parable unveils this very connection. Just as the propriety of a vineyard's destruction (5.5–6) is conveyed through the juxtaposition of the great care a vineyard owner provides to his land, on the one hand, and the abject failure of the vineyard itself, on the other (5.1–4), in the very same manner the wrath of God is rightly executed upon God's obstinately unrighteous people (5.7). At its very darkest, the vineyard is therefore "a setting for the funeral of a nation and its people who had once held such great promise as the chosen and nurtured people of God."[12]

At least two important implications attend. Positively speaking, the unveiling of God alive in this history underscores the necessarily gracious character of all knowledge of God, i.e., that knowledge of God in his perfection is in every respect dependent both upon God's speaking and upon his causing himself to be heard. It also distinguishes divine action, as the true subject matter of this parable, from any mythological account of the source and significance of human suffering as well as from every appeal to an unnamable principle of judgment or force separable from the presence of God himself. Even in the most severe and extreme acts, God does not recede

---

[12] John D.W. Watts, *Isaiah 1–33* (Waco: Word Books, 1985), 56; cf. Childs, *Isaiah*, p. 49.

behind talk of either the righteousness or the wrath, which belongs to his perfection.

The fact that this concrete history—events of divine judgment culminating in a devastating act of dissolution—lies behind the image which Jesus himself invokes, raises a number of critical questions concerning the being and perfection of God. We argued above that, in Matthew's parable, reason is led to operate in anticipation of a false climax, eliciting the expectation of a mundane order of justice in which God will grant goods to his people in direct proportion to their labor. This interpretation, we can now add, would seem to be validated by the unremitting demand for obedience and the severe judgment included in the background of the image of the vineyard.

II. The Righteousness of God: Self-Identical in Every Mode

When all the workers of Jesus' parable are finally paid equally, however, the explanation of the result is even more startling than the result itself. The explanation proscribes dismissing the result either as a fluke or as a simple oversight. With the landowner's twofold assertion of what he wishes or desires [θέλω, Mt 20.14] and of that which he has the right to do [ἔξεστίν, Mt 20.15], not only are we drawn away from something like a classical understanding of justice but likewise there is overturned the lingering suspicion, or perhaps fear, that human obstinacy may have the last word vis-à-vis God's electing grace. The peculiar suggestion in the parable is that the righteousness in which God rules his kingdom, "creating good out of evil,"[13] inverts rather than undergirds the values and presuppositions of even the most honorable of secular orders, settling in the final analysis upon the sovereign freedom of God's love. With the assertion of the owner's wish and right, the narrative crosses over from the mundane and banal to what is controversial and provocative, and uncovers finally the nature of redemption itself. We can examine more closely these two assertions of God's wish and his right as found in Matthew's parable.

On the one hand, the owner's assertion of *what he wishes* acknowledges the genuine differences between the labor of individuals, while simultaneously refusing to capitulate to a normative judgment of what each worker deserves in return. Attention is drawn decisively to the character of the one who owns the vineyard, and so to God, highlighting not the merit of the workers but the depth and texture of divine righteousness. Up to this point, the owner of the vineyard had spoken only to gather his workers. Now the

---

[13] Karl Barth, *Church Dogmatics* II/1, ed. G.W. Bromiley, T.F. Torrance (Edinburgh: T&T Clark, 1957), p. 380.

tenor of his voice changes. He responds to complaints, "as a superior to a subordinate who is in the wrong,"[14] by unapologetically affirming the generosity, which characterizes his dealings with others. This aspect of his character, in fact, is foreshadowed from the outset. The content of the land owner's desire is seen initially in the care with which he goes personally, frequently, and up to the last hour to recruit workers.[15] It is also intimated, as Donald Hagner has observed, in his hiring specifically those—much like the tax collectors and harlots invited into the kingdom by Jesus—who are "regarded as undesirable by others."[16] Divine judgment includes an abounding generosity and the provision of all that is necessary for the fulfillment of righteousness. Interpreting the passage in this manner therefore recommends an equally compelling solution to the problematic of Matthew 19.25, namely "who can be saved" when such a weighty demand for righteousness is placed upon human life. In response, this parable connects the message that "all things are possible" for God with the claim that God is in himself one whose estimation of what is just includes rather than contradicts his mercy and grace. The assertion of God's desire does not stand alone, however.

There is, on the other hand, *the right* through which God acts and so through which his desire is conditioned. God gathers his people and administers his goods not through a capriciousness or by the indulgence of whim; nor does God act because compelled by another. More accurately, the determination itself corresponds to who he is, as the one to whom all things belong and who is, in his very substance, abounding grace. We can highlight, to begin with, the manner in which the parable itself makes this point. The owner of the vineyard presides much like a king over his land. He is the one to whom the land belongs. He determines the work to be done, and chooses those who will do it. Most significantly, because his prerogative determines entirely the grounds upon which workers will be hired, where the giving and receiving of his goods is at issue, the only judgment which matters is his own. Linking this back to the previous point, there is in the parable no other suggested foundation for God's wish than this right, and so it would seem there can be no other justification for his generosity than the fact, simply, that he is the one who gives. We can also set this claim in more formal terms.

---

[14] Boring, *Matthew*, p. 394 n. 449, points to this idiomatic sense of the vocative ἑταῖρε. The word "does not mean 'friend' in the personal sense. It is more like 'mister' when used pointedly without a name." Interestingly, the two other occurrences refer first to those who entered illicitly into the great banquet (22.12), and secondly to Judas (26.50). So too Gundry, *Matthew: A Commentary*, p. 398, and Morris, *Gospel According to Matthew*, p. 503.

[15] Cf. Bruner, *Churchbook*, p. 318; and Boring, *Matthew*, p. 393.

[16] Hagner, *Matthew 14–28*, p. 571.

Perfect Identity of Lord, Law, and Judge

At least three lines of reasoning converge on the fact that consolidating the character of God under a general, legal conceptuality elides the necessarily asymmetrical relationship between human and divine justice. First, both law and judge are identical with the righteous God. An account of the right order, which generosity constitutes for human beings, is neither baseless nor an original product of God's creative act, nor is it a function of an abstractly free will. Were the rule of God's acting not identical with God himself, were it not *right* as the constant maintenance of what is worthy of God from and in his perfection, we would be faced either with the crude notion of a second god, a principle or agent more determinative of God's being than his own perfection, or, as we observed above, we would be faced with the capriciousness of a tyrant.

The solution to these conceptual problems, and the more provocative reading of the scriptural witness, rests in the refusal to divide Judge and law. Righteousness among human beings is rooted in the perfection of God's own life. The claim of God upon creation in its entirety—not only to deal with it in righteousness but correspondingly to have his justice reflected in all its parts and relations—is a divine right precisely because it is "above all grounded in God's nature."[17] God rules as he does because it corresponds to who he is, or better because it *is* who he is, the promised One (Isa 9.6f.), a ruler enthroned in righteousness and justice (Ps 97.2).

It is thus in light of God's utter self-sufficiency and in the plentitude of his own life that the irreversible claim is made: "God is in Himself the law and therefore righteous."[18] The point is well ensconced in Reformed theology. It guides the distinction between, on the one hand, the abstract concept of the "absolute dominion" of the divine will and, on the other, the actual law and right which is grounded in God's "goodness and grace" and so "in the nature of God himself."[19] This identity between Judge and law is also at work in the appeal to the "perfection, eminence, and holiness of God," which lie "naturally antecedent to the divine will" as the limit of all God's commanding and acting.[20]

Second, this means that in every case God's people understand themselves as present to the Electing One, Majesty in perfect presence. Judgment is not

---

[17] Bavinck, *Reformed Dogmatics* III, p. 375.
[18] Barth, *Church Dogmatics* II/1, p. 379. For further references in *Church Dogmatics* IV/1 to the asymmetry between God's proper and God's derivative righteousness: because God is "Himself the origin and basis and revealer of all true law, He is just in Himself" (pp. 530–531); God's love of righteousness as expressed in Psalm 11.7, is "an ontological statement" (p. 531); ". . . the right of God over and to man is grounded in the inward right of His Godhead" (p. 536).
[19] Bavinck, *Reformed Dogmatics* II, pp. 227–228, and III, p. 373.
[20] Turretin, *Institutes of Elenctic Theology*, XI.ii.5.

subjection to cosmic principles, blind moral forces, or the ineluctability of fate. It is rather a matter of remaining constantly in the hands of the righteous God, whether this is actualized now under the mode of generous provision or again under the mode of God's wrathful judgment. Corresponding to this, and just as significant, there is no real distinction to be made between a creaturely act of disobedience and an act of violation against the Judge himself. God is perfect in his judgment and, at the same time, with respect to the antithesis between himself and the sinner, who would assert her own right and so choose to be a god, "he himself is always the offended party."[21] Thus the incoherence of the claim that certain acts of judgment reveal "a God who is far more touchy about personal insults than about subversion of legal systems."[22] Precisely because sin contradicts God in his perfection, the salvation of the sinner and so the disposing of sin itself can only mean that God does this by doing right by himself.

Returning to the image of the vineyard, the negative confrontation is merely hinted at in Matthew 20.14–15, where the grumblings of the workers are met with both an authoritative dismissal (ὕπαγε) and a judgment upon their corrupt motives, as encapsulated in the idiomatic acknowledgment of their envy, ὁ ὀφθαλμός σου πονηρός ἐστιν. Clear at this point, the confrontation is much more direct in the Isaianic announcement of judgment, "and now I will tell you what I will do to my vineyard" (Isa 5.5). The identity of the one before whom the people stand is well established. He is the Lord of hosts before whom a creature of "unclean lips" can no longer assert rights or argue for justification but only cry, "I am lost!" (Isa 6.5). He is the uncompromisingly righteous God who measures sin, whose eyes are "too pure to behold evil" [טְהוֹר עֵינַיִם מֵרְאוֹת רָע] (Hab 1.13). He will not forgive rebellion (Josh 24.19), and "by no means will he acquit" [לֹא יְנַקֶּה] the guilty (Ex 34.5–7; 23.7). God will not stand at a distance from sin, nor seek a middle ground or an equitable resolution.

The Moral Intelligibility of God's Wrath

A juxtaposition of these two passages raises the crucial question as to whether, in fact, the execution of wrath and righteousness do not conflict, whether in attention to God's radical judgment one must leave the sphere of his singular righteousness and conclude, correspondingly, that the victory of

---

[21] D.A. Carson, "The Wrath of God," *Engaging the Doctrine of God: Contemporary Protestant Perspectives*, ed. B.L. McCormack (Grand Rapids: Baker Academic, 2008), p. 45.

[22] Marti J. Steussy, "The Problematic God of Samuel," *Shall Not the Judge of all the Earth do what is Right?: Studies on the Nature of God in Tribute to James L. Crenshaw*, eds. D. Penchansky and P.L. Redditt (Winona Lake: Eisenbrauns, 2000), p. 143. His examples are 1 Sam 3.13 and 8.3.

God's generosity can only be understood as the antithesis of justice. This criticism, a question of the utmost importance to a theology of the divine perfections, may press in at least two distinct directions.

On the one hand, one might argue that where wrath denotes an essentially irrational act of God analogous to a movement of human passion, it demonstrates that the Just One himself is nonetheless subject in his righteousness to external influence and instability. On the other hand, one might argue that righteousness is equally forfeit insofar as wrath denotes exclusively an act of destruction. The superabundance, which God deems right, would in this latter sense be reduced to a wholly tentative matter, strictly contingent on creaturely obedience. The core premise in each criticism is that the foregoing exposition—which argues that the subject matter of both Matthew 20 and Isaiah 5 is the self-same God, both now in his righteousness and again in wrath as the mode of his righteous perfection—moves hastily and unjustifiably from certain concrete divine decisions and biblical language to a unity articulable in terms of a legal motif. Both objections appeal to internal contradiction and, in this section and the section which follows, we will address each in turn—the former as it denies the moral intelligibility of God's wrath, the latter as it isolates wrath as an end in itself.

The first critique, to begin with, accounts for God's wrath in terms of an irrational capacity, "a side of God"—with all the self-contradiction and unpredictability that this connotes—as it is manifested in covenant history. This potentiality and passion, it is claimed, elicits dread and deepest fear. Wrath comes "withering and blasting the rash intruder or those who . . . approach the presence without due preparation, such as spells, fasting, or purification."[23] More pointedly, it has been argued that the exercise of divine wrath involves "no concern whatever with moral qualities . . . [It is] like stored-up electricity, discharging itself upon anyone who comes too near."[24] Where this is claimed in relation to the severity of *The Song of the Vineyard*, however, a number of interpretive problems present themselves.

Close attention to the structure of the song suggests a thoroughly legal confrontation, a measured act in which God calls his people to account for

---

[23] Lewis Richard Farnell, *The Attributes of God* (Oxford: The Clarendon Press, 1925), p. 187.

[24] Rudolf Otto, *The Idea of the Holy: An Inquiry into the Non-Rational Factor in the Idea of the Divine and its Relation to the Rational* (London: Oxford University Press, 1958), p. 18. To speak of God's wrath is therefore to speak of "something supra-rational [which] throbs and gleams, palpable and visible" (p. 19). Apart from a framework of moral intelligibility, "genuinely cognizing and recognizing the holy in its appearances" (p. 144) will depend upon a *faculty of divination* identical with "a direct, first-hand apprehension" or "an intuition and feeling" (p. 155). Cf. the analysis of John Macquarrie, *Twentieth-Century Religious Thought: The Frontiers of Philosophy and Theology, 1900–1960* (London: SCM Press, 1963), p. 214.

their gross inadequacies. Though the passage does not straightforwardly address the operative injunction, evidence, and verdict, each of these elements is distinctly present. Over the course of these verses, a trial takes place (cf. also 3.13). To begin with, the whole of the parable stands under the clear expectation that—consonant with the initial call to "seek justice, rescue the oppressed, defend the orphan, plead for the widow" (1.17)—God's people yield in their midst the justice and righteousness God wills (5.2; cf. 5.4, 7). By design, the moral force of the expectation is not immediately apparent. The call is conveyed in such beauty, in testimony to unqualified provision, that the fulfillment of righteousness suggests itself as beyond doubt. The requirement, in other words, is overshadowed by the generosity of the One who demands. Through the blending of betrothal and vineyard imagery, the song praises the love and fidelity, which an unnamed cultivator shows for his land. Through tender care and at great personal cost, obstructions have been removed, choice materials used throughout the building process, and the owner himself has remained providentially present and at watch (5.1f.).

A few observations follow. First, the parable is in this regard a statement as much on the character of the One in authority as on that which he demands or the ones from whom it is demanded. As with analysis of any of the divine perfections, in fact, so here too it is only on the basis of God as he is alive in his righteousness that one may and must go on to speak of that "very particular form of life that ought to take shape in correspondence."[25] Second, the suggestion that in and with such moral injunctions God provides everything necessary for the flourishing of his people is of decisive importance. In moving between Isaiah and Matthew, one does not move outside the bounds of the self-identical righteousness of God. The movement between passages is not a transition from wrath to graciousness, judgment to generosity, the God of Abraham to the God of Jesus. Unrestricted generosity underlies Isaiah's song. Third, only an abundance of life, a vintage of the highest quality (5.3), can be attributed to the foundation God provides for the life of his people. In fact, precisely because the call to righteousness includes in itself the means to its fulfillment—precisely because the one who demands righteousness is Righteousness itself—in every respect theological reasoning is led to work *once again* in anticipation of a specific outcome, though this time in anticipation of the total fulfillment of righteousness.

Immediately, however, there is a dramatic shift in tenor in which the people of Judah themselves are called as witnesses to judge this as-yet-unidentified vineyard. And the evidence put forward, the concrete result, is decisive. Contrary to every expectation, the vineyard has produced

---

[25] Christopher R.J. Holmes, "The Theological Function of the Doctrine of the Divine Attributes and the Divine Glory, with Special Reference to Karl Barth and his Reading of the Protestant Orthodox," *Scottish Journal of Theology* 61(2) (2008): 207.

nothing delicious. It has produced neither grapes of poor quality nor even merely inedible grapes. Rather its yield is a harvest of "stinking things."[26] This vineyard is Judah, the people of God, and the utter offensiveness and woeful inadequacy of their lives is conveyed brilliantly by the exceptional wordplay of the original. Among them Yahweh had:

> expected justice [מִשְׁפָּט], but saw bloodshed [מִשְׂפָּח];
> righteousness [צְדָקָה], but heard a cry [צְעָקָה] (5.7).

In recognition of their Lord's rightful claim, and in acknowledgement of the actual incongruous results, they arrive at the truth of their own circumstances and futures. As a handful of commentators have helpfully observed, and not unlike the rhetorical reversal of Matthew 20.10, καὶ ἐλθόντες οἱ πρῶτοι, *The Song of the Vineyard* compels its hearers to draw judgment upon themselves in the same forceful manner in which Nathan once confronted David over the poor man's lamb.[27]

Divine judgment and the execution of God's wrath proceed according to this distinct logic. They work not under impulse but in accordance with a full and clear disclosure of the expectations and the evidence, the promise of a fullness of life and the provision of everything which is required for its realization. The undeniable severity of the passage, which Brevard Childs designates a "juridical parable,"[28] is thereby set definitively within the framework of the perfection of divine justice, undercutting the hasty and overly impressionistic conclusion that the wrath manifested therein is an irrational departure from his 'proper' way of being toward his people.[29] To the extent that theological reasoning proceeds from the Christian scriptures as

---

[26] Such is Watts' carefully considered and powerful translation of the obscure Hebrew noun בְּאֻשִׁים—cf. *Isaiah 1–33*, p. 55.

[27] 2 Sam 12.1–15. See Gene M. Tucker, *The Book of Isaiah 1–39* (Nashville: Abingdon Press, 1994), p. 88. So too Christopher R. Seitz, *Isaiah 1–39* (Louisville: John Knox Press, 1993), p. 47; and Watts, *Isaiah 1–33*, p. 56.

[28] Childs, *Isaiah*, p. 46. So too Claus Westermann, *The Parables of Jesus in the Light of the Old Testament* (Edinburgh: T&T Clark, 1990), p. 49.

[29] Similarly, the following prototypical examples have at their base some instance of concrete disobedience set over against morally intelligible divine injunction. For Ex 4.24–26 and the refusal to be circumcised, cf. William Henry Propp, "That Bloody Bridegroom (Exodus iv 24–6)," *Vetus Testamentum* 43(4) (1993): pp. 495–518. For Ezek 18 and 23, where "the clear motivation is infidelity"—Terence E. Fretheim, "Theological Reflections on the Wrath of God in the Old Testament," *Horizons in Biblical Theology* 24(2) (2002): 15 n. 39. And, finally, for the "morally substantiated motive" at work in 2 Sam 6.6–8, cf. especially the summary judgment by Bruce E. Baloian, *Anger in the Old Testament* (New York: Peter Lang, 1992), "[T]he Hebrew mind conceived of Yahweh's wrath as part of His just rulership of the world" (p. 77), as well as his critique of A.T. Hanson (pp. 81–86).

its *positum*—rather than, for example, from a thematizing of profound experience—an interpretation of wrath will be governed by this moral intelligibility.

Furthermore, while the enactment of the righteousness of God is in every respect necessary as the enactment of his own being, the execution of God's wrath is nonetheless derivative of his perfect timing. This crucial point further distinguishes the sphere of divine justice, and so the perfection of God himself, from a generally intuitable concept of what is just. Wrath is not a rash act, but one which is utterly determinate. In chapter 5, we will have occasion to consider this claim in direct relation to the cross of Jesus Christ as an act of divine *patience*. In the present context, we can observe that, given the existence of sin and given the fact that God is none other than he who is essentially righteous, a claim to God's absolute 'freedom' before sin is an abstraction.

God is not free in the sense of a *potentia absoluta* either to deal justly with sin, to turn a blind eye, or to forgive sin by simple force of will. More cogent is John Owen's twofold argument to the effect that, first, because justice in all its modes corresponds to "the very rectitude and perfection"[30] of God himself, where sin is present in reality, God in his wrath will ultimately judge and condemn every sinner.[31] Where righteousness is regarded as an essential divine perfection, attributing to God an antecedent indifference toward sin is nonsensical. A second specification, however, is required. The claim that judgment is necessary is itself thoroughly eschatological: it is determined not by the irreversible sequence of finite time, but in the resources of God's eternity, and so bespeaks that which is *ultimately* necessary. Because wrath is a mode of God's righteous being-in-act, and therefore an act only undertaken in freedom, God is not compelled, so to speak, to act immediately and in every instance but only finally and conclusively with respect to all sin and every sinner, and so in a manner consonant with his nature.[32]

---

[30] Owen, *Dissertation on Divine Justice*, p. 505; also p. 498. Cf. Turretin: Socinians ascribe the egress of justice to the "perfectly free effect of his will" while the orthodox maintain this justice to be an essential property of God which cannot be ascribed solely to his decrees—*Institutes of Elenctic Theology*, III.xix.8–9.

[31] Owen employs the traditional term, "contingent necessity"—cf. ibid., pp. 589, 604–605. Interestingly, he defends here, on the basis of an intellectualist ideal, a matter which five years previous he had refuted on the basis of his own voluntarist leanings. On this shift, see Carl R. Trueman, "John Owen's *Dissertation* on Divine Justice: An Exercise in Christocentric Scholasticism," *Calvin Theological Journal* 33 (1998): 87–103. The relevance for us is Owen's intellectualist conversion: "Goodness and happiness are not arbitrarily dependent on God's will but rooted in his own unchanging being . . . [This] ensures the objective reliability of natural theology and precludes any notion of sin's going unpunished" (pp. 99–101).

[32] Compare ibid., pp. 509–510. See too the claim that justice is not a free act of the divine will but "an essential property requiring in its exercise and egress the intervention of

In Isaiah 5 the necessity, which belongs to God's judgment upon unrighteousness, is included under the fact that the lord of the vineyard not only "expects" results but more specifically that, in light of the fuller meaning of the verb, he acts by 'eagerly looking for' [קָוָה[33]] the production of a fine harvest (5.2, 4) and so, *mutatis mutandis*, God *awaits* fulfillment of righteousness and justice among his people. Thus the lexical breadth commends the patience in which God works and wills. Expectation, evidence, and judgment are thoroughly a function of the time and space God gives for the redemption of his people. This is how the righteous God gathers. We have before us a varied history of God in fellowship with creatures, a history for its variety nonetheless constant in the boundaries and determinations constitutive of God's foundational work of calling to himself a people.

At the same time, one is furnished with little knowledge of the actual pattern of its fulfillment. It may be an utterly surprising act, traveling a completely unforeseen path, the possibility for which there is no scope in creation. To speak of this, however, is to speak of a life unyielding in the maintenance of its own worth and, for that, all the more miraculous as an outworking of God's love in freedom. The triune God may choose to take up this work in a gracious act of passing over sin for a time, dealing with it not on the basis of historical process or in light of the vicissitudes or perceived necessities of creaturely time, but rather out of the resources of his eternity, and so with the advent of τὸ πλήρωμα τοῦ χρόνου (Gal 4.4). By the very fact that God enacts a necessary judgment, yet enacts it in a manner amenable to the whole of his life, God reveals the confluence of his free and necessary action: ὅτι ἐξ αὐτοῦ καὶ δι' αὐτοῦ καὶ εἰς αὐτὸν τὰ πάντα (Rom 11.36). God's confrontation of sin "necessarily comes to expression in the fact that God reacts against it with all his perfections."[34] This coordination of divine will with divine perfection therefore provides the basis for that which Bavinck intends by a "necessity" of action. God always acts

> in harmony with all his attributes . . . And this agreement of the will of God with all his attributes is not coercive, not a restriction for that will, but precisely the true and highest freedom. To will and to act as his holy, wise, almighty, and loving nature itself wants is for God both the highest freedom and the highest necessity.[35]

---

free will, to determine the mode, the time, the degree and the persons upon whom it wills to inflict punishment"—Turretin, *Institutes of Elenctic Theology*, III.xix.18.

[33] See Francis Brown, S.R. Driver, Charles A. Briggs, eds, *The Brown-Driver-Briggs Hebrew and English Lexicon* (Peabody: Hendrickson Publishers, 1999), pp. 875–876.

[34] Bavinck, *Reformed Dogmatics* III, pp. 371–372.

[35] Ibid., p. 371. Emphasis supplied.

God infallibly and with surety judges and destroys sin, while staying true to the flourishing of his righteous order.

For these reasons, an appeal to moral unintelligibility in Isaiah 5 is uncompelling. The history incontestably encompasses a wide variety of action and event, but insofar as God acts always in accordance with his righteousness, any abstract conception of wrath as "a raging indignation" disconnected from the moral intelligibility in which God has his whole life must be contrasted with "the actual and terrible wrath of God which rules [*waltet*] according to God's good-pleasure in the fulfillment of what is from the first his merciful righteousness."[36] Understanding this as God's act of destruction and dispossession, therefore, means decisively situating this happening not within the general cosmic movement but properly within the lordly and good work of the eternal God.

The Restoration of Creation

A second possible critique could concede that a distinct moral intelligibility does in fact belong to the judgment announced in Isaiah 5. Nonetheless, it might be suggested, because the passage envisages total destruction as being for God a viable alternative, the concept of "judgment" according to which the passage must be interpreted is wholly incommensurable with the superabundant generosity at the heart of Matthew 20. Because the Old Testament passage, in other words, proposes a rigid alternative between an enjoyment of obedience and a suffering of punishment, it makes fellowship itself a wholly tentative matter.[37] Destruction and loss of creation are thought equally to serve the ends of God, and the aforementioned thesis that God

---

[36] Barth, *Church Dogmatics* II/1, p. 402; *Kirchliche Dogmatik* II/1, p. 453; cf. p. 410.

[37] From the perspective of the history of dogma, Anselm's atonement theology—cf. "Why God Became Man," in *A Scholastic Miscellany: Anselm to Ockham*, ed. E.R. Fairweather (London: SCM Press, 1956)—offers a most illuminating entry into the meaning of this supposed alternative, according to which "either the honor that was taken away [from God by sin] must be repaid or punishment must follow" (I, 13; cf. 19). He argues it is decisively *not God* who must be set right on account of sin, for God himself is "honor incorruptible and absolutely unchangeable" (I, 15). What must be rectified is *the disorder* resulting when the creature "take[s] away from God whatever he had planned to make out of human nature" (I, 23). It is thus fitting that through the work of God incarnate, the creation, and especially the rational nature, not be lost but rather *restored* to its proper obedience, to its *appointed* beauty (II, 1, 4). Such a perspective on the atonement bears important implications for Anselm's otherwise underdeveloped eschatology. For two excellent essays in interpretation, see Stephen R. Holmes, "The Upholding of Beauty: A Reading of Anselm's *Cur Deus Homo*," in *Listening to the Past: The Place of Tradition in Theology* (Grand Rapids: Baker Academic, 2002). Holmes argues that, for Anselm, it is *creation* "which has been warped and ruined by humanity's failure" and must be restored (p. 48). See also Katherine Sonderegger, "Anselm, *Defensor Fidei*," *International Journal of Systematic*

does what is right precisely by "creating good out of evil" is shown to be hyperbole.

In this instance too, however, several features of the Isaiah text show such an interpretation to be problematic. Placing the onus for the fulfillment of righteousness wholly upon human beings, for example, requires overlooking testimony to the sinfulness of those whom God gathers to himself, or better, that the act of founding new life on the reign of God's righteousness has as its object sinful humanity. The call of God is thus directed to those among whom sin reigns. Just as with those laborers who in Jesus' parable chafe against the goodness of God, demanding fulfillment of their own sense of what is right and begrudging others the grace which God has not begrudged his people (Mt 20.12), and just as the psalmist writes that justice only provokes the wicked to anger and causes them to gnash their teeth (Ps 112.9–10; cf. Lk 15.25–32), so too the prophet Isaiah points to unrighteousness as summarily exemplified in those "who call evil good and good evil, who put darkness for light and light for darkness, who put bitter for sweet and sweet for bitter" (Isa 5.20). The inexplicable and heinous nature of sin is exposed throughout with clarity. Sin does not simply resist the negative aspects of God's just judgment. To reduce it to such is to underestimate sin's power and so too to underestimate God's exhaustive knowledge of his people, their limitations and their determination to resist him. Most radically, sin manifests itself as a rejection of the gratuitous and so freeing gifts of God's just judgment under the guise of upholding righteousness.

The claim that Isaiah presents destruction as an end acceptable in itself likewise underestimates the force of testimony to divine provision with which Isaiah's parable unfolds. The digging and clearing, the selectiveness and watchfulness, all suggest that nothing in the nature of the vineyard allows for failure. God has ensured everything for fruit bearing and has remained providentially present. Crucially, righteousness is in this latter sense not a matter of creation in and of itself. It is not a matter of gifts given and so fellowship made contingent upon their use. This could only be the case were righteousness itself a commodity separable from the triune God. As a perfection of the divine life, however, the reduplication among creatures of God's righteousness, the reckoning of what is right and worthy of God himself, primarily, and creatures, derivatively, is an event based upon the constant presence of God. We will return to this question again in our final subsection. The point here is that on the basis of the *Song of the Vineyard* failure only casts doubt back upon the people themselves, highlighting the absurdity of the turn of events, raising the question of how this could happen and, decisively, leaving little space for the countercharge that God

---

Theology 9(3) (2007), especially the conclusion: "Neither a mediator nor a propitiator, Jesus Christ, for Anselm, is principally a 'restorer'" (p. 348).

has either begrudged his creation righteousness, demonstrated reluctance to fulfill it himself, or revealed any number of divergent outcomes to be satisfactory.

Some care must be taken in proposing such a disjunction, finally, because the underlying presupposition is that "finality"—the end of covenant life—can be clearly perceived in the destruction of Isaiah 5. This criticism regarding the possibility or plausibility of the loss or restoration of creation is therefore closely linked to the broader understanding of how God works redemption for and among his people. The prophetic word of Isaiah 5 might not in and of itself offer an answer to this particular question, precisely because the question itself concerns that which lies beyond the horizon of these events. If indeed the mode of inquiry is to be guided by actualities and not possibilities, if it is to be a descriptive following-after the events of redemption rather than an analytic reckoning of the meaning of such events as generally transparent, one will have to look more broadly to the canon of Christian scriptures. This would include not only a forward glance toward a king whose reign will be forevermore marked by the justice and righteousness—note the hendiadys—which God has appointed (Isa 9.6–7) but, more directly, it will be shown to include a new song of the vineyard, this time as an eschatological vision of hope illuminating Israel's future:

> On that day: A pleasant vineyard, sing about it! I, the Lord, am its keeper; every moment I water it. I guard it night and day so that no one can harm it; I have no wrath [חֵמָה אֵין]. If it gives me thorns and briers, I will march to battle against it. I will burn it up. Or else let it cling to me for protection, let it make peace with me, let it make peace with me (Isa 27.2–5).

Reading the parable of Isaiah 5 in its broader contexts thus suggests the genuine possibility that, for the God who speaks throgh the prophets,

> the call of anger is a call to cancel anger. It is not an expression of irrational, sudden and instinctive excitement, but a free and deliberate reaction of God's justice to what is wrong and evil . . . . There is no divine anger for anger's sake. Its meaning is, as already said, instrumental: to bring about repentance; its purpose and its consummation is its own disappearance.[38]

It is therefore a suggestion of preservation in judgment, a suggestion that, within a well-defined set of concepts, wrath may be considered one form of

---

[38] Abraham J. Heschel, *The Prophets* (New York: Harper & Row, 1962), p. 286; cf. pp. 224–245.

that "pathos" constitutive of "the focal point for eternity and history, the epitome of all relationships between God and man" and therefore in and of itself "neither irrational nor irresistible, [but] result[ing] from a decision, from an act of will."[39]

Coming to some theological clarity on the potent and perplexing discontinuities, which the Christian faith embraces—and this includes the death and destruction merited by sinners and wielded instrumentally by the living God—depends upon discerning the broader patterns of judgment through which scripture speaks of divine perfection. First and foremost, the wrath and righteousness of Isaiah 5 are legible as one concrete moment within the larger plan of creation and redemption, a plan that betrays a distinct flexibility in execution, patience in outworking, and decisiveness in effect. God is One for whom wrath will not in and of itself have the last word because it is a mode of his righteousness.

Such a possibility is held open by a second systematic thesis, namely that God's freedom for creatures is directly rather than inversely proportional to his freedom from them. He does not suffer compulsion, so to speak, in the enactment of either his wrath or righteousness. Sin (as measured against God himself) necessarily concludes in a judgment of condemnation and a final exclusion from the kingdom of God. Yet, as Barth has observed, the cross of Jesus Christ reveals that God, "cannot be denied the right to execute judgment and punishment according to his good pleasure."[40] We will have need to focus specifically on the relationship between wrath and the cross in the next chapter. The crucial point here is that across the whole arc of redemption history not only is God the exclusive source of the righteousness of all life but, over against the opposition of sinful humanity, he is also the ongoing standard and present guarantee of its fulfillment. God's wrath lasts only for a moment precisely because God is perfect in his wrath. Because wrath finds its end, it may finally be turned away (Ps 30.5; 85.5; Isa 54.8; Hos 14.4).

---

[39] Ibid., pp. 229, 298. Pathos is simply "a theological category *sui generis*" (p. 229), and as such cannot be confused with that "common psychological concept" (p. 270), which suggests "the emotional excitement induced by intense displeasure . . . the loss of self-control, compulsiveness, temporary derangement of the mind, and the desire to avenge or punish" (p. 281; cf. pp. 282, 288). Heschel's brilliant analysis nonetheless requires a critical reconsideration of: (1) his unnecessary, exclusivist distinction between legal descriptions of the relationship between God and creatures and those descriptions set in terms of personal involvement, participation, and tension (cf. p. 230), as well as (2) the thesis that the provisional status of divine wrath may be fully conceptualized through a contrast between fleeting wrath and the blessing God gives "with all His heart and all His soul" (p. 287 cf. p. 291). In this second matter, his thesis is perhaps more dependent upon the "psychology of passions" (p. 282)—a contrastive, psychological model—than he himself suggests (cf. p. 226).

[40] Barth, *Church Dogmatics* II/1, p. 401.

III. The Living Parable

Beyond the prophecies of Isaiah, the unity of this singular righteousness is seen in its concrete fulfillment, a new gathering of God's people, mediated by the incarnate presence of the eternal Son in the power of the Holy Spirit. This movement is therefore not wholly unexpected but, once again staying with the image of the vineyard, it is identical with that movement hinted at elsewhere in the prophets. "Just as I have watched over them to pluck up and break down, to overthrow, destroy, and bring evil, so I will watch over them to build and to plant" (Jer 31.28). This movement from the old to the new, from the covenant God's people are able to break to that which secures fellowship in a qualitatively different manner, rests upon the fact that "I will put my law within them, and I will write it on their hearts" (Jer 31.33). We are inquiring, in other words, after that complete manifestation of divine perfection which guarantees for theological reflection the continuity of God's righteousness through judgment and unto boundless generosity. We can conclude this chapter as we began: with the parable of Matthew 20 and the reality of this decisively new act.

We have seen that the prophetic song of Isaiah 5 uncovers the interim results or outworking of God's gathering to himself a people. So too the parable which issues from Jesus' lips must be understood not as timeless but as eminently the work of the eternal God. Both are prophetic illuminations of concrete contexts and events. Having thus considered both pronouncements, we can look to the decisive manner in which God, in new and unexpected ways, gathers to himself a people. We will consider briefly the nature of the injunction to righteousness as it relates to the parable of the workers in the vineyard and, correspondingly, the christological and pneumatological mode of its fulfillment.

Righteousness as Injunction

Righteousness, though properly a perfection of God's life, is derivatively an injunction for God's people to gather under the cover of his life-giving reign. As such, it does not grow out of worldly knowledge, but turns it on its head. It does not reinforce the status quo but provokes upheaval. This is what Jesus Christ does as righteous Sovereign, and his parables are an instrument of this work. They "surprise, they jar, indeed they often shock, in order to foment an evaluation of one's current assumptions and expectations and a reorientation toward a more fundamental and God-given reality."[41] One of the more counterintuitive aspects of the parable of the workers in the

---

[41] Robert J. Sherman, *King, Priest, and Prophet: A Trinitarian Theology of Atonement* (London: T&T Clark, 2004), p. 226. Reflecting on this parable, Sherman suggests that "the single most telling point one may make about the kingdom that Christ proclaims

vineyard, and a good example of its provocative nature, is the manner in which it temporarily entertains suspicion as to whether God's justice has not in fact been compromised. We have already discussed the suspicion it stirs up: if the kingdom of God is indeed "like this," perhaps God does not distinguish honest labor from idle existence. This momentary concession, as counterintuitive as it might seem, serves to dispossess one of an *a priori* impulse toward measure-for-measure compensation. Concepts like "wage" and "reward" are indeed embedded in the image. As Eduard Schweizer tersely summarizes, however, they are employed precisely so that they might be done away with.[42]

In the economy of God's dealings with his creatures, what is due them on the basis of his righteousness is announced as the most original and basic meaning of human life and simultaneously as the most alien, seemingly unjust, and impracticable of orders. Consequently, there arises

> a conflict between two worlds of thought. There are those who insist on being able to calculate how the master's benefits should be distributed. And there is the master, to whom the spotlight now turns, who insists on dealing with employees on the basis of their need and his own reckless generosity.[43]

While the righteousness of God is certainly a kind of "hypergood,"[44] in the sense that it occupies a peculiar moral primacy and so serves as a landmark by which all other moral goods can be weighed or judged, its substance and unique character are dictated solely by the peculiar foundation we have been at pains to describe. This divine judgment, i.e., that there is a *rightness* to generosity, is equivalent neither to a general principle of benevolence nor to an intuited or observed concept of the relative equality of persons. Its source rather is the particularity of God's own life, the benefits of which

---

42 and inaugurates is that it displays none of the characteristics typically associated with worldly kingdoms" (p. 143).

42 Eduard Schweizer, *The Good News According to Matthew* (London: SPCK, 1976), p. 393. Righteousness is thereby revealed as "of such a strange sort that it is lost when men claim it by right, when they compare their own performance with that of others instead of concentrating on the goodness of the Lord, before which all accomplishments vanish" (p. 394).

43 Steven H. Travis, *Christ and the Judgment of God: Divine Retribution in the New Testament* (Basingstoke: M. Pickering, 1991), p. 149; cf. Mk 10.29f. C.H. Dodd's assessment that divine generosity "gives without regard to the measures of strict justice" obscures the central point, namely that the parable judges, condemns, and replaces human notions for the sake of the generosity of God's true justice—cf. *The Parables of the Kingdom* (New York: Charles Scribner's Sons, 1961), pp. 94–95.

44 Charles Taylor, *Sources of the Self: The Making of the Modern Identity* (Cambridge: Harvard University Press, 1989), p. 63.

may be received solely on the basis of the wish and right of the Giver himself and, as we will shortly argue, they are revealed and made manifest in the work of the Son and Spirit. Under the rule of righteousness, our "discriminations of right or wrong, better or worse, higher or lower," are rendered valid as they obey this rule rather than our own desires, inclinations, or determinations.[45] The parable of the workers in the vineyard provides, in this sense, part of that "frame or horizon within which I can try to determine from case to case what is good, or valuable, or what ought to be done, or what I endorse or oppose."[46] In considering as we have the implications of God's righteousness for human life, we have not departed from the foundational claim that the Lord is always the subject of his righteousness. We now need to make this point clearer.

Righteousness in the Son and through the Spirit

The passage under consideration unfolds with the "playful character"[47] of a parable. In response, one option for theological exposition would have been to translate the images into propositional content and, in so doing, to transcend and leave behind the metaphorical apparatus itself. That is not the option we have followed here, and we need to state our reasons. At the first and most general level, there is reasonable doubt as to whether an act of translation like this is capable of preserving the complex meaning of the image. The vital tension in the parable comes to a head as a result of the confrontation of the landowner and his various laborers. Its crux, in other words, is inextricably linked to matters of agential action, concrete context, and the unfolding of a series of irreversible events. As such, the narrative underscores and clarifies a prominent feature of Jesus Christ's concrete ministry. Our own interpretation acknowledges this bond between form and content. Rather than attempt to peel away the packaging, we have sought instead to relish the tangibility of the images, to place ourselves in a posture to hear the narrative diachronically, and to allow it on its own terms to convert our knowledge of God, creature, and kingdom. In moral-theological

---

[45] Ibid., p. 4.

[46] Ibid., p. 27. John Webster draws fruitfully on this notion of a "moral ontology"—cf. *Barth's Moral Theology* (Edinburgh: T&T Clark, 1998) and *Barth's Ethics of Reconciliation* (Cambridge: Cambridge University Press, 1995).

[47] Eberhard Jüngel, *God as the Mystery of the World: On the Foundation of the Theology of the Crucified One in the Dispute between Theism and Atheism*, trans. D. Guder (Grand Rapids: Eerdmans, 1983), p. 291. He describes a parable as "forceful in its non-necessity" (ibid.), a description which, though somewhat opaque, makes the essential point: "[W]hile this story is being told, the listener is being focussed on its point. He is being collected in that the parable collects itself, so to speak. And with the point, the kingdom of God itself in the parable *arrives* in the hearer if he engages himself in the parable and lets himself be gathered by the parable into it" (p. 294).

terms, our resolution should be to remain critical hearers of the parable rather than promote ourselves through the work of interpretation to the status of authors in our own right.

More importantly, there is a second benefit to this interpretive approach. Staying with the parabolic form per se can be understood once more as self-conscious resistance to the idealistic endeavor to distill from the passage its "kernel of truth." Parables can, and indeed have been, harvested for their eternal verities. All along we have followed a line of interpretation which has among its presuppositions the belief that metaphors like these, along with the whole of salvation history, have as their concrete reference God's dealings with Israel and the Church. The significance for us in the present context is that the conversion at which this particular parable aims is a conversion to a reality already concretely established and fulfilled once and for all in the life, death, and resurrection of Jesus Christ. According to Matthew, he is the one who in fulfilling the law (5.17), gives from an expansive generosity, reaching out to restore human worth (8.13) and life (15.28, 37). It is intimated of those who have no need of these, in fact, that they have no need of Christ's presence, his righteousness, or his mediation (9.13). The divine perfection which our parable points to, therefore, does not lie outside Jesus Christ's life as an eternally applicable truth or as an epiphenomenal expression of basic human need. Neither, comparably, does it remain incomplete until fulfilled through human action and obedience. As a parable *of Jesus* it is a description of both what happened then and what continues to happen now and forever as he orders the life of his kingdom and defends his generosity with a vengeance. Schweizer's observation is astute:

> [I]n this parable the strange righteousness of God in giving gifts actually takes place. It takes place as Jesus tells the story: tax collectors and prostitutes come to him and find entrance into the kingdom of God. This is as concrete as the denarius in the parable.[48]

In short, the meaning of the parable does not displace but highlights the acting Lord who stands at its center, resisting human control or adulteration, gathering his people to himself, and producing the righteousness of his kingdom by the gift of his Spirit (Rom 14.17). As with all scientific exposition of the divine perfections, righteousness here has as its subject matter primarily and properly the being of God himself.

---

[48] Schweizer, *Good News According to Matthew*, p. 394. Hagner draws a connection between this parable and "the important theme of the gospel articulated by Jesus in the words 'I did not come to call the righteous but sinners' (9.13) and illustrated in his table fellowship with 'tax collectors and sinners' "—*Matthew 14–28*, p. 573. Compare similar conclusions in Hultgren, *Parables of Jesus*, pp. 11–18, and Snodgrass, "From Allegorizing to Allegorizing," p. 28.

This leads us directly to a third and final point. Just as the concrete, historical meaning of the parable can be distinguished from its idealistic counterpart,
so too can its particular power to convert the human mind be differentiated
from an ordinary process of reasoned persuasion. Considered in and of itself,
the parable shocks, but it does not convince; it suggests but does not secure
an objective and reliable order for life. Its announcement of divine righteousness can be captured, comprehended, and adopted exclusively on the basis
of the illuminating power of God's Spirit. It is the Spirit who knows the
depths of God, and so the Spirit who converts human hearts for service
within God's kingdom by raising God's people up to new life in Christ Jesus
(1 Cor 2.9–13; Gal 5.5).[49] The power of the parable is that which it derives
as an instrument of the Holy Spirit, containing by way of promise not only
the very reality to which it points but the basis for its reception as well.
Therefore, a radically counterintuitive and so potentially offensive call to
gather under the righteousness of God need not depend upon human sympathy, requirement, example, or rationale for its reception.

* * * * *

The transcanonical image of the vineyard of the Lord presents a rich description of the righteous God who is resolute in gathering to himself a righteous
people. As such, we have argued, it is an image which encompasses the generosity which belongs in every respect to God's judgment as well as the
severity and unremitting wrath in which God, in a redemptive mode of his
righteousness, is nonetheless perfectly honoring of both himself and his people. In particular, we have demonstrated the distinctly moral intelligibility
proper to all such acts. Likewise, we have intimated that the question of the
end or purpose of God's wrath also requires for its resolution attention to
the whole scope of God's acts. By this wholeness it is announced that

> in the process of judging, rejecting and punishing, God does not break
> but keeps His covenant, and therefore comforts, helps and saves.[50]

Nonetheless, already in the larger context of Isaiah's prophecies, and
decisively in the incarnate and spiritual fulfillment revealed in Matthew's

---

[49] Mt 20.1–16 suggests that conversion continues among those who have been shown
mercy, received faith, and so have entered already into the fellowship of God's people. The
"first and last" of the parable, thus refer to insiders to the community, both Christians
who have worked long and faithfully and latecomers to faith who, relatively speaking,
have hardly worked. Cf. Boring, *Matthew*, p. 393; Bruner, *Churchbook*, p. 320. Hagner
reads this as a specific reference to Israel and the Gentiles—*Matthew 14–28*, p. 573.
[50] Barth, *Church Dogmatics* II/1, p. 390.

parable, the particular relationship between God's righteousness and wrath means that wrath cannot and will not be made a theme independent of the larger testimony to God's character. This very conclusion and the truth of the depth of God's righteousness, of course, does not complete an analysis of wrath but rather makes requisite a second study, focused upon the pattern in which it is fulfilled.

5

WRATH, RIGHTEOUSNESS, AND THE ACQUITTAL OF THE GUILTY: ROMANS 3.21–26 AND EXODUS 34.6–7

Romans as a whole, and particularly the section stretching from 1.18 to 4.25, comprises a grand theological description of God's righteousness—a matter judged variously the "heart"[1] and "coherent center"[2] of the letter—and it does so by indicating, among other things, the self-sacrificial work in which the righteous One himself becomes the gift of righteousness. In this work, the righteousness of God proceeds toward redemption in the mode of his wrath, for by his wrath God carries out the executing power of his judgment and so brings sin to its determinative end. The present chapter thus complements the claims of chapter four. God is righteous not only as he establishes a righteous order and gathers his people to it, but he is also righteous in Christ Jesus our mediator. Of all the places in which this message is unfolded, Romans 3.21–26 is arguably the most vital. Paul's well known words run thus:

> [21]But now, apart from law, the righteousness of God has been disclosed, and is attested by the law and the prophets, [22]the righteousness of God through faith in Jesus Christ for all who believe. For there is no distinction, [23]since all have sinned and fall short of the glory of God; [24]they are now justified by his grace as a gift, through the redemption

---

[1] C.E.B. Cranfield, *A Critical and Exegetical Commentary on the Epistle to the Romans, vol. 1: Romans 1–8* (Edinburgh: T&T Clark, 1975), p. 103.

[2] John Reumann, "Righteousness (NT)," *The Anchor Bible Dictionary*, ed. D.N. Freedman, vol. 5 (New York: Doubleday, 1992), p. 764. Douglas J. Moo regards the connection between righteousness and faith to be a "leitmotif of the letter"—*The Epistle to the Romans* (Grand Rapids: Eerdmans, 1996), p. 73. Similarly Robert Jewett, *Romans: A Commentary* (Minneapolis: Fortress Press, 2007), p. 272. See Rom 1:16, 3:5.

that is in Christ Jesus, [25]whom God put forward as a sacrifice of atonement by his blood, effective through faith. He did this to show his righteousness, because in his divine forbearance he had passed over the sins previously committed; [26]it was to prove at the present time that he himself is righteous and that he justifies the one who has faith in Jesus.

This passage, along with Exodus 34.6–7, will be the primary material for the exposition which follows. Before undertaking that work, however, we need to pause here at the outset and state the approach of our argument as well as clarify a crucial material decision, namely the reference of δικαιοσύνη τοῦ θεοῦ as it is employed in Romans and will appear in our exposition.

While there are a number of possible avenues for entering a theological exposition of Romans 3.21–26, one particularly strong option—and the option pursued here—is to begin from the last verse, taking the purpose statement of 3.26 as the source for both our guiding question and its answer. Construed in this way, the clause "it was to prove [πρὸς τὴν ἔνδειξιν] . . . that he himself is righteous" focuses attention initially upon the manner in which the fullness of God's righteousness is left an open question in light of the unexpiated, unpunished, and so unresolved sins of his people. In the argument preceding Romans 3.21–26, Paul claims that God manifests his righteousness in two distinct yet interrelated modes. In one respect, it is revealed in the gospel as "the power of God for salvation for everyone who has faith" (1.16–17).[3] Correspondingly, his righteousness is manifest as an act of final judgment, a day of wrath, when the impartial Lord has promised to repay all people for their deeds (2.5).

Doubt over the essential or effective nature of God's righteousness, however, arises as one observes that up to Romans 3.21–26, and so apart from testimony to the sacrifice of Jesus Christ, neither of God's promises have been fulfilled. Because sinners persist in their sin, having received neither definitive judgment nor redemption, love for the righteous God threatens to flag. If righteousness is indeed an attribute of God, an issue which we will consider momentarily, it seems prior to Christ "not to come to manifestation and therefore to be nonexistent."[4] The answer offered in Romans is an event: God's singular act in putting forward Jesus Christ as ἱλαστήριον. This proof vindicates God's righteousness and gives evidence of the inner relationship between his determination to save and the wrath which deals death to sinners in their sin.

Something of the peculiar force of this interpretation is especially apparent alongside an exposition of the righteousness of God like that of Hermann

---

[3] The antecedent of ἐν αὐτῷ (1:17) being τὸ εὐαγγέλιον (1:16).

[4] Bavinck, *Reformed Dogmatics* III, p. 369.

Cremer. Cremer refers lavishly and effulgently to God's righteousness as a *iustitia salutifera* according to which divine forgiveness, and *not* condemnation, constitutes "the highest proof of his judging righteousness." Thus Cremer's pithy summary: the righteousness of God means "not salvation *from* his hand but salvation *by* his hand."[5] As we suggested above, recent revitalization of creativity and interest in the divine perfections is partly indebted to Cremer's work. In this particular context, his research highlights specifically the generosity and self-sacrifice which we have identified as proper to divine righteousness. The Romans passage in question, however, does not argue for forgiveness per se as proof of God's character. Rather it is God's concrete act of putting Christ forward as an atoning sacrifice—in all its dimensions—which proves that he is righteous. Undeniably, this singular act has forgiveness and restoration as its end, but it secures this end precisely as it incorporates, rather than excludes, the punitive or negative dimension to God's righteous work. Whereas Cremer is concerned with expunging the retributive element from "the marvelous righteousness of God" in order to convey that righteousness "is not our terror but our refuge and hope,"[6] our claim will be that the event of the cross demonstrates the unity and difference of mercy and wrath, and thus reveals that God's righteousness is proved as he redeems his sinful people by punishing sin in an utterly free and singular act.

In addition to this overview of our approach to the text, there is a material decision central to this chapter that needs to be defended. As we have already hinted, it is a peculiarity of the interpretation of Pauline theology—at least since Luther "raged with a fierce and troubled conscience"[7] under the burden of the righteous God—that righteousness itself cannot be assumed to refer to God's character or essence. Certain expositions of this passage suggest that, for the sake of precision, δικαιοσύνη τοῦ θεοῦ must be identified with one of three possible meanings: the perfection of God's life, the perfection God produces in his people, or the divine act of creating righteousness itself. One thinks, for example, of Alan Spence's *The Promise of Peace: A Unified Theory of Atonement* and his decision to treat the genitive of Romans 3.21 strictly as a genitive of origin. The result is that he reads Romans 3 as concerned primarily with "the revelation of a different order or type of righteousness."[8] Exegetical decisions are inextricably intertwined with both theological presuppositions and implications. The most significant implication of this particular decision is that, as an overemphasis upon divine action, it may begin to eclipse consideration of who God is as Subject.

---

[5] Cremer, *Die christliche Lehre von den Eigenschaften Gottes*, p. 60.

[6] Ibid., p. 78.

[7] Martin Luther, *Luther's Works, vol. 34: Career of the Reformer IV*, eds. L.W. Spitz, H.T. Lehmann (Philadelphia: Muhlenberg Press, 1960), p. 337.

[8] Alan Spence, *The Promise of Peace: A Unified Theory of Atonement* (London: T&T Clark, 2006), pp. 96–97.

Several more examples of comparably *exclusivist* interpretation could be adduced, particularly from biblical-theological scholarship. This approach, however, has not gone unquestioned. John Reumann, for example, incorporates both the subjective and originating (*genitivus auctoris*) dimensions of righteousness in his claim that "God is *dikaios*, the characteristic feature of whose nature is preserved in the sacrifice of Christ; but he is also a God *dikaiounta*, or 'declaring righteous' men who respond in faith, and saving them."[9] Similarly, if more reservedly, Douglas Moo cautions against exclusivist interpretations. "The jump from the one [God's justifying act, 3.21–22] to the other [God's own integrity, 3.25–26] is not as great as might at first appear," he writes, "since always lurking in 'righteousness' language is allusion to the character and person of God."[10] Robert Jewett, by contrast, counsels judicious restraint in presiding over exclusivist judgments at all. Because "not all genitives can easily be forced into the scheme established by grammarians" and because "there is no reason why a genitive in the author's mind may not have been both subjective and objective," he avers, it is precarious business to erect one's theology on the interpretation of a case ending.[11] That is the literary evidence.

More decisive is the biblical logic according to which, as we have argued, the concrete effects of the life of the triune God must be held together with the perfection God has from himself in an irreducibly asymmetrical unity. Without the formal and material reference to God's immanent perfection, the attempt to attribute certain effects to *divine* action—such as the production of righteousness in human beings—will nonetheless terminate in an analysis of the economy itself. An exposition of the righteousness of God undertaken from within the proposed scientific frame of reference, by contrast, compels an account of Romans 3.21–26, if it is to be in this very specific sense nonreductionistic, to give due place to righteousness as a divine perfection.[12] A more comprehensive and salutary definition of δικαιοσύνη τοῦ θεοῦ commends itself:

> God is just, not indeed as one among many, but as one who contains in Himself alone all the fullness of righteousness. He receives the full and complete praise which is His due only as He alone obtains the name and honor of being just, while the whole human race is condemned of unrighteousness. The other part refers to the communication

---

[9] John Reumann, "The Gospel of the Righteousness of God: Pauline Interpretation in Romans 3:21–31," *Interpretation* 20 (1966): 447.

[10] Moo, *Epistle to the Romans*, p. 219 n. 4.

[11] Jewett, *Romans*, p. 277.

[12] Both Jewett, *Romans*, p. 292, and Cranfield, *Epistle to the Romans*, p. 213, express explicit concern for the divine character.

of righteousness, for God does not by any means shut His riches within Himself, but pours them forth upon mankind.[13]

One clear advantage of this summary by John Calvin is that it places deliberate emphasis upon three dimensions of the righteousness of God, yet without separating them. Just as the parable of the workers in the vineyard invokes the very quality—the wish and right—of God's character as the basis of his action, so too, as Calvin shows, Romans 3 is concerned primarily with the particular claim that "alone"—i.e., above and prior to creation—God himself is righteous. God is this, furthermore, not in poverty or in potentiality but in "all the fullness of righteousness," a fullness which correspondingly exposes the unrighteousness of sinful humanity. Even the strong opposition of which Calvin writes, however, need not imply that God's righteousness excludes his being for and among his people. As Calvin continues, God is also righteous as he works righteousness in the lives of his sinful people. That this encompasses the act as well as its objective result is conveyed by his original idiom: God pours out his riches upon his people in an authentic communication such that, so long as they are united to Jesus Christ by faith, they are credited with the righteousness which he has earned on their behalf.

Similarly comprehensive are Barth's comments on righteousness. He writes in *Church Dogmatics* IV/1 that this Romans passage as a whole testifies to the making righteous of sinners. This is its meaning for us as God's creatures. However, because Romans 3.26 identifies this work specifically as proof of God's righteousness—in the sense that sin will not go unpunished and salvation will not be left empty and incomplete—the meaning for God is "that He Himself is just (in this work)." Barth underscores, lest the central point escape us:

> If it is the case that in our justification God also and in the first instance justifies Himself, then in the knowledge of it we have to do with the knowledge of God Himself, who in the fact that He affirms His right proves that He is the One who neither can nor will deceive.[14]

---

[13] John Calvin, *The Epistle of Paul the Apostle to the Romans and to the Thessalonians*, eds. R. Mackenzie, D.W. Torrance, and T.F. Torrance (Grand Rapids: Eerdmans, 1995), p. 77. This same affirmation underlies Calvin's rejection in the *Institutes of the Christian Religion* of Osiander's radical view. It is Jesus Christ's acquired rather than essential righteousness, which is imputed to the redeemed. The alternative tends to relativize the life, death and resurrection of the Mediator, and so to surrender assurance of salvation by eliding the distinction between justification and regeneration, or by either postulating a "mixture of substances" or a transfusion of deity into human life—cf. III.xi.5–12.

[14] Barth, *Church Dogmatics* IV/1, p. 561.

Our own interpretation follows the approach exemplified by Calvin and Barth, one which is more cogent to the degree that it holds *what God does* together with *who God is*.[15] In the exposition which follows, God will be understood on the basis of Romans as himself righteous, doing righteousness, by declaring the ungodly righteous.

A closer examination of the wrathful and righteous God at work in the cross of Jesus Christ requires, first, an analysis of the judgment under which sinners stand, i.e., the back story to redemption, along with consideration of the direct and personal manner in which God presides over such judgment in his wrath. It requires, second, development of the evidence offered in proof of the righteousness which belongs to divine perfection, namely God's act of setting forth Jesus Christ as ἱλαστήριον. The question of God's righteousness, therefore, entails close attention to the concrete outworking of redemption. Out of the resources of Reformed theology, we will argue that God does what is worthy of himself through an irreducible twofold work of saving his people and punishing sin. This is the simultaneity in which, on the one hand, sinners are made recipients of Jesus Christ's righteousness and have their sin borne for them and, on the other, God shows himself as perfect in his wrath by disposing of sin through the expiatory work of the cross. Our task at each point is to deploy these resources in order better to understand the character of God.

Through an incorporation of the testimony of Exodus 34.6–7, our exposition will enter, third, into inquiry over wrath's place in the harmony of God's life and, fourth, into the significance of God's patience for the outworking of his wrath. Particularly with regard to the latter, because the atoning death of Jesus Christ occurs in particular time and space, and so falls at a single, determinative point within a larger history of redemption moving from promise to fulfillment, we will argue that wrath appears not as a created feature of the universe but as the redemptive mode of divine righteousness, subject to God's patient timing for its enactment. This latter insight is perhaps the most salutary and invaluable point, as well as the most rarely appreciated, which the Romans passage offers a study on the doctrine of divine wrath. In sum, Romans 3 and Exodus 34 together comprise some of the most profound testimony to God's character in the Old and New Testaments. Both passages, whether by anticipation or fulfillment, pivot on the self-sacrificial pattern by which God is righteous and generous, unrelenting

---

[15] Eberhard Jüngel similarly works toward an exposition in which the subjective and objective senses function in a complementary fashion—cf. *Justification: The Heart of the Christian Faith* (Edinburgh: T&T Clark, 2001), p. 76. Alister McGrath judges this strategy fairly common from an historical-theological perspective—*Iustitia Dei: A History of the Christian Doctrine of Justification*, 2 vols. (Cambridge: Cambridge University Press, 1986), I, p. 52.

in his claim upon creatures, unwavering in his wrath toward sin and, in all things, true to his own worth.

I. Sinners under God's Wrath

A conceptualization of wrath as a mode of divine righteousness depends, first of all, upon a consideration of those *for whom* God acts, and so wrath's object and occasion. When Paul writes that all have sinned under the law and so are shut up in alienation from God (Rom 3.23), such that there is no distinction among human beings, he is summarizing the broad discussion of the extent and depth of human guilt which precedes our passage. Even the briefest sampling of Paul's descriptive language from the *Verdammnisgeschichte* of 1.18–3.20 yields a startling picture. The ungodly and wicked (1.18), he writes, are all fools (1.22) and impure (1.24); they applaud the death-meriting sin of others (1.32), bear hard and impenitent hearts (2.5), and live lives marked by hypocrisy (2.21–24), untruth (3.4) and worthlessness (3.12). Though examples from scripture could be multiplied, the summary would remain the same:

> Man is the dark corner where wrong can settle and spread and flourish in all its nothingness as though by right. It is therefore man who evokes the wrath of God, who comes into conflict with the righteousness of God, upon whom it breaks as crisis, as catastrophe, as mortal sickness. He is the one who is impossible and intolerable before God, who cannot remain in His presence but can only disappear.[16]

The claim that human beings, one and all, have proven themselves by their willful denial of God to be this "dark corner" intimates the corresponding judgment which belongs to them. A close reading of Romans 1.18–3.26, therefore, will not bypass the question of judgment, proceeding as it were to the fact that when Paul announces redemption, it is precisely all these people (cf. πάντες, 3.23), in the full extent of their rebellion against God, selfishness, and injustice, to whom the inheritance belongs.

Indeed, "all" are justified by grace through faith in Jesus Christ (3.24–25), but the content and significance of salvation is conveyed partly through analysis of the connection between sin and wrath which Barth's language so effectively highlights. All humanity, as sinful, stands under the definitive judgment of God's wrath (1.18; 2.5; 2.8; 3.5–6). Jew and Gentile alike, having chosen against life in all the ways just named, have made death their part (1.32; 2.12; 3.9; 6.21, 23). In affirmation of his righteousness, God has

---

[16] Barth, *Church Dogmatics* IV/1, p. 539.

determined his wrath for the destruction of all sin. The origin of the wrath introduced in Romans 1.18, however, particularly considered alongside the righteousness of the preceding two verses, is a matter of considerable disagreement. The contemporary debate is shaped by two dramatically opposed positions, and possibly a third intended to mediate between them.

Debate over the Righteousness and Wrath of Romans 1.18

On the one hand, there is the thesis that the righteousness and wrath of Romans 1.17–18 are to be read in parallel. Both, it is argued, are perfections of God, and so each is revealed in the gospel of Jesus Christ as belonging to God's essence as well as to his overarching work of redemption. On the other hand, some argue that a clear disjunction is signaled in this verse. In contrast to divine righteousness, which comprises the wholly positive character of salvation as it is revealed in the gospel, wrath is not related to the perfection of God's life, but is wholly resolvable as a feature of the economy. Wrath is the judgment manifested by virtue of God's "seeing to" the connection between sinful actions and their so-called "natural" consequences. The former interpretation attributes wrath directly to God and so locates its origin *ab extra*, "external to human existence."[17] The latter, immanentist interpretation—by which we denote a disproportionate focus upon the created economy and indirect divine action and, correspondingly, a conscious inattention to God's transcendent freedom-in-relation—creates distance between God and wrathful judgment via secondary causes.

It has been a continual concern of this thesis to highlight the costly systematic consequences of transposing divine qualities into economic occurrence, and the potential for this error perhaps reaches its height in relation to the present scriptural passage. It is therefore eminently important to inquire after the extent to which the variegated arguments for an immanentist interpretation of Romans 1.18 are based less upon clear exegetical work than upon theologically unserviceable philosophical or sociocultural presuppositions.[18] We turn to this task by a critical exegesis. In terms of the overall

---

[17] Simon J. Gathercole argues persuasively for this interpretation of judgment and wrath—cf. "Justified by Faith, Justified by His Blood: The Evidence of Romans 3:21–4:25," *Justification and Variegated Nomism, vol. 2: The Paradoxes of Paul*, eds. D.A. Carson, P.T. O'Brien, and M.A. Seifrid (Grand Rapids: Baker Academic, 2004), p. 170. Over against the fatalism and dualism of first century religion, G. Stählin argues boldly that "nowhere in the NT is ὀργή a principle which operates rigidly and independently of God, but...everywhere it is very closely linked to God . . . who acts personally therein"— "ὀργή," *Theological Dictionary of the New Testament*, vol. 5, ed. G. Kittel, G. Friedrich and G.W. Bromiley (Grand Rapids: Eerdmans, 1985), p. 424.

[18] Of course, Rom 1:18 is not the only relevant scripture passage. For further examples see: "the fruit of their schemes" (Jer 6:19); "pour out their wickedness upon them" (Jer 14:16); "brought evil on themselves" (Isa 3:9); "you have plowed wickedness, you

structure of our argument, our conclusions here will set the background for the nature of the atoning work described in Romans 3.21–26. Our contention is that the act of judgment in these texts cannot cogently be attributed, whether as a *divine* act or as an act of *judgment*, to the fabric of creation itself and so cannot be coherently accounted for within theological exposition by means of mechanical or organic metaphors.

"Immanentist" Interpretations

Through a close analysis of the textual evidence and by focused attention on the underlying theological judgments, we will challenge the notion that immanentist or mechanistic interpretations of Romans 1.18,

> For the wrath of God is revealed from heaven against all ungodliness and wickedness of those who by their wickedness suppress the truth,

> ['Αποκαλύπτεται γὰρ ὀργὴ θεοῦ ἀπ' οὐρανοῦ ἐπὶ πᾶσαν ἀσέβειαν καὶ ἀδικίαν ἀνθρώπων τῶν τὴν ἀλήθειαν ἐν ἀδικίᾳ κατεχόντων,]

best account for the biblical references to divine wrath. So much is Romans 1.18 the center of gravity for this debate, R.V.G. Tasker thought it appropriate to introduce his own monograph on God's wrath—despite a deep-seated disagreement with immanentist interpretation and contrary to the salvation-historical progression of the argument as a whole—with an analysis of this single verse.[19] By way of anticipation, we can note that recent scholarly investment in this passage is, by turns, both surprising and inevitable: the former, on account of the dearth of textual and exegetical support, which Romans 1.18 actually provides an immanentist position; the latter, in light of the strong hold immanentist thought has upon certain schools of late modern theology as well as the new possibilities it is understood to provide theological interpretation in general.[20] One thinks in this respect especially of C.H. Dodd's 1932 commentary on Romans, which, we will argue, has

---

have reaped injustice, you have eaten the fruit of lies" (Hos 10:12–14); "they sow the wind, and they shall reap the whirlwind" (Hos 8:7); "does a lion roar in the forest, when it has no prey?" (Amos 3:3–8, *passim*); "all who take the sword will perish by the sword" (Mt 26:52); "if anyone destroys God's temple, God will destroy that person" (1 Cor 3:17); "because they shed the blood of saints and prophets, you have given them blood to drink" (Rev 16:5–6; cf. also 18:6 and 22:18–19).

[19] See R.V.G. Tasker, *The Biblical Doctrine of the Wrath of God* (London: Tyndale, 1951), pp. 9–12.

[20] John Macquarrie, for example, observes the philosophical rejection of metaphysics, along with the corresponding tendency toward confining religion "to its place in the historical and cultural life of man," in influence upon the theologies of later figures like Otto Pfleiderer, Ernest Troeltsch and Albert Schweitzer—*Twentieth-Century Religious*

exerted widespread and primarily negative influence upon a cogent, systematic understanding of God's wrath.[21]

Important in this debate is the unified nature of Paul's discourse. Taken in its most natural sense, the conjunction γὰρ (1.18) is a marker of continuation and connection best translated as "for . . ." or "you see . . . ."[22] The implication is that, in turning to the wrath of God, Paul does not initiate a contrasting theme, one separate from the gospel which he has just announced, but is continuing via a theme intimately connected to God's righteousness, though it has its own distinct integrity and content. The connection between them can be stated as such: the gospel proclaims both God's perfection in redeeming his people and simultaneously and necessarily God's identity as the one who draws definitive judgment upon all ungodliness and unrighteousness.

This is the crucial point for us, and it may be contrasted with Dodd's oddly unjustified option for disjunction, following the Moffatt translation of the New Testament. Assuming the disjunction, Dodd refers wrath to that "inevitable process of cause and effect in a moral universe" of which God is author and sustainer.[23] This exegesis has contributed to a tradition of immanentist interpretation in which the relationship between God and wrath is conceived in the most limited and indirect fashion.[24] A similar though more

---

Thought: The Frontiers of Philosophy and Theology, 1900–1960 (London: SCM Press, 1963), p. 136; cf. esp. pp. 139–154.

[21] C.H. Dodd, *The Epistle of Paul to the Romans* (London: Hodder & Stoughton Ltd., 1932).

[22] Walter Bauer and Frederick W. Danker, *A Greek-English Lexicon of the New Testament and Other Early Christian Literature*, 3rd ed. (Chicago: University of Chicago Press, 2000), p. 189. Among those who follow this ordinary usage: Cranfield, *Romans 1–8*, p. 106; Steve Finamore, "The Gospel and the Wrath of God in Romans 1," *Understanding, Studying, and Reading* (1998): p. 145. Moo notes that this conjunction intimates Paul's answer to the question implicit in 1:17, namely why righteousness is needed and why it must be acquired solely by faith—cf. *Epistle to the Romans*, p. 99.

[23] Dodd, *Epistle of Paul to the Romans*, p. 23; cf. pp. 18–25. Out of proportion with the weight of the exegetical move, Dodd presupposes, rather than argues, the adversative sense. Among those who have followed Dodd, consult A.T. Hanson, *The Wrath of the Lamb* (London, 1957) and G.H.C. Macgregor, "The Concept of the Wrath of God in the New Testament," *New Testament Studies* 7 (1961): 101–109. I am indebted to Gathercole, "Justified by Faith," p. 170, for the further example of U. Wilckens, "Exkurs: Das Gericht nach den Werken I (Traditionsgeschichtliche Voraussetzungen)," *Der Brief an die Römer (Röm 1–5)*, pp. 127–131. More recently, Gene Tucker argues for a "dynamistic view . . . an understanding of reality in which justice is built in, in which actions entail their consequences"—cf. "Sin and 'Judgment' in the Prophets," *Problems in Biblical Theology: Essays in Honor of Rolf Knierim*, ed. H.T.C. Sun (Grand Rapids: Eerdmans, 1997), pp. 374–375.

[24] Immanentist conceptions of wrath likewise influence systematic theology. For example: wrath is "the emotional symbol for the work of love which rejects and leaves to self-destruction what resists it"—Paul Tillich, *Systematic Theology*, 3 vols. (Chicago:

rigorous position, for example, is worked out by Klaus Koch. For Koch, judgment and wrath operate within the closed system of the economy and so can be accounted for according to the rule, *die Tat ist die Saat* [the deed is the seed].[25] Finally, one thinks of Gerhard von Rad and his organic, quasimystical insistence that:

> Like a stone thrown into water, every act initiates a movement for good or for evil: a process gets under way which, especially in the case of crime, only comes to rest when retribution has overtaken the perpetrator. But this retribution is not a new action which comes upon the person concerned from somewhere else; it is rather a last ripple of the act itself which attaches to its agent almost as something material.[26]

What cannot be underestimated in von Rad's monergistic summary are both the manner in which God is effectively removed as agent and the attendant consequences. The grand biblical theme of God's opposition to all sin is dislocated from its proper place within the biblical understanding of God's manifold, lordly presence to creation. The life of the creature is described not in direct, moral relationship to the Creator but rather as the unfolding of the closed environment in which human beings find themselves. In the case of each of these three scholars, the emphasis lies upon wrath as a predictable feature of the created world.

There is much that is attractive about this emphasis, of course. Its strength lies in its recognition of human sin as the sole occasion for wrath's exercise.

University of Chicago Press, 1976), I, p. 284; the "retribution of God" is what people bring on themselves—J. Denny Weaver, *The Nonviolent Atonement* (Grand Rapids: Eerdmans, 2001), p. 41; most clearly, wrath is "the world in its essential structure reacting against the sinful corruption of that structure"—Reinhold Niebuhr, *The Nature and Destiny of Man: A Christian Interpretation*, 2 vols. (New York: Charles Scribner's Sons, 1943), II, pp. 55–56.

[25] Klaus Koch, "Gibt es ein Vergeltungsdogma im AT?," *Zeitschrift für Theologie und Kirche* 52 (1955): esp. p. 10. He explores the planting and harvesting metaphor in Prov 11:18 as well as Hos 8:4–7, Ps 7:13–16; 141:10; Jud 9:23f.; and 1 Ki 2:32. Unattended to is the *ab extra* dynamic which conditions accounts of plagues (Ex 7–11), disease (Num 11:33), drought (Jer 14:1–7), famine (Ezek 5:12, 16), or earthquake (Isa 29:6).

[26] Gerhard von Rad, *Old Testament Theology*, 2 vols. (Edinburgh: Oliver and Boyd, 1962), I, pp. 384–385. His conception is that of "a sphere of action which creates fate" (p. 385), one related intimately to Yahweh's power, for it was Yahweh "who eventually brought this process to its goal; he carried this connexion into effect; and hence the guilty party could appeal only to him in order to induce him to break this nexus and avert from the agent the disaster already impending" (p. 386). Hans Wildberger replies critically: "Wherever the saving order, which is what is meant by *sdq* [צֶדֶק], is damaged, then Yahweh must step in; then, the punishment of the wicked person would also be part of Yahweh's acting in a righteous way"—*Isaiah 1–12: A Commentary* (Minneapolis: Fortress Press, 1991), p. 207.

Where each manifestation of wrath is viewed as derivative of a concrete human act, the "punishments" and sufferings themselves, however inescapable or disagreeable the process, likewise become part of a predictable experience of cause and effect. In addition, there is much that is attractive in the claim that such suffering is only indirectly ascribable to God. Because God does not inflict such suffering directly, he need not be implicated in any attitude or act of opposition to his creatures. The daunting task of reconciling a loving God with such potent experiences, moreover, loses its urgency. Ostensibly, God is loving and stands on the side of human life even as his people reap the tragic consequences of their actions. Finally, immanentist views of wrath emphasize—even if too strongly—the way in which God can and indeed does work through his instruments. An account of God's character in these historical manifestations of wrath, in fact, will be a central topic of chapter 6.

Before engaging critically with this general immanentist interpretation, we need to consider at least one recent theory which tempers and nuances, even if unsuccessfully, the more extreme positions we have so far considered. In his *Commentary on Romans*, Ernst Käsemann writes that both the threefold reference to God's giving sinners over to their sin (παρέδωκεν αὐτοὺς; cf. Rom 1.24, 26, 28), as well as scripture's thoroughly eschatological perspective (cf. Zeph 1.8; Dan 8.19), sufficiently rules out a stark impersonal-mechanistic explanation. Furthermore, he observes, Paul makes no effort to identify an intermediary through which wrath might be enacted, one which would keep the dubiousness and supposed evil of the act itself comfortably removed from the person and culpability of God. It can be noted, however, that despite Käsemann's insistence on wrath as the secret retribution by which "God himself is at work in a hidden way," the fact that this wrath is conceived of as operating "apart from Christ"[27] compromises the unity of Romans 1 by referring divergently to either the "revealed" or the "hidden" God.

If pressed too far, the appropriation of divine work to individual persons of the Trinity eventuates an ontological distinction, even opposition, between the Father and the incarnate Son. One such overemphasis is found in Emil Brunner's distinction, not merely between the two "modes" or "spheres" in which God is known, but rather in the more radical distinction between the

---

[27] Ernst Käsemann, *Commentary on Romans*, trans. G.W. Bromiley (Grand Rapids: Eerdmans, 1980), respectively, pp. 37, 35. Related but less conceptually sharp is Stephen Travis' argument, in *Christ and the Judgment of God*, that wrath is "the self-imposed—yet divinely controlled—consequence" of human action (p. 51) such that judgment itself must be considered "intrinsic, but from God" (p. 122). The benefit of retaining retributive language in theology, he argues, is its capacity to protect "the supremacy of God as Judge and as the sender of wrath" such that God retains the last word in all matters (p. 38). The plausibility of this intrinsicism, however, is dulled by inattention to Jesus Christ's role in the act of divine judgment.

God who meets us in his alien work and the God revealed in Jesus Christ. Specifically, Brunner argues that the One who "meets us in Nature and in the natural course of this world,"[28] will be known only in the work of his "retributive justice"[29] and so as judge and executioner, darkness and death. Decisively, this work

> is not Salvation, it is not Life, it is not Light; this is the work which He does where He is not known, not loved, not trusted, not recognized. There too He is the Holy God; but His holiness does not express itself as love, but as wrath, as consuming Fire. Where he is *thus* present, as the wrathful God, there he is not present in Jesus Christ, but outside of Him. The witness of the New Testament confronts us unmistakably with this alternative: *either in Christ, the love of God, or outside of Christ, wrath.*[30]

The identity of God, it is thus suggested, includes but also surpasses and encompasses the self-revelation of God in the incarnate Son.[31]

Whereas we have developed the task of the doctrine of the divine attributes as a response to the self-revelation of God, and most especially as a following after christological and pneumatological resources, and while the variation that this self-revelation encompasses has been stated in trinitarian and so distinctly ontological terms, this has been articulated in agreement

---

[28] Brunner, *Christian Doctrine of God*, p. 173.

[29] Ibid., p. 233.

[30] Ibid., p. 230; the emphasis is supplied. With reference to classical trinitarian theology, he argues his own position as a retrieval of a robust emphasis upon the doctrine of appropriations: "There are works of the Father, which are most certainly not the works of the Son" (p. 234).

[31] Ibid., p. 232. The initial inspiration for this distinction, according to Brunner, is derived from Martin Luther's writings; see pp. 168–174. It is not clear, however, that his reading of the Reformer is most accurate at this point. For example, in Luther's commentary on the twentieth thesis of his *Heidelberg Disputation*, he invokes John 14:9 ("Whoever has seen me has seen the Father"): "That person deserves to be called a theologian, however, who comprehends the visible and manifest things of God through suffering and the cross"—*Luther's Works*, vol. 31, ed. J. Pelikan, H.T. Lehman (Philadelphia: Fortress Press, 1960), p. 53. The point of the commentary is to identify the knowledge of God exclusively with the suffering of Jesus Christ. This is where God has hidden himself, in other words, and God has done so for the very purpose of being revealed only by faith. This fuller reading is supported by Gerhard O. Forde, *On Being a Theologian of the Cross: Reflections on Luther's Heidelberg Disputation, 1518* (Grand Rapids: Eerdmans, 1997), esp. pp. 77–81. According to Forde, theologians described in thesis twenty "have eyes only for what is visible, what is actually there to be seen of God, the suffering and despised crucified Jesus." By faith, this is where they *must* look. There is no other place *extra Christus*. "In the cross God actively hides himself. God simply refuses to be known in any other way" (p. 79).

with the indivisibility of the external acts of the triune God. Under this conception, there is no ground for a *deus absconditus* such as Käsemann suggests. "There is only the one God who has revealed himself in Jesus Christ in such a way that there is perfect consistency and fidelity between what he reveals of the Father and what the Father is in his unchangeable reality."[32] Wrath, in short, is a matter of the gracious self-revelation of the triune God and so an object grasped *per solam fidem*.

Two Implications and Intimation of a Third

In anticipation of our positive exposition—which locates the decisive self-revelation of God in his wrath in the cross of Jesus Christ—we can note two of the distinct inadequacies which attend this immanentism. A first point of contention is whether immanentist accounts do not finally collapse all divine action into the outworking of the "natural" order, binding God to a course of action incommensurate with both his freedom and grace. Brian Gerrish argues that Reformed theologies, as with certain others, have generally affirmed the contrary point: "God is the free Lord over the works of his hands and is not irrevocably committed to the natural sequence of events."[33] We have developed at length an account of the subject matter of the divine perfections, which not only allows for divine self-manifestation in a variety of economic events but also rests at each point on a non-competitive understanding of God's presence. In short, God directs "in an irresistible but non-coercive fashion, a history between God and creatures whereby the two are one in act yet remain completely themselves."[34] At every point, God's work of creation and redemption preserves rather than compromises divine and human freedoms.

In relation to our Romans passage, we can recall that the whole of what Paul refers to—righteousness and wrath, salvation, and judgment—is grounded in the central event of God's self-revelation, the cross and resurrection of Jesus Christ. God acts in the economy of creation and redemption without compromising either his own sovereignty or the finitude and goodness of what he has made. In particular, this is specified in the revelation of wrath ἀπ᾽ οὐρανοῦ (1.18). The spatial metaphor, distinguishing the mundane and systemic (*hic et nunc*) from the heavenly and transcendent (that which is *ab extra*), indicates the peculiar immanence by which the transcendent God is present and active. As potent a reality as wrath may be,

---

[32] Torrance, *Christian Doctrine of God*, p. 243.

[33] Brian Gerrish, *Tradition and the Modern World: Reformed Theology in the Nineteenth Century* (Chicago: University of Chicago Press, 1978), p. 148.

[34] Kathryn Tanner, "Creation and Providence," *Cambridge Companion to Karl Barth*, ed. J.B. Webster (Cambridge: Cambridge University Press, 2000), pp. 124–125.

"the cause is actually external to human existence."[35] While secondary causality is not thereby denied—in a context such as that of the Gospels, for example, detailed analysis would have to account for the simultaneity of God's disposing of sin and human culpability in the crucifixion of Jesus—secondary causality is nonetheless prevented from eclipsing the primary mode in which God actively engages the economy as Lord.

Mechanistic theories, by contrast, tend to eclipse "the Lord of history" and, correspondingly, to submit human beings—explicably and predictably—to the compulsive and controlling power of blind force.[36] If God has divested himself of a direct role in this return of evil for evil, it remains particularly unclear and troublesome whether this process can in any way be mercifully interrupted. Tony Lane is particularly attuned to the manner in which immanentist theories of wrath drift toward deism.[37] In support of this judgment, he calls attention to A.T. Hanson's somewhat unfortunate defense of immanentism. "Wrath is part of the natural moral order," writes Hanson,

> and it is no more deistic to conceive of God as allowing the process of the wrath to work impersonally, than it is to conceive his allowing the process of the laws of nature to work impersonally. Just as moral life is erected on a foundation of natural order, so life in the Spirit is erected on a foundation of impersonal moral laws.[38]

The irony is that at least one prominent tradition of Christian theology, as we observed above, has denied even that the laws of nature, once established, are set on their way, and so function independently of the guiding, sustaining, and ruling work of the triune God. Identifying immanentist interpretation as broadly "deistic" is therefore an important starting point for critical engagement.

A still more penetrating critique, however, is that the immanentist perspective offers little evidence that a formal or self-critical concept of divine action is actually at work but rather suggests only *ad hoc* approximations to certain intuitive values and judgments.[39] As a result, the decision to accredit judgment

---

[35] Gathercole, "Justified by Faith," p. 170.

[36] Lesslie Newbigin, *Foolishness to the Greeks: The Gospel and Western Culture* (Grand Rapids: Eerdmans, 1986), p. 63.

[37] Cf. Tony Lane, "The Wrath of God as an Aspect of the Love of God," *Nothing Greater, Nothing Better: Theological Essays on the Love of God*, ed. K.J. Vanhoozer (Grand Rapids: Eerdmans, 2001), pp. 148–149.

[38] Hanson, *The Wrath of the Lamb*, p. 188.

[39] Consider, for example, the twofold claim that, not only is there "universal agreement among civilized people that no human being should perpetuate horrors" like those which scripture occasionally attributes to God but, more to the point, it is clear to "a mind nurtured by the Spirit" that such severe acts cannot even be attributed to God—I.

to cosmic processes but blessing to God appears wholly arbitrary. Even more objectionable is the suggestion that *each* terminates in economic process. If blessing, in other words, as an irreducible dimension of the moral world which human beings occupy, is likewise a matter of mechanistic return—as, for example, with Hanson's identification of "life in the Spirit" with impersonal law—it is no longer commensurate with grace. A theology of divine wrath *ab extra*, by contrast, does not bear this serious weakness. The connection between divine righteousness, human sin and the blessings and punishments of God are, on this account, subjected entirely and as a whole to God's discretion. Without exception and without qualification, wrath and blessing are understood as dependent upon the wish and right of God, and so reflect an essential continuity between creation and redemption.

Second, insofar as such interpretations deny the inner unity of wrath and righteousness, they divest themselves of the genuinely representational nature of the act of judgment required to characterize such adverse experiences as *punishment*. When considered strictly as a feature of the world, in other words, wrath cannot be expounded in terms of an active, legal development, one which relies upon a set of legal norms flowing from the covenant, norms upon which prophetic judgments might be based. Sufficient for such "judgment," it is argued, is "the fate-enacting sphere of action" [*die schicksalwirkender Tatsphäer*[40]], which surrounds each person and effects the consequences "appropriate" to each action. Without the reference to law, however, and apart from the discretion of a judge, an immanentist theory needs either to supply a basis for its moral reference or to abandon the moral reference altogether. Without an inner, juridical foundation, human experiences of divine wrath could only be understood as the unpleasant consequences of personal or corporate action.

Gene Tucker has argued that much of scripture is distinguished by its concern for the juridical rather than the immanentist—or what he refers to as the "dynamistic"—perspective. The particularity of the scriptural witness is directed neither at the connection "between a particular kind of willing and pain," nor at the mysterious sense in which, as Edwyn Bevan has further

---

Howard Marshall, *Beyond the Bible: Moving from Scripture to Theology* (Grand Rapids: Baker Academic, 2004), pp. 66–67. He offers as examples the images of the Himprisonment and torture of the unforgiving servant (Mt 18), the eternal fire (Mt 25; Lk 16), and the brutal killing executed in the presence of the king (Lk 19). An adequate response to this position would have to address, at the very least, how one's capacity for theological judgment is related, one the one hand, to catechesis and, on the other, to formal education and sociocultural inheritance.

[40] Robert L. Hubbard, "Dynamistic and Legal Processes in Psalm 7," *Zeitschrift für die alttestamentliche Wissenschaft* 94(2) (1982): 267.

argued, such a connection *ought* to exist.[41] Rather it is directed at a concrete account of the One who presides over such judgment. In the last chapter, we argued that God's foundational righteousness is recognizable as a function of the wish and the right of God himself, and is intelligible within a judicial framework, which includes injunction, concrete evidence, and corresponding verdict. It is standing before the Judge himself, in other words, which provides for that "major step from recognizing actions as careless or foolish to identifying them as criminal or sinful."[42]

Oliver O'Donovan, though concerned primarily with the sociopolitical dimension of justice, judgment, and punishment, offers valuable guidance. The justice, which belongs to punishment, he writes, is not exhausted by an exchange of suffering for suffering. Exchange theories like this fail to recognize that a return of *the truth* of an offender's crime is inherent to punishment. Punishment does not merely "echo" the crime but rather "answers" the crime in a representative manner. O'Donovan writes:

> the punishment of an offender requires the community to devise a truthful response to the offense, which is a purposive action, not a blind consequence or an instinctive reaction.[43]

This is a crucial observation. The attempt to incorporate moral categories into an overall understanding of punishment as the "echo," which obtains between actions and subsequent experience of the "consequences" of those actions is deeply misguided. It subverts the inextricably personal dimension of righteousness by excising the ruling judge. Judgment and punishment, rather, should be presented decisively as acts of personal agency. They are not merely events but rather interpreted events, and as such they are best understood as "answers" offered by the one in authority.

O'Donovan comes very close to our particular concern in offering two additional warnings:

> The concept of punishment as an automatic and impersonal return of evil to the doer is a seductive but dangerous one. Seductive, because it offers to relieve us (and God) of the responsibility for fashioning hostile judgments, so permitting us (and God) to be wholly friendly towards offenders while the just desserts of crime are worked out behind our backs with the rational impersonality of a law of nature.

---

[41] Edwyn Bevan, *Symbolism and Belief* (London: G. Allen & Unwin, Ltd., 1938), pp. 243–244. Thus his analytic account concludes: wrath "is what the law of *karma* becomes if the nexus is regarded as willed by a personal God" (p. 245).

[42] Tucker, "Sin and 'Judgment' in the Prophets," p. 375.

[43] O'Donovan, *The Ways of Judgment*, p. 113; cf. pp. 110–113.

Dangerous, because it carries the high price-tag of a despairing fatalism about evil. There will be no forgiveness or escape in a world where cosmic justice operates apart from anyone's intention; we will quickly be given over to the implacable Furies. The best theological tradition asserts God's responsibility even for what look like chance occurrences of justice.[44]

Dubious suggestions of moral distance between Judge and judgment and an inherent tendency toward fatalism and quasikarmic notions of reality raise serious questions concerning the adequacy of immanentist interpretation of God's wrath *as punishment*. At this point, it seems, the road of interpretation forks, and the profound consequences of following to the left or the right are eminently clear. At the end of one path lie the closed, inescapable, and morally unintelligible consequences inherent to one's actions—the implacable Furies. At the other await "the hands of the living God" (Heb 10.31), the Judge who is both full of wrath for the sinner as he returns punishment by word and deed, and yet also fully alive in generosity.

By drawing out these two negative implications—the naturalization of both curse and blessing and the loss of a coherent concept of judgment—the theological costs of allowing God to be lost behind his livingness are made clear. A criticism of immanentist theories of wrath therefore begins effectively from these two observations. Nevertheless, this is merely a beginning—a sharpening of the larger question concerning the exact character of God in his wrath. Our goal, in this respect, is not to isolate Romans 1.18 and make it the center of our exposition. As we have already intimated, we intend to avoid this common reductionism by demonstrating that the most provocative and compelling argument against mechanistic theories of wrath or, positively stated, the most reliable foundation for locating wrath among the perfections of God's life, is provided in Romans 3.21–26. In turning to an analysis of the patience with which God's redemptive work unfolds as well as its center in the cross of Jesus Christ, we are not, as some would have it, turning to a "counterposed"[45] theme but rather to wrath's very center and fulfillment.

---

[44] Ibid. Likewise, Barth insists that God's reaction to wrongdoers cannot be compared to "a mechanism which functions . . . independent of His free ruling and disposing . . . God is the Lord in all His rule, even in that of his wrath"—*Church Dogmatics* IV/1, p. 221. This claim is clearly conditioned by Barth's description of divine patience in *Church Dogmatics* II/1, pp. 407–422, a topic that will be taken up below.

[45] Peter Stuhlmacher, *Gerechtigkeit Gottes bei Paulus* (Göttingen: Vandenhoeck & Ruprecht, 1965), pp. 80–81, argues on the basis of OT parallels that the wrath of God must always be "counterposed" against God's righteousness. This sharp disjunction, as we have already noted, is little warranted on the basis of Paul's usage. Far from

II. *The Gift of Jesus Christ: Wrath and the Exchange of Death for Life*

In Romans 3.21–26, a number of themes converge: the atrocity of universal sin, the severity of the wrathful God before whom sinners are judged, the sacrifice of Jesus Christ for the sake of God's people, and the offer of proof that throughout his dealings with humankind God maintains his righteousness. Having drawn out the implication of the first two for a doctrine of God's wrath, we can begin an analysis of the third—Jesus Christ in the place of sinners—by noting that, in our passage, all is subsumed under the freedom in which those who believe are justified δωρεὰν τῇ αὐτοῦ χάριτι (3.24).

The meaning and significance of the term δωρεὰν for dogmatic reflection is a matter of some dispute. Its adverbial form indicates the manner of divine action and so deepens an understanding of how God *gives* as grace the justification and redemption, which therefore may only be *received.* At the very least, δωρεὰν should be understood in the present context as a positive form of the claim that no antecedent ground exists in sinful human life for the grace which sinners receive. Because righteousness is indeed the focus of the Romans passage as a whole, the gift-nature of redemption is *the* instance of the generosity which God reveals as essentially right. Despite the judgment under which all sinful humanity stands, human beings do not receive what is "due" them but by faith receive the blessing of Jesus Christ's death and resurrection. The passage offers no indication that God's gift is given grudgingly or partially, but that it is rather the intentional outworking of his gracious initiative, completely sufficient to the redemption it is meant to effect.

Observations like these are helpful in thinking through what it might mean for a gift of God to be genuine and perfect. By contrast, they might also tend toward speculation and so the endorsement of an abstract concept of gift. Recent expositions of God as a giver of good gifts, in fact, have taken the notion in a more radical direction than we ourselves intend and so demand careful attention. Kathryn Tanner, for example, argues that in order to resist "worldly expectations and patterns of commodity exchange," the basic claim that divine gifts are "not obligated by prior performance" must be supplemented and deepened by a subsequent recognition that neither are such gifts "conditional upon a return."[46] We have argued for the former. By contrast, however, the latter appears not only inaccurate in its core criticism but, where it is made axiomatic for a systematic presentation of the gospel,

---

doing justice to the dramatic tension of the gospel, terms like "counterposed" tend to create *strife.*

[46] Kathryn Tanner, *Jesus, Humanity and the Trinity: A Brief Systematic Theology* (Edinburgh: T&T Clark, 2001), p. 84.

wholly inadequate to an account of God's wrath. We can expand upon both assertions.

First, the criticism is misplaced because, identical with the work of the Holy Spirit, it should be understood that the gifts of God themselves provide the ground for their reception and so, in our specific case, produce the righteousness of God in creatures. A high pneumatology, in other words, is able to hold forensic imagery together with that of union with Christ. According to J. Todd Billings, precisely this feature of John Calvin's theology is largely misunderstood. While critics of the Reformer's theology are quick to charge him with an illegitimate reliance upon the logic of debt and repayment, Calvin actually follows a middle position, "a multifaceted doctrine" in which both legal and transformative imagery are held together.[47] While this tendency is likewise traced through his theology of prayer and sacraments, perhaps the case in point is the inextricable link between participation in Christ and obedience to the law. Billings writes,

> For Calvin, knowledge of God through *pietas* . . . always involves communion and reunion with God. Both tables of the law *function* so as to lead persons to find this salvific communion and righteousness in Christ. Yet, along with this dynamic movement out of oneself, Calvin's emphasis upon the prelapsarian role of the law [i.e. its "third use"] means that a renewal by the Spirit is also an *internal* renewal into the creature that God created one to be. Thus, Calvin's insistence upon the necessity of the Spirit for regeneration does not mean that God must violently intrude upon the "natural," fallen human.[48]

This indivisibility means that faith does not displace love, and divine agency cannot be understood to overpower free human response.[49] Asserting the perfection of divine gifts does not *of necessity* preclude a direct, moral relationship between Creator and creature.

Were the criticism accurate, however, the alternative proposal would nonetheless be inadequate to an account of God's wrath. Where a radicalized theology of divine gifts is brought to bear upon soteriology, as it is in Tanner's theology, it will lead away from the expiatory nature of the cross and toward the peculiar assertion that "*the incarnation* is the very means by which the

---

[47] J. Todd Billings, *Calvin, Participation, and the Gift: The Activity of Believers in Union with Christ* (Oxford: Oxford University Press, 2007), p. 23.

[48] Ibid., pp. 155–156.

[49] For example, even where Calvin speaks of union with Christ in terms of an "infusion" rather than an "imputation," e.g. *Institutes of the Christian Religion* III.vi.2, he nonetheless maintains the unity-in-distinction proper to the *duplex gratia*—cf. ibid., pp. 157n. 59.

fight is waged and won."[50] The incarnation is thought decisive because it centers on God's self-giving, his cleaving to creation. There is no exchange, no reckoning of the obedience of Jesus Christ as righteousness, and no expiatory judgment upon sin. Rather the connection between God and cross is thought through strictly in terms of its horizontal dimension, i.e., its significance for human relationships. Every act of righteousness—including the cross of Christ—is thus considered a good deed owed to the world rather than one owed to God on the basis of the relationship between Lord and servant.[51] This diverges significantly from a twofold analysis of biblical righteousness as both a realization of "covenant relationship with God (by repentance, faith, and obedience), and with the covenant community (acting unselfishly)."[52]

The implications for our study on wrath are correspondingly momentous. Within this account, wrath too is interpreted in exclusively horizontal, immanentist terms. Tanner herself offers little in the way of constructive development. Nonetheless, she twice quotes Ricoeur's *Conflict of Interpretations* on the topic:

> If sin . . . is the expression of . . . separation, then the wrath of God can be another symbol of the same separation, experienced as threat and active destruction . . . punishment is nothing more than the sin itself . . . it is not what a punitive will makes someone undergo as the price of a rebel will . . . punishment for sin is sin itself as punishment, namely, the separation itself.[53]

Punishment is thus what one suffers in disrupting the web of relationships constitutive of human life. It is a conclusion, moreover, heavily indebted to a radical development of what is entailed in God's act of giving gifts to his people. We are committed to a far less radical concept. In what follows, we will understand grace as a gift precisely in the sense that in the lives of sinful and rebellious human beings, there is for this gift absolutely no merit, no fittingness, and no correspondence.

The Justice of an Incarnate Representative

Having clarified what is meant by the claim that redemption comes to God's creatures as a gift, we can now continue by filling out the significance and

---

[50] Kathryn Tanner, "Incarnation, Cross, and Sacrifice: A Feminist-Inspired Reappraisal," *Anglican Theological Review* 86(1) (2004): 41. Emphasis supplied.

[51] Ibid., *Jesus, Humanity and the Trinity*, p. 89.

[52] P.J. Achtemeier, "Righteousness in the NT," *The Interpreter's Dictionary of the Bible: An Illustrated Encyclopedia*, ed. G.A. Buttrick, vol. 4 (New York: Abingdon, 1962), p. 92.

[53] Kathryn Tanner, "Justification and Justice in a Theology of Grace," *Theology Today* 55(4) (1999): p. 517 n. 7; and also *Jesus, Humanity and the Trinity*, p. 86 n. 39.

historical shape of the gift itself. First, as presented in Romans 3.21–26, the gift of God's righteousness is the concrete, sacrificial death and new life procured by God himself *pro nobis* in the incarnation of his Eternal Son. The trepidation and agony of Gethsemane and Golgotha are not, in other words, a general experience of suffering and death. To suggest this would be fundamentally to mistake both the curse and guilt under which Jesus Christ places himself and the concrete history into which he enters as man for the sake of humankind.[54] This curse, guilt, and history of perdition were unfolded above precisely so we could understand the significance of Jesus Christ as the one "whom God put forward [προέθετο] as a sacrifice of atonement [ἱλαστήριον] by his blood" (3.25).[55]

This work is to be interpreted as an expiatory sacrifice in the tradition of the Old Testament witness. Increasingly, contemporary commentators recognize a distinct connection between the atonement ritual of Leviticus 16.11–22 and the cross of Christ as it is described in Romans. Understanding them together, Douglas Moo suggests, is both "theologically sound and hermeneutically striking."[56] For our purposes, we need only observe one implication of this comparison, namely that the place of atonement, the mercy seat at which God meets his people (cf. Ex 25.22; כַּפֹּרֶת), is identified in Romans with the gracious, personal presence of Jesus Christ. Via a dramatic revelation of God's intention and work, the righteousness of his people

---

[54] In his *Wrath of the Lamb*, A.T. Hanson writes: "Christ never endured the wrath, but by his self-offering through faith culminating in his death he submitted to it in its aspect as the consequences of men's sin; and transcended it, and thereby proved the law, the principle whereby it worked, ineffective" (p. 110). It is on this basis that he can express essential agreement with Dodd's immanentism (p. 69) as well as emphasize the profound truth that wrath is revealed on the cross as the most terrible consequence of sin (pp. 178ff.). Interestingly, Tanner's understanding of incarnation as Jesus' ongoing assumption of human experience—and so death 'in general'—is likewise open to this criticism; cf. *Jesus, Humanity and the Trinity*, p. 31. For a similar critique of Ritschl's theology, see Bavinck, *Reformed Dogmatics* III, p. 397.

[55] In a related passage, it is "Jesus Christ the righteous," as a "sacrifice of atonement," who stands as the assurance of salvation "if we should sin." He is given not for a few people, but "for the whole world" (1 Jn 2:2). Twice more, John roots this sacrificial work in the overall context of God's *missio*, his sending of the Son, who undertakes this work "so we might live" (4:9–10).

[56] Moo, *Epistle to the Romans*, pp. 232ff.; also Jewett, *Romans*, pp. 284–287. Käsemann is disinclined toward this reading. Striking, however, is the conjecture upon which his views are based. He believes the most substantive arguments against Rom 3:25 as a linking of Jesus Christ with the cultic mercy seat are that: (1) Gentile-Christian communities would not have understood "so ambiguous an allusion," and (2) the Jewish-Christian tradition "would probably have clarified it" had Paul meant it in this sense—cf. *Commentary on Romans*, p. 97.

is now (Rom 3.21; νυνὶ δε[57]) made manifest in the living ἱλαστήριον. The conclusion is that what was once veiled—the righteousness of God in dealing with sin—is now unveiled to faith. Jesus Christ is the mercy seat. God's effective judgment upon transgression is no longer accessible through the ongoing observance of the cultic order, with its appointed means, times, and locations, but has been disclosed once and for all (Rom 3.21; πεφανέρωται) in his Son. In him the redeeming presence of God is celebrated, for by the blood of his sacrifice God deals definitively with the sin of his creatures.

While it is not quite accurate to assert, as does Simon Gathercole, that the righteousness of God is "constituted" in this event—since the prevenience of God's life requires that divine action *pro nobis* is only ever the exercise, the proof, of his perfection—the conclusion is absolutely crucial: God's righteousness encompasses "not only . . . his saving deliverance, but also . . . the fact that he has now punished the sin that had previously been passed over."[58] This particular judgment is at the heart of Romans 3.21–26, and is likewise present everywhere scripture indicates that God κατέκρινεν τὴν ἁμαρτίαν ἐν τῇ σαρκί (Rom 8.3), or that Christ was made sin for us (2 Cor 5.21), or became a curse for us (Gal 3.13), or τὰς ἁμαρτίας ἡμῶν αὐτὸς ἀνήνεγκεν ἐν τῷ σώματι αὐτοῦ ἐπὶ τὸ ξύλον (1 Pet 2.24). It is not into the death of a merely finite, mortal life that Christ steps, but the death of condemnation for which, correspondingly, there is in his own history of perfect obedience no just basis. A dogmatic account of God's wrath is largely determined by that particular intercession wherein God sacrificially takes upon himself the destructive power of his own oppositional work.

The ground for conveying the rightness of this act is the singularity of the incarnation by which God in Christ comes to stand in the place of humanity. According to Hebrews 2.17, the atoning sacrifice through which Jesus Christ brings sinners before God for forgiveness [εἰς τὸ ἱλάσκεσθαι τὰς ἁμαρτίας τοῦ λαοῦ] rests on the fact that in every way he was made like them [ὁμοιωθῆναι]. In his priestly work Christ is Very Man and Very God, one able to "represent all and make Himself responsible for the sins of all" so that through the exercise of "the almighty righteousness of God," sin will cease to be ours.[59] The Son of God Incarnate, in other words, is not simply

---

[57] As we will see in relation to the time and space God provides for redemption, i.e., his patience, the "now" does not distinguish a new salvific dispensation, but the revelation of the righteousness which has always been effective for God's people. Cf. Rom 4:3 and Gen 15:6. "For Paul . . . the law served not to distinguish the incorrigibly 'wicked' from the basically 'righteous,' but to show that *all* are 'sinners,' the 'ungodly,' God's 'enemies'"—cf. Stephen Westerholm, "The Righteousness of the Law and the Righteousness of Faith in Romans," *Interpretation* 58(3) (2004): 262. See Rom 3:23; 4:5; and 5:6–8.

[58] Gathercole, "Justified by Faith," p. 169.

[59] Barth, *Church Dogmatics* IV/1, p. 236.

an individual (*anhypostasis*) but the *central* individual (*enhypostasis*), and this is irreducibly necessary to an account of his redemptive work. This theme bears comparable emphasis in Calvin's writings:

> [O]ur common nature with Christ is the pledge of our fellowship with the Son of God; and clothed with our flesh he vanquished death and sin together that the victory and triumph might be ours. He offered as a sacrifice the flesh he received from us, that he might wipe out our guilt by his act of expiation and appease the Father's righteous wrath.[60]

An attempt to grasp the righteousness of Christ's substitution does not fittingly begin from the notion of Jesus Christ as one individual among many. The argument proceeds rather from the premise that only as the Incarnate Son and second Adam is he eminently able and worthy to undergo the punishment of our sin, to represent us before the judgment seat of God, and so to impart to us his own righteousness as a free gift [δώρημα and χάρισμα; cf. Rom 5.15–17]. Thereby, Bavinck writes, Jesus places us "at the end of the road that Adam had to walk, not at the beginning."[61]

Incarnation and the Spirit as Lord over Life and Death

Second, it is on the basis of Jesus Christ's person as the God-man that he is uniquely able to bear the severity and to endure the efficacy of wrath's exercise. A robust doctrine of the incarnation is likewise the basis for asserting that no other human, not even humanity in its entirety, could undergo the judgment and destruction of God's wrath both justly and without being lost to death. Karl Barth therefore refers to the cross of Christ as "that double proof of omnipotence in which God did not abate the demands of his righteousness but showed himself equal to his own wrath"; he submitted to it but was not consumed.[62] John Calvin writes similarly that it was a mark of the power and victory of Jesus Christ that he himself was not overcome by the curse of the cross; rather "he crushed, broke, and scattered its whole force."[63] Neither God alone does this, nor man alone, but God as man. Whereas a mere human being "can only cast himself headlong and be swallowed up in the abyss" of God's wrath,[64] the incarnate Son of God can not only bear it

---

[60] Calvin, *Institutes of the Christian Religion*, II.xii.3.
[61] Bavinck, *Reformed Dogmatics* III, p. 395.
[62] Barth, *Church Dogmatics* II/1, p. 400.
[63] Calvin, *Institutes of the Christian Religion*, II.xvi.6.
[64] Barth, *Church Dogmatics* II/1, p. 401. In fact, as Barth structures this section of the *Church Dogmatics*, §30.2, it is the cross of Christ, which finally supports his assertion that mercy and righteousness cohere as perfections of the divine life: "It [reconciliation]

in the potency which is true to God's judgment upon sin without himself being annihilated, but by it he also brings sin to its end. McNicol makes precisely this point in relation to our Romans text:

> On the cross Jesus Christ, the Righteous One, was set forth in the sight of God as the representative of sinful man. And there, in that supreme hour, the righteousness of God met the wrath of God and, 'in his blood', became 'the redemption that is in Christ Jesus'.[65]

McNicol's is an astute and helpful summary. It also helps clarify two correlative points. In the first place, the event of the cross should be construed broadly enough to allow for the inclusion of those prior moments in which Jesus Christ stands already under the alienation and estrangement, which only *concludes* on the cross. While it is most certainly unwise and perhaps impossible to draw decisive boundaries around this event,[66] we want to suggest that it encompasses, at the very least, his suffering in the Garden of Gethsemane. In this latter event is discernable a point of no return; the moment in which our Mediator asks whether he might be spared "this cup" [τοῦτο τὸ ποτήριον[67]] of God's wrath, and so whether there is not in fact another way through to the reconciliation and redemption which is his mission.

Correspondingly, God shows himself equal to his own wrath neither through the power of the Son once made man—as if he were subsequently left to his own resources—nor in the compatibilist sense that Father and Son agree on the necessity of this righteous act of self-sacrifice. While there is an element of truth in each, neither assertion reflects adequately the thoroughly trinitarian nature of Jesus Christ's priestly work. The same Spirit who binds God to flesh in Jesus Christ (Mt 1.20; Lk 1.35) sustains him under the outworking of

---

could take place only in Him because only He as this one person could be both subject and object in this history, uniting the antithesis of it in Himself: Himself the full end which is made in it; and Himself also the new beginning which is made in it"—*Church Dogmatics* IV/1, p. 550.

[65] John McNicol, "The Righteousness of God in the Epistle to the Romans," *Evangelical Quarterly* 6(3) (1934): 305. In "Justified by Faith," Gathercole relates penalty, wrath, and the destruction of sin thus: "Christ's death is punitive precisely in the sense that he bore the act of divine condemnation of sin in his own death" (p. 179). The schema with which he works, however, unpersuasively sets his own position over against Barrett's and Dunn's nonpunitive interpretation of the cross as "God's action in wiping out sin" (p. 178). Our argument clearly incorporates aspects of both views, suggesting that divine wrath is concerned not simply with the execution of judgment upon wrongdoing but also with restoration through the destruction of obstacles and opposition.

[66] There is, for example, an intimation of impending conflict and a demonstration of Jesus' intentional, conscious move toward it, for example, when he "set[s] his face to go to Jerusalem" (Lk 9:51).

[67] See Mt 26:39, Mk 14:36, Lk 22:24, Jn 18:11, and Rev 14:10.

God's wrath and the death which it effects. We have attempted to follow scripture by characterizing Christ's suffering as a once and for all [ἅπαξ] atonement for our sins, and as a handing over of the righteous for the unrighteous. Jesus Christ—as sin—stood before the God who is full of wrath and so suffered the purity and potency of God's opposing power. What makes it a unique act, however, is that the Spirit of life ministered to him at each and every point and raised him up to new life (1 Pet 3.18; cf. Rom 8.11).[68] The limit of death was itself decisively limited.

Wrath as the Destruction of the Old Adam

Third and finally, we can draw out explicitly that union with Christ, sealed in baptism as God's Spirit claims us *per solam fidem* (1 Cor 6.11; Rom 7.6; 8.10; 1 Jn 2.2), entails for God's people both a great act of destruction and a new creation, their death and their rebirth. The death which one receives through the work of the Spirit is the result of Christ's having exchanged[69] places with the sinner. We have argued above that human beings are neither worthy nor fit to stand before the wrathful God and survive. It is only as Jesus Christ παρεδόθη διὰ τὰ παραπτώματα ἡμῶν, therefore, that sinners are restored (Rom 4.25). By his obedience, δίκαιοι κατασταθήσονται οἱ πολλοί (Rom 5.19). Most forcefully, 2 Corinthians 5.21:

> For our sake he made him to be sin who knew no sin, so that in him we might become the righteousness of God.

Whereas Jesus Christ himself perishes under God's wrath, for us, the unconditional declaration of justification "*is our death and our life*," such that the *simul iustus et peccator* is truly also a *simul mortuus et vivus*.[70] There is no

---

[68] See Bavinck's discussion of the Holy Spirit as the agent of Christ's resurrection—*Reformed Dogmatics* III, pp. 435–436.

[69] Hans Urs von Balthasar identifies "the great exchange" as one of the five central elements of a biblical theology of atonement. To say that *God is for us*, he writes, is to acknowledge that in our helplessness, Jesus Christ becomes sin (2 Cor 5:21) and a curse (Gal 3:13) *so that we can share in God's covenant righteousness* and receive the blessing. The cross is an "ontological transfer" (cf. Col 1:13), or an "expropriation" of human sin into the very life of God (cf. 1 Cor 6:19, 2 Cor 5:15, and Rom 14:7). In Jesus Christ's body, human sin and hostility are condemned (Rom 8:3; Eph 2:14). On the basis of this objective exchange, we are reconciled to the Lord even before and without our consent (Rom 5:18)—cf. *Theo Drama: Theological Dramatic Theory* IV, trans. G. Harrison (San Francisco: Ignatius Press, 1994), pp. 241–242.

[70] Gerhard Forde, *Justification by Faith: A Matter of Death and Life* (Mifflintown: Sigler Press, 1990), p. 35. Bavinck writes, according to "this realistic-mystical view of Christ's substitution . . . believers have been crucified with Christ, have died, been buried, been raised with him, and been made to sit with him in heavenly places"—*Reformed Dogmatics* III, p. 405. Cf. also Rom 6:8; Gal 2:20; Eph 2:6; Col 2:11; 3:3; etc.

separating the righteous declaration of God based on the death and resurrection of the incarnate Son.

Wrath, as the redemptive mode of God's righteousness, is not first and foremost a chastening, not an instigation of human discomfort or an elicitation of discontent in order that humanity might be guided into a more perfect obedience. Viewed from the perspective of our gracious participation in Christ's cross by the Holy Spirit, we are presented rather with the totalizing work of God's wrath, God's "engagement on man's side *against* sin and *for* the creature," which because it is everywhere a mode of the righteousness of the living God, means both "the sentence of death and the provision of life, the fatal no and the quickening yes."[71] That faith calls creatures into this crisis, that a building up into faithfulness involves this self-sacrifice as the foundation of human life, means, as Gerhard Forde so concisely states, "it is not that one must merely live to avoid dying, but that unless we die we shall not live."[72]

If God's yes is most often given the bulk of the attention in Christian theology, proclamation, mission, etc., this is both understandable and proper. It has been our argument, in fact, that the oppositional work of God's life cannot be construed as an end in itself; it is a distinguishable theme of the gospel, but not an independent theme. More precisely, God's wrath should not be understood as a perfection of his eternal life, but rather belongs to his perfection as a mode of his righteousness. While, therefore, we cannot do justice in this space to the numerous positive benefits communicated in God's creative and redemptive work, we can more adequately account for at least one benefit, negative in form, namely God's decisive act in disposing of sin and sinners. Forde's claim is particularly illuminating, for it directs one to the genuinely irreplaceable work of God's wrath. The destruction of the old Adam is a vital consequence of God's will to redeem.

In chapter 4, we examined the significance of God's foundational righteousness for his response to sin. Given a fallen creation, we asked whether God's attention to his own worth isolates him from the work of his hands or constitutes a statute of limitations to the generosity, which he reveals as essentially *right*. Just as our conclusion there was that God both does right by himself and provides for his people by restoring a righteous order, the conclusion in the present chapter is that this restoration is worked out in a pattern of purposeful self-sacrifice. With respect to the Mediator:

> The decisive thing is not that He has suffered . . . [but] that in the suffering and death of Jesus Christ it has come to pass that in His own

---

[71] Weber, *Foundations of Dogmatics* I, p. 436. Similarly, Barth writes of "the radical nature of the divine love, which could 'satisfy' itself only in the outworking of its wrath against the man of sin, only by killing him, extinguishing him, removing him"—*Church Dogmatics* IV/1, p. 254.

[72] Forde, *Justification by Faith*, p. 18.

person He has made an end of us as sinners and therefore of sin itself by going to death as the One who took our place as sinners. In his person He has delivered up us sinners and sin itself to destruction.[73]

The righteousness of God, and the wrath which fittingly and justly accompanies it, are therefore properly unfolded from this central act, from this fullness of time which God has appointed out of the resources of his life above and prior to the irreversible succession of temporal moments. The objective of the cross is more than an act intended to 'set aside God's wrath', a notion which tends toward equilibrium or resolution of internal discord. Wrath, in the context of Romans 1.18–3.26, is only "extinguished" through its perfect execution; God ceases in his destructive and disposing work when there is no sin remaining to be judged.

In this gracious and unexpected event, there is unveiled neither compromise nor contradiction in God's life but rather proof of his everlastingly righteous character. In light of the problem and mystery which sinful human beings constitute, God acts in ways worthy of himself by destroying opposition to his goodness and maintaining his righteousness. This casts significant light on why wrath may only be grasped in close relation to the content of God's righteousness. If the latter is manifested in that "act by which God brings people into right relationship with himself,"[74] wrath, precisely as God's death-dealing opposition, bears a peculiar and indispensable role in thinking through Jesus Christ's act of atonement. The triune God takes up this work freely as a fulfillment of what is right, and thereby justifies the ungodly, acquits the guilty, and raises the dead into newness of life. In order more fully to defend this seemingly outrageous claim, we will turn from our exposition of Romans to the Book of Exodus. The benefits of this second movement in exposition are clear. Attention to both passages in their thematic unity highlights the harmony of God's life—the co-inherence of his righteousness and wrath, the determination to uphold his own worth, and the work of opposition, which is its redemptive mode—and it highlights this harmony by close attention to the patience in which God acts to redeem his creatures.

III. Acquittal of the Guilty

We attempted in the last chapter, in relation to the biblical image of the vineyard, to evoke the counterintuitive nature of God's righteousness as it is manifest in and through his wrath for the sake of redemption. We can now note for similar reasons that, from the perspective of those who depend

---

[73] Barth, *Church Dogmatics* IV/1, p. 253.
[74] Moo, *Epistle to the Romans*, p. 74.

upon the righteousness of God, the message of Romans may be equally shocking. Within the canon of the Christian scriptures, however, there is strong precedent for the claim that God acquits the guilty, and the single most significant instance is arguably that of Exodus 34.6–7. The text reads:

> [6]The Lord passed before [Moses], and proclaimed, "The LORD, the LORD, a God merciful and gracious, slow to anger, and abounding in steadfast love and faithfulness, [7]keeping steadfast love for the thousandth generation, forgiving iniquity and transgression and sin, yet by no means clearing the guilty, but visiting the iniquity of the parents upon the children and the children's children, to the third and the fourth generation."

As a classic constellation of the perfections of the divine life, this passage is particularly germane to our investigation. The material continuity between Romans 3.21–26 and the striking testimony of Exodus 34.6–7 commends, in turn, the harmony in which God has both his righteousness and wrath, as well as the patience which is irreducibly a part of their execution.

Turning to Exodus, immediately apparent in our passage is the twofold witness to God's character. There are, on the one hand, those qualities in 34.6b, which together convey the length to which God goes to maintain a right relationship with his people. The words for merciful [רַחוּם] and gracious [חַנּוּן] are, according to Donald Gowan, special forms of common roots, used in scripture only with reference to God.[75] Particularly relevant to our subject matter is the additional claim that God is slow to anger. The Hebrew idiom means, literally, "long nostril" [אֶרֶךְ אַפַּיִם], and suggests that whatever fury there is in the breath of Yahweh has time to cool off before being breathed out upon his people. Finally, there is the pivotal assertion of God's great loving-kindness [רַב־חֶסֶד], the meaning of which includes "an element of spontaneous freedom in the demonstration of goodness or in kindly conduct."[76] Taken together, this encapsulation of the goodness of God's will and ways is repeated frequently throughout the Old Testament.[77]

Just as pronounced, on the other hand, is the concern of 34.7b for the worthiness of God's action in response to sin, a worthiness that includes visiting [פָּקֵד] judgment upon those who have earned it for themselves. Anything less, it is believed, would be an abomination of justice (cf. Ex 23.7; Prov 17.15; also Isa 5.23; Deut 25.1). Both themes are present in what is, particularly within the Old Testament, a rich description of God's character.

---

[75] Donald E. Gowan, *Theology in Exodus: Biblical Theology in the Form of a Commentary* (Louisville: Westminster John Knox Press, 1994), p. 236.

[76] Ibid.

[77] See particularly Jonah 4:2. This knowledge of God's character, as discussed above, caused the prophet much anguish. Cf. also Num 14:18; Ps 86:15; Neh 9:17 and Joel 2:12–14, and modifications as in Mic 7:18–20.

On the basis of this testimony, the question arises once again as to how God can be disposed toward his people in both regards, and so precisely how wrath may be related in systematic perspective to the righteousness of God.

The Life of God and the Question of Strife

This singular description of God's perfection lies at the theological center of Exodus 32 to 34, a passage which itself constitutes the climax of the book. At one end is the heinous event of the Golden Calf, on account of which Yahweh desired "to consume" his people by his wrath (כָּלָה; 32.10). The lasting effect of this incident upon Israel's conscience cannot be underestimated. As Terence Fretheim has pointed out, in many ways this episode functions for Jewish theology as "a fall story."[78] At the other end, however, and arguably for the first time in Israel's history, this narrative describes the manner in which Yahweh manifests himself as a God who forgives his stiff-necked people and shows them mercy. Opposite the dreadfulness of their idolatry, in other words, is juxtaposed Yahweh's unforeseen pledge, "I hereby make a covenant" (34.10). It is a peace-making pronouncement, one which marks "a decisive turning point" in the history of the people of God.[79]

In order rightly to interpret the movement of this passage, we propose that both confidence and modesty are required: the former, insofar as the impetus for the redemption of God's people is indeed traceable to God and God alone; the latter, because it is not apparent within the confines of the passage itself how this act of mercy harmonizes with the corresponding claim that God, in his righteousness, does not fail to visit iniquity upon the guilty. We can expand these two points in turn.

A first point suggests that because redemption has its source and occasion in the self-sufficiency of God's righteousness, one is rightly confident that God lives his life for the redemption of his people. Only initially, in other words, does Moses himself appear responsible for bringing about or mediating God's resolve to save. While, as Childs notes, in *requesting* to be left alone (32.10) God indeed "leaves the door open" for Moses to contribute something to his decision,[80] in the dialogue between the two, what Moses finally contributes is a mere reiteration of God's past deeds. God has already delivered his people out of slavery; he has been glorified before the Egyptians; and in doing so he has remained faithful to his promise to Abraham (32.11–13). The reminders offered by Moses are thus reminders that the basis for God's actions is wholly located in his own gracious resolve and so in the perfection which these acts manifest. Because this grace is not dependent on anything

---

[78] Terence E. Fretheim, *Exodus* (Louisville: John Knox Press, 1991), p. 279.
[79] Walter Brueggemann, *The Book of Exodus* (Nashville: Abingdon, 1995), p. 949. Cf. also Gowan, *Theology in Exodus*, p. 217.
[80] Brevard S. Childs, *Exodus: A Commentary* (London: SCM Press, 1974), p. 567.

outside of God himself, its enactment—whatever its historical shape might be—neither depends upon nor finds its source in creaturely merit.

A second point follows. In reaching back into the Exodus story, we have moved into the soteriological open-endedness and incompleteness which, according to Romans, characterizes the entire situation prior to the life, death, and resurrection of Jesus Christ. This moment falls under the shadow of the unrighteousness and ungodliness of humanity and, as such, demands a certain modesty from theological judgment. An account of God's character works decisively from the concrete events of God's self-revelation, but as such these events are not isolatable affairs. As we have argued at length, it is only when they are understood as intentional divine action, and so as acts in complex interrelationship and pattern, that God is known. One implication is that judicious inquiry into the harmony or strife implicit to Exodus 34.6–7, should recognize the provisional nature of this isolated witness and so refuse to draw absolute conclusions on either side.

In concluding in favor of internal divine conflict, for example, Walter Brueggemann is as quick to claim a definitive shape for God's character as the systematic arguments that he criticizes. The events of Exodus 32–34, he argues, reveal the "profound and durable incongruity" proper to the life of God, a tension between God as he "inclines to be utterly for the other" and God as he is "characteristically . . . for God's own self."[81] Consonant with his commitments to both the irreducibility of the text's historical boundedness and its existential quality, he concludes that God's presence to Israel is "marked by an open-ended, unresolved two-sidedness."[82] At the other extreme, however, it is equally immodest to consolidate the thematic overlap between Exodus 34 and Romans 3 in such a way that an element of capriciousness is introduced into God's gracious character. Donald Gowan, for example, indelicately expresses the central theme of both of the passages as "God's freedom to forgive whomever he wills and . . . the triumph of mercy over justice within the divine will."[83] Following the brilliant theological analysis of G.C. Berkouwer, the first extreme tends through a process of historicization to detach temporal, discursive events from their foundation in God's electing love. The second, by contrast, tends through a process of eternalization to compromise the irreplaceable work of Son and Spirit in history.[84] In terms of the divine perfections, the former position favors strife, while the latter favors an empty identity. Neither, we argue, gives due consideration to the canonical perspective and so to the inner logic of Romans.

[81] Brueggemann, The Book of Exodus, p. 947.
[82] Ibid., p. 951. More constructive debate would address (1) Brueggemann's reduction of divine attributes to essentially non-relational claims about God's character *in itself*, and (2) his corresponding claim that Israel was never concerned with such concepts (p. 947).
[83] Gowan, *Theology in Exodus*, p. 251.
[84] Berkouwer, *The Work of Christ*, p. 270.

The identity of God is rendered in and across the canon of Old and New Testament writings, and so should be understood irreducibly as a matter of the eternal One as he is present to and active in history. Without this basis, one lacks sufficient ground for following after the acts of God as being single-minded in origin, uncompromising in execution and unvarying in goal. Once again, Berkouwer is finely attuned to that overemphasis upon historical reality, which misinterprets, in particular, the event of the cross as being the *cause* of God's turn toward creatures. The reasoning behind the *Umstimmung Gottes* is viciously circular and so quite simple to summarize: God, it is thought, turns from wrath to love by an act of his love. Historically speaking, Berkouwer sees this as a dilemma presupposed and introduced by certain critics of satisfaction theories of the atonement—specifically, Korff and Harnack—and cites a number of biblical and historical resources in support of his own position.[85] A passage like Romans 3.21–26, however, includes in itself an adequate response. The divine act of setting Jesus Christ forward as ἱλαστήριον does not generate God's love over and against the potent reality of his just wrath but, as we have argued at length, is itself based on the gift-character of God's everlasting love (cf. Rom 3.24). The cross is not an event constitutive of divine perfection, but rather the manifestation of God's life or, as Berkouwer more elegantly summarizes it, the "mysterious harmony between God's love *from eternity* and Christ, whom he appointed as the means of reconciliation."[86] An adequate account of the divine identity requires attention to the whole of God's self-revelation.

While Exodus 34.6–7 indeed comprises "an astonishing disclosure of God, which tells Moses (and us) as much about the God of the Bible as any verse can,"[87] the reasons for cautious consideration of Brueggemann's thesis are near to hand. Were this twofold witness lifted from scripture, christened an irresolvable duality, and so made a limit for interpretation of the text, at the very least, the impetus behind God's saving actions would no longer be discernable. If human beings have constituted themselves enemies of God, if

---

[85] Amongst the relevant biblical texts, Berkouwer cites 2 Cor 5:19; Jn 3:16; and Lk 1:78 (p. 261). He likewise cites John Calvin's insistence, first, that one must ascend to God's ordaining grace for the source and beginning of salvation and, second, that John 3:16 and Romans 3:25 together clarify that it is by his love that God chooses to act as ἱλαστήριον in the person of Jesus Christ (pp. 268–269). Finally, the Reformed Confessions speak both to the appeasing of God's wrath and to God's initiative in this work, and they do so without any awareness of a dilemma and so without any desire to resolve the supposed tension. For examples, cf. *Belgic Confession*, arts. 21 and 26; *Canons of Dort*, v, 7 and i, 2–3 (pp. 258–259).

[86] Berkouwer, *The Work of Christ*, p. 277.

[87] Brueggemann, *The Book of Exodus*, p. 947. It is significant too that Calvin, who so consistently avoids the "vain speculation" of traditional descriptions of the divine attributes, regards these verses as genuine expressions of God as he is toward his people—*Institutes of the Christian Religion*, I.x.2.

they have thus rendered themselves helpless in this terminal condition, and if God's righteousness (given the duality) is such that it cannot be reconciled with a determination to "create good out of evil" but has already pronounced humanity's death and damnation a fitting and right end, then there is ostensibly nothing within or without God, which could change their fate. In his righteousness and wrath, the one God himself would be torn between two equally strong impulses.

Even in this respect, however, simply by virtue of what God has done, the passage bespeaks a confidence in the loving-kindness, which is God's life and the mercy in which he returns to his people in the most unexpected of ways, reliant only upon the resources of his own life, and saves. This brings us to a closely related second point. Just as redemption has its source and occasion in the self-sufficiency of God's righteousness, so too its form and content are determined by God alone. In newly instituting the covenant with his people, Yahweh surpasses in both degree and kind Moses' plea that somehow the Lord might accompany the people without consuming them (כָּלָה; cf. Ex 33.3). Whereas the prophet had been trying to keep the people from death, Yahweh responds with that fellowship which gives fullness of life. While Moses and the people indeed receive back something significantly greater than that which they had sought, this divine gift should be described more penetratingly than as "the immensity of divine grace that lies beyond justice."[88] Once again, construals like this sacrifice God's justice to his mercy, and they do so in a costly and ultimately unnecessary manner.

The demonstration of God's grace does not entail the nullification of his promise to judge in wrath. In and through his mercy, God may yet deal rightly with sin. Tying this point into our exposition of Romans, when Paul declares that God proves his righteousness by justifying the ungodly (4.5; 5.6) and reckoning sinners as righteous in Christ (4.6–8, 11, 22–25), he hearkens back to a much older theme.[89] From this perspective, Romans is an account of redemption, which concerned to preserve the righteousness of God both in relation to salvation and judgment, stands in a much longer history of God's ways with his people. Thus the irreducibility of the conclusion: "justification of the fallen human being . . . takes place only in conjunction with condemnation."[90] This is

---

[88] Lou H. Silberman, "You Cannot See My Face: Seeking to Understand Divine Justice," *Shall Not the Judge of all the Earth do what is Right?: Studies on the Nature of God in Tribute to James L. Crenshaw*, eds. D. Penchansky and P.L. Redditt (Winona Lake: Eisenbrauns, 2000), p. 95.

[89] Gowan points out that in Ex 34:7, the qal participle "forgiving" (נֹשֵׂא) can be translated as either lifting up, bearing, or carrying. The vicarious salvific overtones have been irresistible for some Christian interpreters of the text—*Theology in Exodus*, p. 238. Cf. similar uses Ezek 4:4 and Isa 53:4.

[90] Mark A. Seifrid, "Righteousness, Justice and Justification," *New Dictionary of Biblical Theology*, eds. T.D. Alexander and B.S. Rosner (Leicester: InterVarsity, 2000), p. 744;

based upon the claim, positively, that wrath and judgment are borne fully only by Jesus Christ. Negatively, this has as it corollary the claim that all other divine judgment undertaken in history—which would encompass the slaughter and plague of Exodus 32.27–29, and 35—should be regarded as mere tokens or shadows of the fullness of God's wrath, a notion we will consider closely in chapter 6 (cf. Rom 1.32; 4.25; 8.3). Where Jesus Christ is revealed as the center of the whole sweep of salvation history, a history moving from promise to fulfillment according to the timing of God the Almighty, there is revealed the objective continuity of divine action, a continuity which obviates recourse to a divine double-mindedness and preserves confession of God as "uncompromisingly all things which he is."[91]

The cross of Christ is therefore itself identical with "the harmonization in historical outworking of attributes that are united in the eternal nature of God."[92] In the absence, however, of an attentive and carefully developed understanding of how God is revealed in scripture as alive in his perfection, without an account of his singular presence, and apart from a theologically chastened notion of eternity and the variety and constancy of divine action, which it commends, one must seemingly choose whether God is fully committed to his mercy or uncompromising in his determination to judge. In short, God will either be righteous or full of wrath. Whatever the precise form of the reductionism which results—having observed in Brueggemann's critique at least one concrete example—the implication is the same. Where the judgment of God's wrath is understood as a disposition contradictory to the self-sacrificial work of Christ, the end result will be some variation upon a "divine schizophrenia."[93] Here our argument comes fully around to the decisive proof of wrath's reference.

The Patience of All God's Works

The various lines of inquiry converge here. We have argued that God's wrath is discernable in the context of that singular self-sacrificial act in which God disposes of sin in order to redeem sinners, the cross of Jesus Christ. In relation to this history, we have finally to clarify the single most compelling reason for attributing wrath to the presence and activity of God rather than to an impersonal capacity of the created order. In short, God is alive in his

---

cf. esp. 2 Cor 3:4–11. So too Gathercole: "God saves the righteous precisely *by* his punitive removal of the wicked"—"Justified by Faith," p. 181.

[91] Bavinck continues: "He is righteousness in person, [and so] does not need to restore justice or nullify it by grace, but lets both justice and grace come to expression in the cross of Christ"—*Reformed Dogmatics* III, p. 373.

[92] Lane, "The Wrath of God as an Aspect of the Love of God," p. 163.

[93] Hans Boersma, *Violence, Hospitality and the Cross: Reappropriating the Atonement Tradition* (Grand Rapids: Baker, 2004), p. 48.

righteousness as well as in the wrath which is its redemptive mode, but he is such in his own peculiar timing. These identity descriptions, in other words— whether centered on blessing or curse, affirmation or divine opposition— display neither a mechanical nor an organic character. According to scripture, they are at their heart determined by the perfection of God's forbearance or patience (ἀνοχῆ, Rom 3.25; paired with μακροθυμία at 2.4; cf. the LXX of Ex 34.6).

We can expand upon this claim. In the broadest possible terms, patience is that perfection of God's will,

> deep rooted in His essence and constituting His divine being and action, to allow to another . . . space and time for the development of its own existence, thus conceding to this existence a reality side by side with His own, and fulfilling His will towards this other in such a way that He does not suspend and destroy it as this other but accompanies and sustains it and allows it to develop in freedom.[94]

As with every divine perfection, therefore, so too patience cannot be reduced merely to a mode of God's presence to sinful human beings. At the very least, it likewise characterizes God as he is present to the finite creatures who are created good and blessed with the freedom to "be fruitful and multiply, and [to] fill the earth and subdue it" (Gen 1.28). In the perfection of his patience, God allows even sinners "to stand before him without their having provided an adequate 'satisfaction' of the demands of his holy justice."[95]

First, then, patience is not indeterminate; it does not lack the eternal foundation from which all God's plans flow. In his patience, God anticipates the cross of Christ and so, amidst the ongoing work of redemption—even amidst the history of perdition so forcefully summarized in Romans 1.18–3.20—he withholds the full measure of his wrath. Second, neither is divine patience a special restraint exercised toward those outside the covenant who do not have the temple cult.[96] Such an interpretation would miss entirely the impressive force of the "all people" which conditions Romans 1.18–3.20, as well as the uniqueness of the act in which the triune God himself offers a sacrifice by his own blood in Christ Jesus. Third, God's act of holding history open for redemption does not anticipate a facile act of clemency,

> his *wiping away* of sin at a later date. Rather, the concept inevitably refers to a gracious delay, on God's part, of judgment . . . The divine

---

[94] Barth, *Church Dogmatics* II/1, p. 410.

[95] Moo, *Epistle to the Romans*, p. 240; also Jewett, *Romans*, p. 291, and Gathercole, "Justified by Faith," p. 180.

[96] Cf. Sam K. Williams, "The 'Righteousness of God' in Romans," *Journal of Biblical Literature* 99 (1980): 277.

> verdict upon humanity in Romans 1.32 and the fate of Jesus in Romans 3.25 are identical, with the result that people are saved from that verdict.[97]

God overlooks the sins of humankind for a time precisely because "the intention has been all along to deal with them once and for all, decisively and finally, through the Cross."[98] The sense of God's patience is not consecutive but final.[99]

Fourth, while God's patience provides time and space for a human response, a repentance which corresponds to God's own gracious initiative (2 Pet 3.9, 13–15), this cannot eclipse the utter freedom of God's life and so the manner in which God is eminently at work in his waiting. Wolfhart Pannenberg, for example, focuses in an unusual and provocative manner upon the close relationship between divine patience and wrath, suggesting that one can speak of the former only in light of the threat that the latter constitutes. Nonetheless, on the basis of Romans 1.18–3.26 it is inaccurate to suggest that, in his patience, God simply "waits for the response of creatures to fulfill their destiny."[100] Because promise and fulfillment belong equally to the work of God, conversion is a matter of a larger history of provision—by the law, the prophets, the incarnate presence of Jesus Christ and the gift of the Holy Spirit. In the context of Romans, most decisively, God's patience is not the anticipation of a possibility but, in the most particular and proper respect, the anticipation of the actual obedience of the Incarnate Son. "Jesus Christ is the meaning of God's patience."[101]

* * * * *

We have attempted to show that the movement in which Romans 3.21–26 is rooted testifies to the relationship between wrath and righteousness as they flow from God's own life. And we have offered Exodus 34.6–7 as an example of the mysterious open-endedness clarified by the evidence of God's righteousness. It is thus the peculiar perfection of God's patience, which signals most fully and forcefully the character of his wrath. Wrath does not spring automatically and uniformly into effect, as does natural law or

[97] Gathercole, "Justified by Faith," p. 181.

[98] Cranfield, *Romans 1–8*, p. 212. Positively construed, this is consonant with a reading of Rom 3:20–21 in which two "ways" of receiving God's righteousness are contrasted, "one real and one imagined," namely faith in Jesus Christ and obedience to the law—Gathercole, "Justified by Faith," p. 151.

[99] Käsemann, *Commentary on Romans*, p. 100; also Jewett, *Romans*, p. 291.

[100] Pannenberg, *Systematic Theology* I, p. 439.

[101] Barth, *Church Dogmatics* II/1, p. 432.

mechanism. Its immediate reference is rather God himself as acting Subject, and its fundamental character is revealed in the fact that it may be withheld until fulfilled primarily and properly by God in Jesus Christ.

Stephen Westerholm has identified this as the single most significant aspect of the threefold Pauline use of δίκαιος. While the ordinary usage indicates the universal requirement to do good and avoid evil, and while the extraordinary usage, he continues, denotes the paradox in which sinners are declared righteous, the divine usage designates how God postponed the condemnation of human wrongdoing "until it could be channeled onto the crucified Christ rather than onto the wrongdoers themselves . . ..[H]is rightness and commitment to goodness were never more apparent" than in this act. By it "the divine endorsement of good and hostility to evil are given triumphant expression."[102] The righteous God is Lord too of his wrath.

Precisely in view of the bleakness in which sin denies to God his glory, disrupts and mars creation, and so commits itself to death; precisely in view of God's promise not only to condemn sin in just judgment but likewise, in that judgment, to be the gracious and generous God of his promises; precisely in the essential continuity between the delay in and exercise of God's wrath, it is intimated that there belongs to self-sacrifice and so to genuine righteousness and to God's concrete wrath the perfection of his patience. The time and space, which this opens up for the proclamation of the truth of the gospel, is the subject matter of our final exegetical section.

---

[102] Stephen Westerholm, *Perspectives Old and New on Paul: The "Lutheran" Paul and his Critics* (Grand Rapids: Eerdmans, 2004), pp. 284–285.

6

PUBLICATION OF SALVATION AND FINAL JUDGMENT: REVELATION 14.14–20 AND AMOS 3.2

In the two preceding chapters we attended, first, to the foundational work of God's righteousness and the generosity, which is its proper depth and, second, to the pattern of self-sacrifice by which God accomplishes what is right by saving sinners and disposing of sin. We turn now to a third and final moment in the relationship between divine righteousness and the wrath, which is its redemptive mode, namely the end which God's wrath serves.

This chapter unfolds initially through close attention to Revelation 14.14–20 and the twofold message of triumph[1] in which truth is vindicated and falsehood condemned.[2] In particular, we will argue that this passage

---

[1] Left unread and uninterpreted by the gospel, the notion of divine *triumph* may suggest heroes and villains, seemingly insurmountable obstacles, and tentative outcomes— cf. G.C. Berkouwer, *The Work of Christ* (Grand Rapids: Eerdmans, 1965), p. 327. Consistent with a robust understanding of the eternal resources from which God gives space and time to history, however, we will use the term simply to designate the genuine confrontation in salvation history between asymmetrical and opposing forces.

[2] Our argument is indebted to Richard Bauckham's analysis of the prophetic-apocalyptic genre, *The Theology of the Book of Revelation* (Cambridge: Cambridge University Press, 1993). J.P.M. Sweet, *Revelation* (London: SCM Press, 1990), fittingly describes the imagery as "vague and evocative" (p. 229). Eduard Schweizer considers the author "overpowered by an abundance of images that describe the nature of the coming of God"—*A Theological Introduction to the New Testament* (London: SPCK, 1992), p. 164. The analysis in which we are engaged is thus by no means a complete program for reading first-century prophetic apocalyptic literature. Rev 14.14–20 is complicated. Within this pastiche of images, one counts the winepress and juice-spattered garments of Isaiah 63.1–6, the Son of Man from Daniel 7, as well as the central image of harvest and vintage taken from Joel 3.9–14. For background, see both Bauckham's monograph

bears a redemptive depth. First, we contend that the truth published in final judgment is identical with the judgment manifest once and for all in the life, death, and resurrection of Jesus Christ. Because the wrathful God is in the eschaton none other than who he is on the cross, the cross of Christ publishes what is *even now* if *only then completely* true of God's people.[3] Second, we will unfold the evangelical import of all proclamation of God's opposition to sin by distinguishing wrath's chastising power from the power to bring enemies of God to faith. In exploring the horrible clarity with which the light of divine judgment shines upon wrongdoing and wrongdoer as well as its power to illumine godly hope amidst judgment, the words of Amos 3.2 will figure prominently.

Subsequently, we will examine the claim that, in his wrath, God works from within the life careers of human beings for the purpose of their purification, and so for the education of his people in righteousness. Though a number of resources could be drawn upon, we will focus upon the merits and drawbacks of John Calvin's robust distinction between the *iudicium vindictae* and the *iudicium castigationis*. Requisite to this will be, on the one hand, consideration of certain inadequate theories in which wrath is presented as a means to the maintenance of society and, on the other, attention to the work of the Spirit of God as the irreducible presupposition of redemption.

I. The Righteous God, the Hope of the Persecuted

For a church whose witness and existence are threatened by repeated persecution and suffering, salvation takes the form of a decisive announcement of vindication, an uncovering of their righteousness and the righteousness of God at work in the world. In the Book of Revelation, the possible paths for human life are reduced to two. There are those who have followed the beast and accepted his sign (13.3b–4, 16–17) and so, in being seduced by his "haughty and blasphemous words" (13.5) stand wholly deceived (13.14). Juxtaposed to them are those who have taken their place at the side of the Lamb (14.1, 4). Reflective of the leading motif of the struggle between light and darkness, or truth and falsehood, the faithful are distinguished by the

---

and Margaret Barker's interesting—if not somewhat idiosyncratic—commentary, *The Revelation of Jesus Christ: Which God Gave to Him to Show to His Servants What Must Soon Take Place* (Edinburgh: T&T Clark, 2000), esp. pp. 254–258, 302–309. The latter section treats the non-canonical influences.

[3] Eberhard Jüngel, "The Last Judgment as an Act of Grace," *Louvain Studies* 15 (1990): 391. In contrast with a *not yet—but then* paradigm, this schema applies to the relationship between history and eschatology Jüngel's accent on the "still greater correspondence" between God and world. See also his "Theses on the Relation of the Existence, Essence and Attributes of God," trans. P. Ziegler, *Toronto Journal of Theology* 17(1) (2001): 55–74.

fact that in their mouths οὐχ εὑρέθη ψεῦδος (14.5). In this concrete state of persecution and violence, the church is offered in 14.14–20 the twofold truth of divine triumph. The text reads:

> [14]Then I looked, and there was a white cloud, and seated on the cloud was one like the Son of Man, with a golden crown on his head, and a sharp sickle in his hand! [15]Another angel came out of the temple, calling with a loud voice to the one who sat on the cloud, 'Use your sickle and reap, for the hour to reap has come, because the harvest of the earth is fully ripe.' [16]So the one who sat on the cloud swung his sickle over the earth, and the earth was reaped. [17]Then another angel came out of the temple in heaven, and he too had a sharp sickle. [18]Then another angel came out from the altar, the angel who has authority over fire, and he called with a loud voice to him who had the sharp sickle, 'Use your sharp sickle and gather the clusters of the vine of the earth, for its grapes are ripe.' [19]So the angel swung his sickle over the earth and gathered the vintage of the earth, and he threw it into the great wine press of the wrath of God. [20]And the wine press was trodden outside the city, and blood flowed from the wine press, as high as a horse's bridle, for a distance of about two hundred miles.

For the community of God's people, the imagery of Revelation 14 speaks to the vindication of God with an unmistakable clarity. Absent are any moral shades of gray, false starts in God's workings, or existential anxieties concerning the outcome of history. John's announcement is precisely and concretely *the end of the story*, that toward which all of God's dealings with humankind, sin and falsehood drive.

Dual Images of Triumph

On the one hand, the image is one of the triumph in which God claims and vindicates his people. He harvests the righteous in the dramatic advent of Jesus Christ.[4] The suddenness of the event and its transparently objective quality are indicated by ὅμοιον υἱὸν ἀνθρώπου coming on the clouds (14.14). His authority, like the angels of 14.15 and 17, issues from God

---

[4] G.B. Caird, *A Commentary on the Revelation of St. John the Divine* (London: Black, 1984), p. 190; George E. Ladd, *A Commentary on the Revelation of John* (Grand Rapids: Eerdmans, 1972), p. 199. See Mk 13.27; Mt 24.31; 1 Thess 4.15–17; also Isa 27.12; Hos 6.11; Mt 9.37f.; Lk 10.2; and Jn 4.35–38. While both David E. Aune, *Revelation 6–16* (Nashville: Thomas Nelson, 1998), p. 800, and G.K. Beale, *The Book of Revelation: A Commentary on the Greek Text* (Grand Rapids: Eerdmans, 1999), pp. 770–771, argue that the figure is Jesus Christ, they conclude that the image is most likely one of pure judgment. We explore the cogency of this claim below.

himself and is rooted in God's very presence. The appearance of the Son of Man leads into the event of harvest, a reiteration of the "first fruits" [ἀπαρχή] redeemed from humankind (14.4) now made definitive in scope. It is important that, as Bauckham has argued, had this been intended instead as an image of God's condemning judgment, it would most certainly have been complemented by an act of threshing or winnowing.[5] Here, the harvest is testimony to the redemption in anticipation of which God's saints are called to endure in their witness.

On the other hand, this twofold picture of triumph is also the divine triumph in which falsehood is decisively condemned and destroyed by God. As such, the severity of 14.17–20 can hardly be overstated. In the first place, the announcement originates with the angel who possesses ἐξουσίαν ἐπὶ τοῦ πυρός,[6] a reference which directs our hearing to previous announcements of God's consuming (8.7; 11.5) and death-dealing power (9.18).[7] From a slightly different perspective, of course, the image may not suggest "pain as retaliation" but "pain as purification," a renewal of God's people analogous, for example, to the smelting of iron.[8] The multiple layers of meaning, which belong to the image, are together extremely provocative for reflection on

---

[5] Bauckham, *Theology of the Book of Revelation*, p. 97. See Jer 51.33; Mic 4.12f.; Hab 3.12; Mt 3.12; and Lk 3.17. Caird agrees, observing that though θερισμός and θερίζω include in their lexical scope the mowing down of enemies, they are never so used in the LXX, and in the NT are used most often for the ingathering of the righteous, e.g. Mt 9.37f.; Mk 4.29; Lk 10.2; and Jn 4.35–38—*Commentary on the Revelation of St. John*, p. 190. Though he finally opts for the alternative, Aune too acknowledges that the absence of the language of threshing "makes it possible (though not necessary) to construe this grain harvest as a metaphor referring to the eschatological salvation of those 'harvested'"—*Revelation 6–16*, p. 845. Beale opposes a "harvest as salvation" reading for four reasons. First, salvation is indicated solely, if at all, by the "first fruits" redeemed in 14.3f.; the image most likely refers to "the totality of believers throughout the ages who finally receive their full and final redemption"—*Book of Revelation*, pp. 742, 777. Second, the absence of threshing imagery is inconclusive. Beale suggests Mt 13.30 as a parallel example (though, it might be added, without explanation of the fire imagery). Third, the Son of Man in Dan 7.22 is associated with judgment in the earliest interpretations of the prophecy. Fourth and most important, John would not have altered the basic thrust of Joel's prophecy. At each and every point he "uses the OT consistently with its contextual meaning" (p. 778).

[6] More broadly, compare ἐν πυρὶ ἀποκαλύπτεται, i.e., the terrors and revelation of Final Judgment (1 Cor 3.13, 15), τὴν γέενναν τοῦ πυρός (Mt 5.22; 18.9), and τὸ πῦρ τὸ αἰώνιον (Mt 18.8; 25.41; Jd 7).

[7] God's messengers bear only a derivative and instrumental authority, here indicated by the fact that they act from the temple of God's dwelling (14.15, 17), and so on his authority alone. That the Son of Man himself does not announce "the hour to reap" (14.15, 18) comports with testimony elsewhere that such knowledge belongs solely to the Father (cf. Mt 24.36; Lk 10.22; and Mk 13.32).

[8] Niels Henrik Gregersen, "Guilt, Shame, and Rehabilitation: The Pedagogy of Divine Judgment," *Dialog* 39(2) (2000): 114.

God's wrath, and we will explore the supporting evidence and implications in greater detail below. Of the utmost significance is the description of judgment in 14.17–20 as a trampling of τὴν ληνὸν [winepress] τοῦ θυμοῦ τοῦ θεοῦ τὸν μέγαν (14.19; cf. also Joel 3 and Isa 63). Without yet exploring the specifics, the singular severity and intensity of this judgment seems undeniable—it turns the surrounding land into a lake of blood (14.20).

John's witness is a revelation of the goal of God's redemptive work, the victory of his righteousness, and also the vindication of those martyred for their faith in Jesus Christ. A christological reading of the passage, one which reads vindication and condemnation together rather than in antithesis, reveals significant features of both God's righteous judgment and the wrath in which he judges. There is a redemptive depth to the passage crucial to understanding the unique way in which God opposes those who would oppose him. What follows is an elaboration of the scriptural conviction that publication of final judgment, even at its most severe, obviates neither hope for God's mercy nor the gospel call to repentance. It is to these two themes that we now turn.

Unity of Cross and Final Judgment

To speak of a redemptive depth, first, in terms of the soteriological features of the passage, is to draw attention to those elements of the event of Jesus Christ's cross, which appear here and so to root the decisiveness of the judgment of the vintage and the winepress in the objective event of his atoning death. Little appreciated is the fact that the blood imagery culminating, as we have observed, in the final verse of the chapter is best interpreted in the light of the book as a whole.[9] Whether the author is referring here to the enemies of God, to the blood of the martyrs who serve the Lamb, or to the slaughtered Lamb himself is of tremendous import. Most out of place within the Apocalypse would be the first interpretive option. Of the nearly two dozen occurrences, none refer to the blood of God's *enemies* spilled as a result of judgment. The second possibility can likewise be ruled out on the grounds that such instances comprise merely a varied set of circumlocutions for referring to the martyrs themselves.[10] The blood here is symbolic of their deaths, but bears no independent significance. An independent significance and effective capacity, however, is *consistently* attached to the blood of Jesus Christ. By his blood "he freed us [λύσαντι ἡμᾶς] from our sins" (1.5) and "ransomed for God [ἠγόρασας τῷ θεῷ] saints from every tribe and language

---

[9] But compare Christopher C. Rowland, *The Book of Revelation* (Nashville: Abingdon, 1994–2002), p. 668.

[10] Rev 6.10; 16.6; 17.6; 18.20; and 19.2. The remaining instances are inanimate objects—moon, rivers, hails, etc.—turned into blood or mixed with it as expressions of judgment; cf. 6.12; 8.7; 8.9; 11.6; 16.3; and 16.4.

and people and nation" (5.9). In his blood, a great multitude have "washed [ἔπλυναν] their robes and made them white [ἐλεύκαναν]" (7.14). It is by his blood—and derivatively the testimony of the blood of the saints which bears witness to it—that "the accuser has been thrown down [ἐβλήθη]" (12.10f.). So important is this image to his very person that, at his advent, Jesus Christ himself is clothed in a robe dipped in blood (19.13), an image to which we will shortly return.

What is to be made, therefore, of this relationship between this larger testimony and the blood of Revelation 14.20, which is said to flow from the winepress of the wrath of God "as high as a horse's bridle, for a distance of about two hundred miles"? One option for interpretation is to adopt a thoroughly skeptical attitude toward the unity of the book as a whole and conclude, for example, that the images have been brought together in ad hoc fashion with little concern for the overall structure of the book and its themes. Whatever the commonalities among other references to "blood," therefore, the case of 14.20 could be adjudicated an isolated description of the destruction of all God's enemies. Another option for interpretation— and this is for us the more provocative and compelling route—is to accept that however "wonderfully varied" the imagery of Revelation might be, the images nonetheless comprise a "coherent account" of divine victory.[11] The blood spilled in judgment is best read in continuity with the whole and so identified with that of Jesus Christ. This blood is identical with God's victory over the wickedness of his enemies made effective through his own redemptive self-sacrifice.

Another clear indication that this judgment is to be understood in terms of its redemptive significance is that the event itself is placed ἔξωθεν τῆς πόλεως (14.20).[12] Not only in the Apocalypse but more broadly within the whole New Testament, this ignominious location is closely tied to the meaning of the cross and its benefits for sinners gathered in the name of Jesus Christ. The space outside the city, for example, is the point of assembly for those who would distinguish themselves in their redemption from the temple cult: "Jesus also suffered outside the city gate in order to sanctify the people by his own blood. Let us then go to him outside the camp" (Heb 13.12–13). Likewise, it is thought that Matthew the evangelist adapted the parable of the wicked tenants from its earlier form as found in Mark 12, in order to reflect more accurately that Christ's own crucifixion occurred outside the city (Mt 21.37). The latter version describes the death of the son taking place within the city before he is thrown outside its walls. Altering the parable in this way, by locating the death itself outside the city walls,

[11] Bauckham, *Theology of the Book of Revelation*, p. 21.

[12] Note that the city is unspecified in the text, except for the definite article in 14.20, i.e., ἔξωθεν τῆς πόλεως, which according to Aune indicates Jerusalem—cf. *Revelation 6–16*, p. 847.

better reflects the narrative of Christ's crucifixion.[13] The land outside the new Jerusalem, finally, is described as filled with "dogs and sorcerers and fornicators and murderers and idolaters, and everyone who loves and practices falsehood," a fitting place for the death of one whom God made sin itself (Rev 22.14f.; cf. 2 Cor 5.21).

In each case, the description is neither incidental nor dispensable but rather suggests the consistent use of a symbol derived from the crucifixion narrative. Its kerygmatic force is to bring the ignominy of that which lies outside Jerusalem together with the particular circumstances under which Jesus Christ's atoning death took place and locate eschatological judgment there. Against this background, Revelation 14.19–20 calls powerfully to mind the specific event in which Jesus Christ is both subject *and* object of God's righteousness and wrath, and suggests that the judgment of the winepress of Revelation flows directly from Golgotha.[14] More poetically, G.B. Caird notes that the winepress, while horrible as a picture of God's definitive judgment upon sin, is also "the place where grapes are made into wine."[15]

Third and finally, we can ask after the identity of the one who treads the winepress. Whereas four agents in these verses, the one like the Son of Man and three angels, are clearly identified, the fifth and remaining actor (cf. 14.20) goes unnamed. The *passivum divinum*, ἐπατήθη, intimates that we have here to do with God himself, and this is further confirmed by the more expansive description provided in 19.11–16. This latter passage is much more explicit, invoking for a second time the winepress as an image of Jesus Christ's victory over the beast and his army. The whole pericope merits repeating:

> [11]Then I saw heaven opened, and there was a white horse! Its rider is called Faithful and True, and in righteousness he judges and makes war. [12]His eyes are like a flame of fire, and on his head are many diadems; and he has a name inscribed that no one knows but himself. [13]He is clothed in a robe dipped in blood, and his name is called The Word of God. [14]And the armies of heaven, wearing fine linen, white and pure, were following him on white horses. [15]From his mouth comes a sharp sword with which to strike down the nations, and he will rule them with a rod of iron; he will tread the wine press of the

---

[13] The alteration hypothesis is well documented by Robert H. Gundry, *Matthew: A Commentary on His Handbook for a Mixed Church Under Persecution* (Grand Rapids: Eerdmans, 1994), p. 427; Donald A. Hagner, *Matthew 14–28* (Dallas: Word Books, 1995), p. 618; and Eduard Schweizer, *The Good News According to Matthew* (London: SPCK, 1976), p. 414.

[14] Similar proposals are made by Sweet, *Revelation*, pp. 227, 230, and Boring, *Revelation* (Louisville: John Knox Press, 1989), p. 171; cf. too Rowland, *The Book of Revelation*, p. 668.

[15] Caird, *Commentary on the Revelation of St. John*, p. 193.

> fury of the wrath of God the Almighty. [16]On his robe and on his thigh he has a name inscribed, "King of kings and Lord of lords."

This blood stained warrior, familiar to tradition, is in its Christian context identified with Jesus Christ in his atoning death.[16]

This figure comes to the task of pressing the vintage already soaked in blood. Once again, it is unlikely that such an image simply foreshadows what becomes of God's enemies. More likely it is a recapitulation of the leading theme of Revelation 5.9, "You are worthy to take the scroll and to open its seals, for you were slaughtered and by your blood you ransomed for God saints from every tribe and language and people and nation." Its reference is the cross as the content of final judgment. Next, this rider judges with a messianic righteousness (cf. esp. Isa 11.4 and Ps 96.13), and wages war solely on the might of his Word. This sword, which peculiarly issues from his mouth, suggests the inadequacy of militaristic expectations of judgment and victory.

While the victory secured here is depicted in forensic terms as a victory of truth over falsehood, this should not in any way lessen the threat it poses to sinful human life. "There is no more severe illumination of our lives," writes Eberhard Jüngel, than is possible with this light.[17] Our whole existence is illuminated, measured by God's grace, and so called into question. But the goodness of the prophetic word of judgment, exactly in its destruction of falsehood, is that it speaks the truth about the criminal, that it makes public all wrongdoing so that, where it is owned as such by faith in Jesus Christ, it can be borne away and decisively dealt with. Oliver O'Donovan's observation is penetrating: there is "one good always owed to the offender in punishment: the truth about his offense."[18] The revelation of final judgment and the execution of God's wrath is not a mute or opaque event. Much the opposite: the clarity in which God speaks is exhaustive and inescapable, and in this it is an act of generosity.

Being both righteous and wrathful, the judgment operative in this passage does not refer exclusively to "the destruction of the rider's enemies . . . but also has the positive connotation of the salvific action of Christ toward his

---

[16] Aune, *Revelation 17–22* (Nashville: Thomas Nelson, 1998), p. 1057. Significantly, the parallel of Isa 63.1–6 was typically interpreted by early Jewish commentators as a messianic reference (p. 1049). The author of Revelation is eminently attentive to the multidimensional work of Jesus Christ (e.g. the *munus triplex*). Jesus Christ is worthy [ἄξιος] to proclaim definitive and just judgment precisely because he was slaughtered [ἐσφάγης] and by his blood conquered the deceiver of the world and ransomed [ἠγόρασας] the saints (5.2, 4, 9; cf. 12.9, 11; 13.8). To him belong ἡ δόξα καὶ τὸ κράτος εἰς τοὺς αἰῶνα (1.6). He is the Alpha and Omega, sharing God's throne (11.15; 21.5; 22.3) as he establishes and maintains his kingdom (5.10).

[17] Jüngel, "The Last Judgment as an Act of Grace," p. 397.

[18] Oliver O'Donovan, *The Ways of Judgment* (Grand Rapids: Eerdmans, 2005), p. 118.

people, i.e., as judge of his Church."[19] This observation, typifying as it does the righteousness of God found in Matthew 20 and Romans 3, goes straight to the heart of our argument. It suggests not that wickedness might remain unpunished, but rather that God's exacting, scrutinizing, and uncompromisingly just judgment upon sin will not exclude his acting through grace for the salvation of his people. Even in face of the reality of God's deadly word and the lethal light of his judgment, hope abides. Thus the exclamation:

> Come, let us return to the Lord; for it is he who has torn, and he will heal us; he has struck down, and he will bind us up. After two days he will revive us; on the third day he will raise us up, that we may live before him (Hos 6.1–2).

A much different conclusion would be required were the bloodstained warrior not he who died on the cross as an atoning sacrifice for human sin, and if the sword with which he struck down were not the truth, which is grace to a deceiving and self-deceived people.

The final judgment of Revelation 14.14–20, though challenging in its use of apocalyptic imagery, nevertheless speaks with clarity to the unity of cross and final judgment. Even in this cataclysmic event of wrath, God is in his character *nothing other than* that revealed on Golgotha.[20] The author of the Apocalypse "has not forgotten the definitive picture of the nature of Christ's conquest already given in 5.1–14. The death by which he conquers is his own."[21] Particularly important in the larger context is the blood imagery, the location of judgment, and the mutual conditioning of winepress and sword. Together these features betray the coherence of the richly evocative and varied imagery of Revelation 14. They suggest that God, in the perfection of his singular life, works toward an end beyond the pure destruction of his enemies.

Within this picture of judgment there are genuine hints and intimations of a salvation that gives room for hope to thrive amidst faith and love. In the end, this suggestion does not nullify the terrors of judgment but, as M. Eugene Boring has astutely observed, makes "it possible to take them seriously by

---

[19] Aune, *Revelation 17–22*, p. 1053. See agreement at Sweet, *Revelation*, p. 282, who also notes significantly that the verb ποιμαίνω, usually translated "rule" in 19.15, is the same word reckoned as "shepherd" in Rev 7.17, and so hints at the tender care conveyed by Ps 23 and Jn 10.11. A.T. Hanson is critical of commentary which does not attain to John's high conception of Christ as both Redeemer and Judge—cf. *The Wrath of the Lamb*, p. 177. In this regard, contrast the one-sidedness of Beale's exposition: "Christ's conviction of the impious will lead to his destruction of them, which will be as thoroughgoing as the crushing of grapes in a winepress"—*Book of Revelation*, p. 963.

[20] Cf. Jüngel's claim that ". . . there is no suggestion that the last judgment represents either a rival or a hindrance to justification"—"The Last Judgment as an Act of Grace," p. 395.

[21] Boring, *Revelation*, p. 196.

readers who also affirm the ultimately redemptive purpose of God expressed elsewhere in the Bible, including elsewhere in Revelation."[22] Where such hope is allowed space, however, we would expect the presence of a correlative call to repentance and an invitation to respond to the prophet's sobering announcement. This is our second theme.

Warning and Invitation

To speak of the redemptive depth of this passage once more, this time in terms of its evangelical content, is to point to the living and dynamic function of the imagery. The picture of vintage and the pressing of grapes does not portray something like the ineluctable destruction individuals must accept. The announcement does not, in that sense, destroy history. Rather it marks the singular manner in which the present is held open by God as a time for repentance. Richard Bauckham's view that the world of the Apocalypse "is a kind of court-room in which the issue of who is the true God is being decided" brings us nearer to this point.[23] The pastiche of images is constantly moving the hearer to a decision concerning the truth of its claims. Openness here need not indicate an element of uncertainty, which threatens God's victory. Openness is a matter of the number of those who will finally be given to hear God's truth and to live in his light. Expressing openness in this way gives due place to the all-encompassing and universal goal of God's redemptive work, his self-proclamation, while simultaneously relegating the particular question of who or how many will be saved to the realm of hope, rather than knowledge.

In chapter 14, the prophetic shape of the text is signaled in "the eternal gospel" proclaimed to "every nation and tribe and language and people" (14.6; 5.9; contrast 13.6f.). The gospel consists of an invitation to renounce falsehood, through repentance, and join the side of truth. There are those who have followed the Lamb wherever he goes, even to martyrdom, having both his name and that of his Father written on their foreheads. Discerning in these redeemed ones, however, the limit of the saving power of the gospel would be hasty. While they are indeed the "first fruits" (14.4) of the Lamb's work, they do not seem to constitute a closed community of the saved.

---

[22] Ibid., p. 172. Sweet writes that ". . . John does not separate the two [judgment and salvation], and we should be open to the possibility that he sees Christ's final coming not simply as classificatory, like the judgment of 20.11ff., but as creative, bringing to final effect what his first coming initiated, as 'first fruits'"—*Revelation*, p. 226. Alongside this, he suggests negatively that a purely destructive notion of judgment would make nonsense of passages such as Rev 1.7, 11.13, 15.4, and 21.24ff. (p. 230). Similarly, Caird interprets the vintage, like the harvest, as an image of the ingathering of God's people: "Whatever element of judgment there is in the vintage, it is analogous to the judgment of the world achieved once and for all on the Cross"—*Commentary on the Revelation of St. John*, p. 192; cf. pp. 192–194.

[23] Bauckham, *Theology of the Book of Revelation*, pp. 72–73.

This point is made most clearly by the outgoing entreaty to "Fear God and give him glory, for the hour of his judgment has come" (14.7), a word which stands prior to the announcement of Babylon's fall and the defeat of those who follow the beast.

Like all gospel prophecy—cf. "Seek good and not evil, that you may live" (Amos 5.14) as well as "I have set before you life and death, blessings and curses" (Deut 30.19)—the message of Revelation 14.7 maintains a dual function. *Its warning is invitation.* Whereas the function of biblical prophecy is sometimes relegated to a foretelling of what will come to pass, more important is the manner in which the prophets address their own contexts, and so our own present circumstances. Eduard Schweizer contends, in fact, that this is a prophet's most basic purpose: to speak "God's message ever anew in concrete situations, so that decisions are made."[24] In the prophetic call is included all the severity and definitiveness we have tried to voice, but not in such a way as to remove or obviate the hope of the gospel. God judges his creatures, and sin is condemned, but not in a manner that gives the final word to death. At the conclusion of this chapter, we will return to the question of the right reception of this message and the role of the Spirit. We turn now to further exploration of the claim that divine favor excludes the severity of God's judgment.

The Severity of Divine Favor: Amos 3.2

We have seen that God is righteous precisely as he refuses human beings the right to cast final judgment—whether upon him or themselves. An interpretation of the imagery of the Book of Revelation receives significant direction, however, from those pronouncements of God's righteousness upon his own community, those judgments are drawn out precisely because God is determined in his grace to set his people right. In this respect, the prophecies of Amos are distinctive. They connect the exposure and condemnation of sin specifically with God's giving himself to the people as their salvation. In what follows, we will consider this material, and specifically the significance of Amos 3.2, observing first that covenant fellowship includes the severity of divine judgment and second, that such events are not silent but rather stand under the self-revelation of God in his wrath, a revelation without which such events can have no redemptive value.

The opening chapters of Amos announce judgment upon all the peoples surrounding Israel on account of their unrighteousness and injustice. Yet only Israel is finally addressed on the basis of the intimacy with which God has bound himself to them: "You only have I known of all the families of the earth; therefore I will punish you for all your iniquities [אֵת כָּל־עֲוֹנֹתֵיכֶם עַל־כֵּן אֶפְקֹד עֲלֵיכֶם]" (3.2). Salvation is not contentless, formless harmony

---

[24] Schweizer, *Theological Introduction to the New Testament*, p. 162; cf. 1 Cor 14.24–25.

between parties but a dynamic, purposeful and concretely given life founded at every point in God's judgment. Israel is indeed God's chosen people, but their election entails the scrutiny of his righteousness and the burning opposition of his wrath.

The most obvious feature of this "programmatic saying"[25] is its reversal of common expectations. Whereas the intimacy in which God knows his people (יָדַע[26]; cf. Hos 2.20; Deut 9.24; Jer 1.5) and covenants with them typically suggests the bestowal of salvific favor and prosperity, here the stress is on the stringent accountability which such favor entails.[27] As we have seen all along the line, fellowship with God finds its end in fulfillment of and in witness to his gratuitous righteousness. Where self-preservation and benefit are asserted, by contrast, righteousness is secured as God acts in his wrath. As the three-fold use of all [כֹּל] in Amos 3.1–2 indicates, the Lord returns judgment [אֶפְקֹד] on his people in unmitigated and all-encompassing fashion. Just as the *whole* family of Israel was chosen from among *all* the families of the earth, so *all* their sins will be accounted for and punished. It is judgment seen to be all the more acute in comparison with those surrounding nations who receive punishment only for the grossest of their atrocities.[28]

The iniquity for which God's people are held responsible is a wholehearted disregard for the justice and righteousness, which God has laid out for them. The people have twisted God's righteousness into a tool of self-promotion and self-gain, and this at the height of their territorial expansion and national affluence. Precisely when generosity had every conceivable reason to flourish, the people were willing to "sell the righteous for silver, and the needy for a pair of sandals" (2.6; 5.12). Instead of being God's people, they became in their wealth those "who oppress the poor, who crush the needy" (4.1; 8.4, 6). Justice and righteousness are invoked as the benchmark of Israel's failure: "Ah, you that turn justice to wormwood, and bring righteousness to the ground" (5.7, 6.12).

---

[25] Jörg Jeremias, *The Book of Amos: A Commentary* (Louisville: Westminster John Knox, 1998), p. 48.

[26] On the intimate character of God's knowledge of his people, see J. Bergman and G.J. Botterweck, "יָדַע," *Theological Dictionary of the Old Testament*, ed. G.J. Botterweck, H. Ringgren, and H.-J. Fabry, vol. 5 (Grand Rapids: Eerdmans, 2006), pp. 468–469.

[27] Shalom M. Paul, *Amos: A Commentary on the Book of Amos* (Minneapolis: Fortress Press, 1991), alerts the reader to the counterintuitive nature of both Amos 3.1f. and 9.7f. (pp. 102–103). The argument moves, in the former, from chosenness to punishment and, in the latter, from un-chosenness to restoration.

[28] Ibid., p. 102. While Paul translates פָּקַד as "call to account," he notes that "to punish" lies well within the lexical scope of the word. Terence E. Fretheim, by contrast, critiques translations of פָּקַד, which suggest any direct, personal, or unmediated punishment. He suggests "to visit" as a more accurate translation, acknowledging an indebtedness to the immanentism of von Rad—cf. "Theological Reflections on the Wrath of God in the Old Testament," *Horizons in Biblical Theology* 24(2) (2002): 22.

This is the society into which the prophet Amos speaks the truth of God's judgment. Their predilection for wrongdoing, furthermore, is made particularly odious as they attempt to cloak it in piety. The people presume upon their worship practices in order to assuage pangs of conscience but, in doing so, they show "they abhor the one who speaks the truth" (5.10). None of this escapes the Lord's attention. Judgment, in fact, will "begin with the household of God" (1 Pet 4.17). God lives among his people and will execute his wrath in order that life in all its economic, political, and cultural complexities might flourish rather than be lost in sin's dark shadow. Election to fellowship with God does not insulate a people from the severest of just judgments but rather guarantees God will be fittingly present wherever sin and sinners threaten covenant fellowship.

Closely related to this is a second point. The notion that God undertakes the blessing and punishing of human action in order to maintain a just society may suggest the possibility that close attention to history yields insight into where and why God acts. By contrast, we have argued at length that God does not reveal himself in historical occurrence per se. While God does reveal himself through concrete acts of creation and redemption, such events are revelatory on account of the free and gracious presence of his interpretive Word and illuminating Spirit. Without Word and Spirit, in other words, history is silent and, as one theologian has observed, "humans cannot live meaningfully with that which is visible only, nor with that which is invisible alone."[29]

A distinction rather should be drawn between the sufferings of Israel in and of themselves and these same events as they are taken up, interpreted, and spoken by the prophet for the salvation of God's people. Principally in Amos 4.6–11, we are presented with a litany of the calamities that have befallen Israel. Each effort has come up vain and fruitless, however, and the whole enterprise has apparently failed. Neither hunger and thirst, nor ruined crops and illness, nor the violence of war have succeeded in turning God's people back to him. In and of themselves, *silent events* do not convert the human heart to God. As revelation, however, they are objective pronouncements upon sinful human life before a righteous God. As part of the word of Amos' prophecy, furthermore, these events are fittingly described as "a history with a rationale,"[30] manifestations of God's working for and among his people.

This also upends general expectations of the coming day of the Lord as something desirable. Ironically, the people place their hope in a meeting with God himself in his glory. Amos conveys the danger of such hope through another reversal. He asks, "Why do you want the day of the Lord? It is

---

[29] Kōsuke Koyama, *Mount Fuji and Mount Sinai: A Critique of Idols* (Maryknoll: Orbis Books, 1985), p. 55. The concrete object of his analysis is the event of Word War II and the claim that "the destruction of Japan had not just military reason but a 'theological' cause" (p. 56).

[30] Mays, *Amos*, p. 79.

darkness, not light; as if someone fled from a lion and was met by a bear" (5.18). The day on which all shall be uncovered and exposed is a day of terror according to the prophet. Its light does not vindicate the lives which his hearers indulge in. Because they are the ones whom God has known from among all the nations, this light scrutinizes and lays them bare as sinners. For them, the appearance of the righteous God "can only end in death."[31] The force of the prophecy of Amos is thus to lay bare the truth of their actions and God's judgment in order to change them. This feature of Amos' prophecy underscores the inadequacy of any attempt to relegate fear of wrath and judgment solely to those outside the fellowship of God's people. Karl Barth, in his discussion of divine righteousness, grasps acutely the counterintuitive nature of the relationship which Amos describes: "According to scripture it is as the merciful God that God is to be feared, and as the righteous that He is to be loved."[32]

II. Wrath, History, and the Divine Pedagogy

It must be explored more closely whether and how God's confrontation of the world, the preservation of his own worth, and so his oppositional work might likewise bear this dual end such that, on the basis of faith or lack of faith in Jesus Christ, God might strike down the enemy to the left but chasten his child to the right. Answering this question in the negative might start from the premise that ὀργή, particularly in Paul's writings, is a purely eschatological mode of God's presence and therefore, more radically, that it affords no remedial opportunity. Universalism is proscribed because wrath, at least in its eschatological form, and in strict contrast to pre-exilic Old Testament writings, bears no relationship to God's love and has no restorative, chastising end. This is the conceptual way of securing eternal damnation or annihilation. It relies upon a distinction between an inadequate definition of eschatology as that which follows "after" history rather than that which is the goal of history and so, as we have argued with the cross of Christ, may nonetheless be present proleptically even in the unfolding of history itself. Left unexamined is the blithely speculative assumption that this final event has "true anger [which is] . . . the opposite of love" as its content.[33] In the end, ostensibly, God no longer loves the wicked.

---

[31] Jeremias, *Book of Amos*, p. 100.

[32] Karl Barth, *Church Dogmatics* II/1, ed. G.W. Bromiley, T.F. Torrance (Edinburgh: T&T Clark, 1957), p. 381. Cf. Elizabeth R. Achtemeier, *The Old Testament and the Proclamation of the Gospel* (Philadelphia: Westminster Press, 1973): "the very fact of election increases the necessity for the judgment" (p. 66).

[33] William V. Crockett, "Wrath that Endures Forever," *Journal of the Evangelical Theological Society* 34 (1991): 200.

There are in scripture, however, references to the purposefulness and intentionality of God's oppositional presence to a people mired in sin. Among the more significant passages:

> When we are judged by the Lord, we are disciplined [παιδευόμεθα] so that we may not be condemned along with the world (1 Cor 11.32).
>
> Endure trials for the sake of discipline [παιδείαν]. God is treating you as children; for what child is there whom a parent does not discipline (Heb 12.7)?
>
> Now, discipline [παιδεία] always seems painful rather than pleasant at the time, but later it yields the peaceful fruit of righteousness to those who have been trained [γεγυμνασμένοις] by it (Heb 12.11).
>
> By rejecting conscience, certain persons have suffered shipwreck in the faith; among them are Hymenaeus and Alexander, whom I have turned over to Satan, so that they may learn [ἵνα παιδευθῶσιν] not to blaspheme (1 Tim 1.19f.).
>
> I reprove [ἐλέγχω] and discipline [παιδεύω] those whom I love (Rev 3.18).

Given such testimony, and presupposing the gracious gift of faith, we can ask whether wrath remains in some measure upon human life in order to chastise God's people and so train them up into righteousness.

In the Christian tradition, and particularly within the patristic period, one finds the Christian life and conversion imaged in just these categories. According to Werner Jaeger, this aspect of early theology is an adoption and transformation of the Greek philosophical ideal, παιδεία. While the genetic question cannot be investigated within the bounds of this essay, we can offer a brief summary of Jaeger's findings. In the hands of theologians like Clement of Rome, Origen and Gregory of Nyssa, he observes that παιδεία (τοῦ κυρίου) came to be regarded as "the great protective force in the life of the Christian," "the greatest educational power in history," "the gradual fulfilment of the divine providence," "identical" with the Bible, the "will of God," "assimilation to God," and "the lifelong effort to ... approach perfection."[34] In short, παιδεία was regarded as the return of the soul to God and to man's original nature.

This emphasis upon the pedagogical work of God in early Christian theology intersects a range of human experiences and conceptualizes salvation in terms of a divine work in which the life history of individuals is of fundamental importance. Included in this was a reconceptualization of how the presence of God in judgment irreplaceably contributes to this process.

---

[34] Werner W. Jaeger, *Early Christianity and Greek Paideia* (London: Oxford University Press, 1969), respectively, pp. 25, 65, 67, 92, 89–90, and 99.

Several examples commend themselves, not the least of which is found in Gregory of Nyssa's *On the Soul and the Resurrection*. He writes, "[T]he foreign matter, which has somehow grown into [the soul's] substance, has to be scraped from it" by divine judgment.[35] Similarly, according to Clement of Alexandria, divine anger is God's benevolent artifice (τέχνη), meant to prevent sin through fear. Appreciating his extended metaphor requires quoting it at length:

> Reproof is, as it were, the surgery of the passions of the soul; and the passions are, as it were, an abscess of the truth, which must be cut open by an incision of the lancet of reproof. Reproach is like the application of medicines, dissolving the callosities of the passions, and purging the impurities of the lewdness of the life; and in addition, reducing the excrescences of pride, restoring the patient to the healthy and true state of humanity.[36]

If we turn now and focus upon the significance of a pedagogical dimension to God's wrath through the theology of John Calvin, it is not because he was the first theologian to develop this notion.[37] His conception, however, is arguably the fullest and most orderly available.

John Calvin on Wrath and Divine Vengeance

Both in the theology of the *Institutes of the Christian Religion*, and in the exegesis of the commentaries on the Old and New Testaments, the subject of the wrath of God is treated consistently under a twofold distinction. There is, on the one hand, the *chastisement* of the heavenly Father, employed as an instrument for correction and restoration. There is, on the other, the *vengeance* of the divine Judge, which works toward punitive and destructive ends. Van der Kooi observes that the duality within God's eternal counsel, running like "a hidden thread through all history," is decisive for Calvin's interpretation of all human life-experience, and the experience of wrath, at

---

[35] Gregory of Nyssa, "On the Soul and the Resurrection," *Nicene and Post-Nicene Fathers of the Christian Church, Series II*, eds. P. Schaff and H. Wace, vol. 5 (Grand Rapids: Eerdmans, 1983), §7.

[36] Clement of Alexandria, "The Instructor," *The Ante-Nicene Fathers: Translations of the Writings of the Fathers Down to A.D. 325*, eds. A. Roberts, et al., vol. 2 (Edinburgh: T&T Clark, 1986), I.viii.

[37] I owe the initial idea for this reading of Calvin to Ellen T. Charry. In *By the Renewing of Your Minds: The Pastoral Function of Christian Doctrine* (New York: Oxford Univ. Press, 1997), Charry refers to Calvin as being primarily "an aretegenically oriented teacher of the church who understands the implications of theology for public life" (p. 199). By contrast, I will pursue the specific topic of *divine judgment* as pedagogy.

least initially, would seem no exception.[38] Each of these two manifestations of God's wrath requires careful consideration.

Calvin's most sustained treatment is found in *Institutes* book three, particularly chapters 2 through 4. In considering these chapters alongside his scriptural exegesis, we enter into a core facet of this discussion. Indeed, this section attends to the topic of the Christian life. But unlike much of the secondary literature, which gravitates toward descriptions of the human life of obedience through repentance and prayer,[39] our concern will remain largely the identity of God as he reveals himself in acts of refinement and discipline. The task is not to penetrate to the divine essence—a task of which Calvin himself would not approve—but to persist in bringing our attention, again and again, back to God's nature in act in order better to understand his wrath.

The first end, what Calvin calls God's *vengeance*, might be glossed as the just confluence of divine punishment and indignation. It is essentially just in the sense that God's work is neither irrational nor founded upon capricious emotion; rather it is an act of weighing transgressions and executing penalties. In Calvin's own verbiage, vengeance is that destructive mode in which God "pursues the impious and the reprobate with his indignation," and in so doing, "he exercises his wrath against them, he confounds them, he scatters them, he brings them to nought" (III.iv.31). In the presence of this vengeful God, the wicked remain obstinately opposed to the Lord and bound to a servile fear in which their own destruction is anticipated. In contrast to God's elect people, the wicked fear him "not because they are afraid of incurring his displeasure . . . but because they know him to be armed with the power to take vengeance, they shake with fright on hearing of his wrath" (III.ii.27).

Calvin reads in scripture that an experience of nakedness before this righteous Lord yields a peculiar kind of repentance, a "repentance of the law," as seen in figures such as Cain, Saul, and Judas. In the deceit of his heart, for example, Cain "desires to be esteemed just, and even arrogates to himself

---

[38] Cornelis van der Kooi, *As in a Mirror: John Calvin and Karl Barth on Knowing God— A Diptych* (Leiden: Brill, 2005), p. 138. Francois Wendel, *Calvin: The Origins and Development of His Religious Thought* (London: Collins, 1963), agrees that this presupposition not only determined Calvin's understanding of the church as *corpus per mixtum*, a teaching Calvin had inherited from Augustine's *City of God*, but was carried thorough the whole of his theology (pp. 282–283).

[39] For example, when Wendel turns to consider "Regeneration and the Christian Life" (pp. 242–255), the focus is on what man does—prayer, repentance, etc.—rather than the action of God in bringing about this growth. Similarly, William J. Bouwsma summarizes Calvin's view of the Christian life under the essentially human-centered themes of (1) the struggle culminating in victory, where one faces enemies, learns patience, acceptance, and suffering, and is assailed by doubts, and (2) the pilgrimage toward a goal, i.e., as the unceasing, single-minded, travels of a stranger in a strange land—*John Calvin: A Sixteenth-Century Portrait* (New York: Oxford University Press, 1988), pp. 182–188.

the first place among the saints," demanding to deal with God strictly on his own terms (Gen 4.5).[40] Therein lies the basic conflict. Calvin improvises a divine reply:

> Though thou shouldst have nothing to do with me, thy sin shall give thee no rest, but shall sharply drive thee on, pursue thee, and urge thee, and never suffer thee to escape (Gen 4.7).

This reply is particularly interesting as it explicates the consequences of Cain's obstinacy through the larger context and concern of right relationship to God himself rather than, for example, through a concern for the maintenance of society in general. We will shortly return to this feature. Crucial here is that Cain does not muster genuine repentance but looks merely to hold onto his life. Genuine repentance, Calvin concludes, shares little with a "blind and astonished dread of punishment, which is without any hatred of sin, or any desire to return to God" (Gen 4.13).

Cain, and those like him, both acknowledge the gravity of sin and demonstrate fear of God's ensuing wrath. The key point for Calvin is that, "since they conceived of God only as Avenger and Judge, that very thought overwhelmed them" so that they were unable to trust the Lord for their salvation (III.iii.4). From the concrete effects of the administration of such divine wrath, there is distilled the axiom that God can sometimes act in wrath for the sake of his just vengeance alone (*iudicium vindictae*), which is to say, without redemption in view. Apart from the grace of redemption, the wrathful presence of the Lord can only mean "great distress" (III.iv.31–33).

Wrath and the Maintenance of Society

Affirmation of God's dynamic concern for the just order of the world has long been one of the central theological standpoints from which to analyze and account for divine wrath. Were God not righteously concerned with and involved in this sinful world, proceeds the logic, were he not a God of wrath, two implications would follow. The first is the little-discernable difference between an uninvolved God and a God who has surrendered creation to dissolution, anarchy, and non-being. This concern treats as self-evident both the destructive nature of sin and the relative inadequacy of God's foundational work to deal with the challenge it poses. Second and correspondingly, to the extent that this *Deus otiosus* fails to protect justice and righteousness in the economy, it is wide open to doubt whether righteousness and wrath are in fact perfections of God himself. Both these implications need to be

---

[40] See chapter and verse from John Calvin, *Commentaries on the Book of Genesis*, vol. 1, trans. J. King (Edinburgh: Edinburgh Printing Co., 1847).

mentioned. The concern is not only God's idleness and its implications for creation but also an idleness, which compromises God's perfection.

The notion that by his wrath God governs and provides for the broad fabric of human society is fundamentally correct. One encounters this supposition in contemporary theological discussions on matters as varied as the nature of justice and Christian theories of history. In elaborating on social justice, for example, Rufus Burrow Jr. observes the contradiction involved when one claims both "that God truly is love and loves truly, and yet does not become angry or wrathful when persons behave in ways that demean and disrespect the value of others."[41] God's wrath is necessary as righteous opposition to human wrongdoing. Burrow develops from this certain moral consequences, not least of which is his belief that to work passionately for social justice is to act "in accordance with the truth expressed in divine wrath."[42] In an early essay, Kōsuke Koyama argues that the concept of wrath has a unique power to "historicize" God, to show God as meaningfully and potently present in history and, in that activity, to lie beyond the reach of human domestication.[43] Isolated accounts of divine love, by contrast, "lack the *disturbing* and *critical* imagery which the wrath of God carries;" everywhere the Gospel has imposed upon it a *theologia gloriae* or the picture of God as *non perturbationes animi*, it requires the "openly contradicting force" of God's wrath "in order to break through the front line of the anti-historical."[44] In each case, the treatment of the topic of wrath reveals uncertainty as to the broader theological foundation requisite to their respective claims. The primary concern, however, is clear: God is neither closed in upon himself, nor characterized by sentimental love. Rather God is active in history, and active precisely as the one who maintains his own will over against injustice. Elaborations on God's wrath in the maintenance of society, however, are much more ancient than these.

In Christian theology, the relationship between God's wrath and the maintenance of society first receives dedicated attention in the writings of the gifted rhetorician, Lactantius (ca. AD 240–320). Unlike pagan writers of his day, who attempted to distance God from the passion of wrath either by claiming that he is "altogether beneficent" or by concluding radically that God "takes no notice of us at all,"[45] Lactantius writes in *De ira Dei* of love's

---

[41] Rufus Burrow Jr., "The Love, Justice, and Wrath of God," *Encounter* 59 (1998): 396.

[42] Ibid., p. 406.

[43] Kōsuke Koyama, "The 'Wrath of God' and the Thai Theologia Gloriae," *Christ and the Younger Churches: Theological Contributions from Asia, Africa, and Latin America* (1972): p. 43.

[44] Ibid., p. 48.

[45] Lactantius, *De ira Dei*, §1. We are quoting from the text found in *The Ante-Nicene Fathers: Translations of the Writings of the Fathers Down to A.D. 325*, ed. A. Roberts, et al., vol. 7 (Edinburgh: T&T Clark, 1986); subsequent parenthetical citations refer to

requirement that God confront sin and evil. The reasoning is straightforward and easily encapsulated. On the one hand, a concern for moral coherence leads him to assert that "if God is not angry with the impious and the unrighteous, it is clear that He does not love the pious and the righteous" (§5). On the other hand, Lactantius inquires into the societal implications. "If God takes no trouble, nor occasions trouble to another, why then should we not commit crimes as often as it shall be in our power to escape the notice of men and to cheat the public laws" (§8)? By removing God from active and personal—even passionate—interest in creation, the claim is that one both cheapens divine love and legitimizes a society in which individuals are left wholly unaccountable for their deeds. By contrast, in the wrath of the Christian God one is provided the principle of governance necessary to the ongoing maintenance of society.

Equally important, perhaps, the distinctly teleological character of God's wrath provides Lactantius with the basis upon which to distinguish his own position from those which ascribe illegitimate *passio* to God. As forms of *affectus*, lust, fear, avarice, and grief all lack in and of themselves any constructive capacity. They play no part in bringing the world to its goal. Though these forms of *affectus* are alien to God's life, Lactantius argues, the attributes of love, compassion and anger—anger being understood as "an emotion of the mind rousing itself to curb sins"—may all be understood as contributing to salvation (§§16–17). While the serviceability of such general concepts of virtue and vice for theological reflection may be questioned, his own sense for the conclusion is clear: wrath is not "a violent tempest," which washes over God. In God's great excellence "he controls his anger, and is not ruled by it, but he regulates it according to his will" (§21). Wrath, therefore, is neither ephemeral, irrational, nor erratic.[46] It plays an important role in ordering society and preserving history toward its goal.

This teleological criterion for a concept of wrath both complicates and adds depth to our argument. On the one hand, Lactantius' focus corresponds nicely to the line of reasoning we have pursued, for it suggests a concrete ratio by which wrath is executed within salvation history. The unfolding of God's purposes for creation is affirmed here as a genuinely historical process, and he believes it necessary that the moral state of creation be measured in relation to God alone. On the other, it is clear that in his concern for the

---

the chapter. So much was the substance of wrath at the center of Lactantius' thought, he wrote a second treatise entitled *On the Manner in Which the Persecutors Died*, an historical recounting of the fate which the Roman Empire suffered due to its unjust assault upon faithful Christians.

[46] Poignantly, R.V.G. Tasker offers the prodigal son's brother (Lk 15.25ff.), as one "angry with the wrong people, at the wrong time, and for the wrong reasons," as an example of the frailty and destructiveness of human anger—*The Biblical Doctrine of the Wrath of God* (London: Tyndale, 1951), p. 11.

maintenance of society in general, and the intellectually respectable role which God plays in this, Lactantius does not adequately secure the content and form of God's wrath in history. Our exposition of the cross of Jesus Christ challenges the notion either that genuine wrath is to be found outside that event or that wrath may be defined apart from it. Lactantius never perceives the problem, and the corresponding lack of attention to christological or pneumatological resources, at least according to our criteria, is gravely inadequate to the task of developing a theology of God's wrath.[47]

By contrast, we suggest that wherever God himself identifies historical events through his prophetic word as being manifestations of his own wrath, we are dealing only with tokens of the wrath properly and fully manifested in the cross. Were they not mere tokens, were God fully to manifest his wrath against sin, such an act would constitute the end of the story rather than the announcement of its end. It is not only in God's anticipation of the cross that we know his patience but likewise in his determination to hold back full judgment—without idleness or rest from his governance—in order to bring redemption to its goal. Final judgment, as we will see below, and the accompanying publication of the content of Christ's cross bring the history of sin to its end.

The objectivity of the cross grounds rather than dissolves human history. By the once and for all enactment of the stringent demands of God's righteousness and the full expression of his wrath, God gives time and space for the redemption of human life. But in doing so—and this is the key point—he does not give up the proper work of opposing all opposition to himself.

> [A]longside the cross of Christ there is our own cross, alongside his suffering our suffering, alongside his death our death. They are not the judgment of God that we have to fear, but the judgment of God that we have to see as vanquished and ended if we are to continue in penitence and obedience. . . . the shadow would not fall if the cross of Christ did not stand in the light of his resurrection.[48]

Life is given in Christ precisely so that the sinner may live and be made perfect, and this living and perfecting includes God's ongoing opposition to sin.

---

[47] To my knowledge, in the whole of *De ira Dei* there is no reference to "Jesus," "the Word," "the Son," or the like, but only a single allusion to "God's Servant and Messenger" who teaches truly, frees others from error, forms us in right worship and teaches righteousness (§2). The disappearance of the NT insistence that it was Jesus Christ—and therefore God himself—who bore divine wrath is conspicuous. For Lactantius, redemption from divine anger requires simply "a reformation of the morals" (§21). Correspondingly, his emphasis is on the unity of the one God and his one will and power—cf. *Divinae institutiones* 1.3.11, 1.3.2–3, as well as the *Epitome* 2.6.

[48] Barth, *Church Dogmatics* II/1, p. 406. The emphasis is original.

John Calvin on Wrath and the Education of God's People

While all people experience the wrath of God, not all experience it in the same way. The difference between knowing God as Judge and knowing God as loving Father constitutes, for Calvin, all the difference in the world. As Father, the chastising wrath of God (*iudicium castigationis*) means that God desires to teach his people and render them more cautious. In it "[God] is not so harsh as to be angry, nor does he take vengeance so as to blast with destruction"; rather the goal is solely the correction and admonition of his people (III.iv.31). Corresponding to the previous destructive mode of divine wrath, there is this productive, pedagogical mode.

To speak of the chastising wrath of God is therefore to speak about God's act of electing individuals to particular ends. This concrete relationship is marked on one side by trust, for to live under grace is to know the faithfulness of the God who is present to those within covenant fellowship, and on the other by restraint, since God chooses to live among a sinful people so that they may be preserved until his work is perfected. Even in this eminently secure existence, however, Calvin maintains space for that peculiar kind of fear which befits God's children. It has two interrelated aspects: the elect "both fear offending God more than punishment, and are not troubled by fear of punishment, as if it hung over their necks" (III.ii.27). Whenever God reveals himself, the encounter elicits the prayers and worship of his creatures. In circumstances like these, the child of God cares more for honoring the Father than for protecting her own well-being. When scripture witnesses to "gospel repentance," it is therefore not the crying out of those who do not know the mercy of God and so fear for their lives. Rather it is the act of those "who, made sore by the sting of sin but aroused and refreshed by trust in God's mercy, have turned to the Lord" (III.iii.4).[49] Figures such as Hezekiah, the Ninevites, and David should come to mind. In commenting on the book of Jonah, for example, Calvin writes:

> The Ninevites, no doubt, derived from the words of Jonah something more than mere terror: for had they only apprehended this—that they were guilty before God, and were justly summoned to punishment, they would have been confounded and stunned with dread, and could never have been encouraged to seek forgiveness. Inasmuch then as they suppliantly prostrated themselves before God, they must certainly have conceived some hope of grace.... [T]hough they were aware that

---

[49] So too: "the sole purpose of God in punishing his church is that the church may be brought low and repent" (III.iv.33). This is the jealousy in which an unfaithful lover is yet pursued: "the more holy and chaste a husband is, the more wrathful he becomes if he sees his wife inclining her heart to a rival" (II.viii.18).

they were most worthy of death, they yet despaired not, but retook themselves to prayer (3.5).[50]

Note that it is not the threat itself which produces this humility among the Assyrians. If that were the only criteria, so too would Cain, Saul, and Judas have found peace with God. Instead, on the basis of their genuine prostration and return to prayer, Calvin draws the conclusion that they had "conceived some hope of grace," and so had heard the promise of mercy. Whether or not one finds this particular exegetical move convincing, Calvin's distinction stands.

The chastising wrath of God, which plays a peculiar role in gospel repentance, can be straightforwardly contrasted with the wrath of vengeance. The elect do not know the Lord as Avenger and Judge, but rather as Father, the one who in reproving them leads them into a life of righteousness. Chastisement is thus not a curse but a blessing which bears witness to God's love, as taught in scripture (III.iv.32).[51] The elect know themselves as chastised by God—even as beaten with the rod—but they are never given over to death but confess always that the Lord has humbled them so that they might learn his statutes. In such a relationship, affliction and scourgings are a reality for the saints; such experiences may even be confounding in their "extreme and deadly terror" (III.iv.32). In his commentary on Hebrews 12.6, this theme appears once again: "However severe and wrathful a judge God shows Himself to be towards unbelievers whenever He punishes them, in the case of His elect He has no other purpose than to take counsel for their salvation." Whereas unbelievers, out of ignorance, attribute their affliction to chance, believers find in such chastisement "a sure pledge" of God's loving concern.[52]

At the same time, Calvin can confidently say that because of the end to which this wrath is directed, we experience it as only a "slight severity" when compared with the full power of the Lord's judgment and wrath; as experiences of wrath go, experiences of God's chastisement are characterized by "moderation and gentleness" (III.iv.32). The grounds for Calvin's assertion are compelling. Because "there is a covenant still in force," he writes, God will not remove mercy from his people. Rather they will be preserved, justified, and sanctified even in those works of chastising judgment (cf. Ps 89.30–33). This restoration

---

[50] See chapter and verse from John Calvin, *Commentaries on the Twelve Minor Prophets, vol. 3: Jonah, Micah, Nahum*, trans. J. Owen (Edinburgh: Edinburgh Printing Co., 1847).

[51] Calvin points to Job 5.17, Prov 3.11f., and Heb 12.5f.

[52] See chapter and verse in John Calvin, *The Epistle of Paul the Apostle to the Hebrews and the First and Second Epistles of St. Peter*, trans. W.B. Johnston (Grand Rapids: Eerdmans, 1994). Also, the examples from *Institutes* III.iv.32: "O Lord, although thou wert angry with me; thine anger turned away" (Isa 12.1); "when you are angry, you will remember mercy" (Hab 3.2); and "I will bear God's wrath, for I have sinned against him" (Mic 7.9).

does not take place in one moment or one day or one year; but through continual and sometimes even slow advances God wipes out in his elect the corruptions of the flesh, cleanses them of guilt, consecrates them to himself as temples renewing all their minds to true purity that they may practice repentance throughout their lives and know that this warfare will end only at death . . . God assigns to them a race of repentance, which they are to run throughout their lives (III.iii.9).[53]

The event in which Jesus Christ assumes our flesh and once and for all destroys sin by subjecting himself to the destructive work of divine wrath is *singular* in nature. For those in Christ, however, it has the significance of an event both complete in the past and being completed in lives of instruction and disciplined conformity to Christ. Said another way, salvation is God's again-and-again process of training his people through vengeance and chastisement, both of which are founded in the already accomplished fact of Jesus Christ's self-sacrificial life, death, and resurrection.

Two words of qualification are in order. The first is that, if God's wrath is in fact to be identified with the manner in which he trains up humankind into right-relatedness—if it is, in other words, to bear *a pedagogical dimension*—it does so under the rule of redemption. Wrath is a salutary helper where it finds an already imparted faith and redemption, but a debilitating and deadly enemy in confrontation of unbelief. In the end, God's saving work remains objective such that everything required is given by God. Wrath, therefore, should not be conceived of as adversity sufficient to prompt self-redemption. Nothing but God's righteousness given graciously is able to save humankind. The fact that God lives out his righteousness in the redemptive mode of wrath suggests not only that before the eschaton we are occupied with mere tokens of judgment, but even more profoundly, that God is Lord of his wrath without compromise. Unlike earthly fathers, his acts are governed by "the wisest purpose and the highest wisdom."[54] They are "not merely the consequences and punishments appointed by God's justice but, from another perspective, also all without exception appointed means of grace, proofs of God's patience and compassion."[55]

Equally important is a second qualification. Calvin's theology is unfolded under the guidance of a robust doctrine of double predestination. As such, it more closely reflects the option for interpretation which Revelation 14 initially presented us: two groups of people, wrath for the condemned, and blessing

[53] In *The Theology of Calvin* (London: Lutterworth Press, 1956), Wilhelm Niesel offers the following summary: "Because He accepted death as the wages of sin and offered up his life, the old nature common to all of us can no longer subsist but must perish. So we must be slain by the piercing sword of the Spirit and brought to nought" (p. 127).

[54] Calvin, *Epistle of Paul to the Hebrews*, commentary on Heb 12.9.

[55] Bavinck, *Reformed Dogmatics* III, p. 160.

and love for the elect. Our interpretation of Revelation 14, however, just as the whole of our exposition up to this point, has sought to hear and repeat the perfection of God's life as it is properly and primarily manifest in the life of Jesus Christ, God incarnate. This commitment, linked as it is to the representative understanding of atonement iterated above, would require modifying Calvin's position in order for it to be incorporated into our larger argument. Such modifications, however, despite the profundity of their consequences, do not necessarily require radically recasting Calvin's fundamental insight. To offer one possibility, the basic distinction between chastisement and vengeance, which in Calvin's theology is conditioned by divine election, could plausibly be carried over and connected more modestly to theological reflection on the Christian life. Such a move may prove a coherent and cogent manner of reading scripture and accounting for the wrath present wherever opposition to God's goodness gains a foothold. God is wrathfully present to Christians who are, in anticipation of the eschaton, redeemed by faith yet still assaulted by sin. Niels Henrik Gregersen goes so far as to apply this to final judgment itself. "[N]ot everything is granted entry into the reign of God," he writes.

> The final mortification of sin in the purgative crucible of judgment preserves the legitimate motif of separationism. On the annihilationist account, the double end may be a double destiny for each and anybody. The pivotal issue with divine judgment is learning—including learning to unlearn!—and each creature will have to give up what cannot find entry into the reign of God.[56]

Assurance of salvation is thus not located in the fact that human beings are made stewards of the gifts they are given, but in the firm foundation of the grace of the One who gives.

Reliance upon the Seven Spirits

The message of Revelation 14, therefore, "stresses with the utmost seriousness the choices we make and the consequences of those choices . . . [I]ts function is to move readers and hearers to think anew."[57] Speaking concretely of the inherent attraction of the gospel, however, and the assurance in which its truth claims human life, depends entirely upon the presence of God's Spirit. From a broad perspective, "the seven Spirits" (1.4; 3.1; 4.5; 5.6) are

---

[56] Gregersen, "Guilt, Shame and Rehabilitation," p. 118.
[57] Rowland, "The Book of Revelation," p. 670; cf. Bauckham, *Theology of the Book of Revelation*, p. 20. See, once again, Beale's contrasting assessment: " . . . the angel [of 14.6] is not primarily a messenger of grace but of judgment" and therefore, consonant with Mt 24.14, his gospel "is not to result in the conversion of masses throughout the world"—*Book of Revelation*, pp. 748–749.

the presence of God himself, sent out into the world. By this "power of divine truth" God brings about the Lamb's victory on earth and also upholds the church's faithful witness to God's righteousness.[58] In a narrower sense, however, John also refers to "the Spirit" (before each of the letters to the churches, and at 1.10; 4.2; 17.3; 21.10) as the occasion for his own vision. He speaks in this way of the Spirit as the voice of God's prophet broadcasting both judgment and invitation (cf. 14.13 and 22.17; 19.10), events related primarily to specific communities.[59]

Where the seven Spirits are depicted as living and acting by grace in creation, it is difficult to construe their truth as something grasped by humankind, taken, weighed, and finally decided upon. It is indeed knowledge, but it is knowledge which once received, demands not merely the intellectual assent of its hearers but a conversion and reorientation of one's life, for it effects a death for everyone and everything that does not belong to it. As judge, Jesus Christ bears this Spirit. The Father has chosen him and said of him, "I will put my Spirit upon him and, and he will proclaim justice to the Gentiles . . . and in his name the Gentiles will hope" (Mt 12.18–21, *passim*; cf. Isa 42.1–4). In the final analysis, God is present not only in the prophetic utterance of his truth, but also in its hearing. In this fallen economy, the gospel message of judgment and God's impending wrath does not depend upon the capacity of human beings to make something of it. Neither does it work through fear, requiring human despair over life and the wrath under which all humanity stands as a preparation for the word of the gospel, the shelter of God's grace. Neither even does its again-and-again work of mortification dissolve assurance and leave open the final outcome. By his seven Spirits, God alone effects redemption, proclaims it, secures it and, as we have seen, unites his people to the crucified Judge.

* * * * *

Acts of wrath are not silent but verbal and clear; the self-revealing word of God occupies a place of pre-eminence. Its condemnation of sin (one made eschatologically final), furthermore, does not preclude an invitation here and now to repentance. The destruction and death threatened throughout the writings of scripture does not follow incomprehensibly upon the offences of the guilty. The prophetic word warns. It makes clear the grounds on which all will be settled. It is not disinterested, but includes even in the darkest of judgments a flicker of hope—"For thus says the Lord to the house of Israel: Seek me and live" (Amos 5.4, cf. 14)—a hope that God's judgment

---

[58] Bauckham, *Theology of the Book of Revelation*, pp. 111–114.
[59] Ibid., p. 115.

might finally be gracious, that in disposing of sin the sinner might be saved, and that God's word of wrath may not in fact be the last word.[60]

Prophets speak to warn, and so perhaps redeem, those who in their sin oppose the truth of divine righteousness.[61] In this sense, "the Lord God does nothing, without revealing his secret to his servants the prophets" (Amos 3.7). Significantly, because the prophetic message—דְּבַר־יהוה—saves by establishing fellowship, Amos can and does suggest that deprivation of it, a famine as it were (Amos 8.11), itself constitutes the gravest of divine judgments. In this message one hears echoed a warning central to both law and gospel alike, namely that "one does not live by bread alone but by every word that comes from the mouth of God" (cf. Deut 8.3; Mt 4.4). Divine judgment is not only to be described as the visitation of punishment and death, but it may also be articulated as God's act of withholding all that is good, withholding his Word of blessing, and therefore the fullness of blessing.[62] Unless God's prophetic word is sought out, received and responded to in obedience, the future of human life disappears.

These passages from Amos and Revelation together publish in palpable form the already certain *telos* of God's righteousness. God's plan will not be vexed nor will his truth remain hidden. The promise is secure that even in the midst of so great a turmoil as the church faces, her Lord is free and loving. Just as with the prophecies of Amos, the severe imagery of Revelation 14—as with the imagery of all of chapters 6 to 20—is subordinate to the two bookends of creation and atonement (Rev 4.1–5.14) and restoration and fulfillment (Rev 21.1–22.5). Within this greater work, by God's sovereign grace, even "carnage and chaos . . . lead through into the fulfilment of man's destiny in final union with God."[63] Even more significantly, this insight leads us to ask whether these works are not merely complementary acts of righteousness—being, as it were, two sides of the same coin[64]—but, with respect to the creature, two ever-simultaneous aspects of God's single work of redemption.

---

[60] Amos 8.2; cf. Mic 7.18. See too Wolf Krötke, *Gottes Klarheiten: Eine Neuinterpretation der Lehre von Gottes 'Eigenschaften'* (Tübingen: Mohr-Siebeck, 2001), pp. 184–185.

[61] See Jeremias, *Book of Amos*, pp. 54–55.

[62] Though it requires more extensive development, and at least one important correction (i.e., the rigid separation of *divine absence* and *divine action*), Mays' insight is an important one: "God's wrath has two expressions, his absence and his action; both are equally terrible manifestations of his judgment"—*Amos*, p. 150.

[63] Sweet, *Revelation*, p. 47. Cf. also Ladd, *Commentary on the Revelation of John*, p. 200.

[64] Bauckham, *Theology of the Book of Revelation*, pp. 40, 67; Ladd, *Commentary on the Revelation of John*, p. 195.

BIBLIOGRAPHY

Achtemeier, Elizabeth Rice, *The Old Testament and the Proclamation of the Gospel* (Philadelphia: Westminster Press, 1973).

Achtemeier, P. J., "Righteousness in the NT," in *The Interpreter's Dictionary of the Bible: An Illustrated Encyclopedia*, ed. G.A. Buttrick, vol. 4 (New York: Abingdon, 1962), pp. 91–99.

Albrektson, Bertil, *History and the Gods: An Essay on the Idea of Historical Events as Divine Manifestations in the Ancient Near East and in Israel*, vol. 1 (Lund: Gleerup, 1967).

Aloysia, M., "The God of Wrath?" *Catholic Biblical Quarterly* 8(4) (1946): 407–415.

Alston, William P., "Substance and the Trinity," in *The Trinity: An Interdisciplinary Symposium on the Trinity*, eds S.T. Davis, D. Kendall, G. O'Collins (Oxford: Oxford University Press, 2001), pp. 179–201.

Anselm of Canterbury, "Monologion," in *Anselm of Canterbury*, eds J. Hopkins, H. Richardson (Toronto: E. Mellen Press, 1974).

—, "Proslogion," in *A Scholastic Miscellany: Anselm to Ockham*, ed. E.R. Fairweather (London: SCM Press, 1956).

—, "Why God Became Man," in *A Scholastic Miscellany: Anselm to Ockham*, ed. E.R. Fairweather (London: SCM Press, 1956), pp. 100–183.

Ashmon, Scott A., "The Wrath of God: A Biblical Overview," *Concordia Journal* 31(4) (2005): 348–358.

Aune, David Edward, *Revelation 17–22*, Word Biblical Commentary, vol. 52C (Nashville: Thomas Nelson, 1998).

—, *Revelation 6–16*, Word Biblical Commentary, vol. 52B (Nashville: Thomas Nelson, 1998).

Bachman, James V., P.L. Senkbeil, K.L. Thomsen, "God's Wrath Against Sin: Echoes in Contemporary Culture?" *Concordia Journal* 31(4) (2005): 411–424.

Bader-Saye, Scott, "Violence, Reconciliation and the Justice of God," *Cross Currents* 52(4) (2003): 536–542.

Baloian, Bruce Edward, *Anger in the Old Testament* (New York: Peter Lang, 1992).

Barker, Margaret, *The Revelation of Jesus Christ: Which God Gave to Him to show to His Servants what must Soon Take Place (Revelation 1.1)* (Edinburgh: T&T Clark, 2000).

Barth, Karl, *The Epistle to the Romans*, trans. E.C. Hoskyns (London: Oxford University Press, 1953).

—, *Der Römerbrief, 1922* (Zurich: EVZ-Verlag, 1940).

—, *Church Dogmatics*, 14 vols, ed. G.W. Bromiley, T.F. Torrance (Edinburgh: T&T Clark, 1956–1975).

Bauckham, Richard, *The Theology of the Book of Revelation* (Cambridge: Cambridge University Press, 1993).

Bauer, Walter, F.W. Danker, *A Greek–English Lexicon of the New Testament and Other Early Christian Literature*, 3rd ed. (Chicago: University of Chicago Press, 2000).

Bavinck, Herman, *Reformed Dogmatics, Volume 3: Sin and Salvation in Christ*, trans. J. Vriend, ed. J. Bolt (Grand Rapids: Baker Academic, 2006).

—, *Reformed Dogmatics, Volume 2: God and Creation*, trans. J. Vriend, ed. J. Bolt (Grand Rapids: Baker Academic, 2004).

Bayer, Oswald, "Eigenschaften Gottes: Christentum," in *Religion in Geschichte und Gegenwart: Handwörterbuch für Theologie und Religionswissenschaft*, 8 vols, ed. H.D. Betz, 4th ed., vol. 2 (Tübingen: Mohr Siebeck, 1998), pp. 1139–1142.

Beale, G.K., *The Book of Revelation: A Commentary on the Greek Text*, The New International Greek Testament Commentary (Grand Rapids: Eerdmans, 1999).

Bergman, J., G.J. Botterweck, "yāda'," in *Theological Dictionary of the Old Testament*, 15 vols, ed. G.J. Botterweck, H. Ringgren, H.-J. Fabry, vol. 5 (Grand Rapids: Eerdmans, 2006), pp. 448–481.

Berkouwer, G.C., *The Work of Christ* (Grand Rapids: Eerdmans, 1965).

Bevan, Edwyn, *Symbolism and Belief* (London: G. Allen & Unwin, Ltd., 1938).

Billings, J. Todd, *Calvin, Participation, and the Gift: The Activity of Believers in Union with Christ* (Oxford: Oxford University Press, 2007).

Blocher, Henri, "Yesterday, Today and Forever: Time, Times, Eternity in Biblical Perspective," *Tyndale Bulletin* 52(2) (2001): 183–202.

Boersma, Hans, *Violence, Hospitality and the Cross: Reappropriating the Atonement Tradition* (Grand Rapids: Baker, 2004).

Boring, M. Eugene, *The Gospel of Matthew*, The New Interpreter's Bible (Nashville: Abingdon, 1994).

—, *Revelation*, Interpretation (Louisville: John Knox Press, 1989).

Bouwsma, William J., *John Calvin: A Sixteenth-Century Portrait* (New York: Oxford University Press, 1988).

Brown, Francis, S.R. Driver, C.A. Briggs, eds, *The Brown-Driver-Briggs Hebrew and English Lexicon* (Peabody: Hendrickson Publishers, 2001).

Brueggemann, Walter, *The Book of Exodus*, The New Interpreter's Bible (Nashville: Abingdon, 1995).

Bruner, Frederick Dale, *Matthew: A Commentary, Vol. 2: The Churchbook* (Grand Rapids: Eerdmans, 2004).

Brunner, Emil, *The Christian Doctrine of God*, trans. O. Wyon (Philadelphia: Westminster Press, 1950).

Buckley, Michael J., *At the Origins of Modern Atheism* (New Haven: Yale University Press, 1987).

Burrow, Rufus, Jr., "The Love, Justice, and Wrath of God," *Encounter* 59 (1998): 379–407.

Busch, Eberhard, "Reformed Strength in its Denominational Weakness," in *Reformed Theology: Identity and Ecumenicity*, eds, W.M. Alston, M. Welker (Grand Rapids: Eerdmans, 2003), pp. 20–33.

Caird, G.B., *A Commentary on the Revelation of St. John the Divine* (London: Black, 1984).

BIBLIOGRAPHY

Calvin, John, *The Epistles of Paul the Apostle to the Romans and to the Thessalonians*, eds, R. Mackenzie, D.W. Torrance, T.F. Torrance (Grand Rapids: Eerdmans, 1995).

—, *The Epistle of Paul the Apostle to the Hebrews, and the First and Second Epistles of St. Peter*, trans. W.B. Johnston, eds D.W. Torrance, T.F. Torrance (Grand Rapids: Eerdmans, 1994).

—, *Institutes of the Christian Religion (1559)*, 2 vols, trans. F.L. Battles, ed. J.T. McNeill (Philadelphia: Westminster Press, 1960).

—, *Commentaries on the Book of Genesis*, vol. 1, trans. J. Owen (Edinburgh: Edinburgh Printing Co., 1847).

—, *Commentaries on the Twelve Minor Prophets, vol. 3: Jonah, Micah, Nahum*, trans. J. Owen (Edinburgh: Edinburgh Printing Co., 1847).

Campbell, Alastair V., *The Gospel of Anger* (London: SPCK, 1986).

Carson, D.A., "The Wrath of God," in *Engaging the Doctrine of God: Contemporary Protestant Perspectives*, ed. B.L. McCormack, (Grand Rapids: Baker Academic, 2008), pp. 37–63.

Charry, Ellen T., "The Soteriological Importance of the Divine Perfections," in *God the Holy Trinity: Reflections on Christian Faith and Practice*, ed. T. George (Grand Rapids: Baker Academic, 2006), pp. 129–147.

—, *By the Renewing of Your Minds: The Pastoral Function of Christian Doctrine* (New York: Oxford University Press, 1997).

Childs, Brevard S., *Isaiah*, The Old Testament Library (Louisville: Westminster John Knox Press, 2001).

—, *Exodus: A Commentary*, The Old Testament Library (London: SCM Press, 1974).

Clarke, Samuel, *A Demonstration of the Being and Attributes of God and Other Writings*, ed. E. Vailati (Cambridge: Cambridge University Press, 1998).

Clement of Alexandria, "The Instructor," in *The Ante-Nicene Fathers: Translations of the Writings of the Fathers of the Christian Church, Down to A.D. 325*, vol. 2, eds A. Roberts, et al. (Edinburgh: T&T Clark, 1986).

Cranfield, C.E.B., *A Critical and Exegetical Commentary on the Epistle to the Romans, vol. 1: Romans 1–8*, International Critical Commentary (Edinburgh: T&T Clark, 1975).

Creel, Richard E., *Divine Impassibility: An Essay in Philosophical Theology* (Cambridge: Cambridge University Press, 1986).

Cremer, Hermann, *Die christliche Lehre von den Eigenschaften Gottes*, ed. H. Burkhardt (Giessen: Brunnen Verlag, 2005).

Crockett, William V., "Wrath that Endures Forever," *Journal of the Evangelical Theological Society* 34 (1991): 195–202.

Dalferth, Ingolf U., *Becoming Present: An Inquiry into the Christian Sense of the Presence of God* (Leuven: Peeters, 2006).

Davis, Stephen T., "Universalism, Hell, and the Fate of the Ignorant," *Modern Theology* 6 (1990): 173–186.

Dodd, C.H., *The Parables of the Kingdom*, rev. ed. (New York: Charles Scribner's Sons, 1961).

—, *The Epistle of Paul to the Romans* (London: Hodder & Stoughton Ltd., 1932).

Dorner, I.A., *Divine Immutability: A Critical Reconsideration*, ed. R.R. Williams (Minneapolis: Fortress Press, 1994).

—, *A System of Christian Doctrine*, eds A. Cave, J.S. Banks (Edinburgh: T&T Clark, 1880).

Ebeling, Gerhard, "Schleiermacher's Doctrine of the Divine Attributes," in *Schleiermacher as Contemporary*, ed. R.W. Funk (New York: Herder and Herder, 1970), pp. 125–162.

Eichrodt, Walther, *Theology of the Old Testament*, trans. J.A. Baker (Philadelphia: Westminster Press, 1961).

Farnell, Lewis Richard, *The Attributes of God*, The Gifford Lectures, 1924–25 (Oxford: The Clarendon Press, 1925).

Farley, Edward, *Divine Empathy: A Theology of God* (Minneapolis: Fortress Press, 1996).

Feinberg, John S., *No One Like Him: The Doctrine of God* (Wheaton: Crossway Books, 2001).

Feuerbach, Ludwig, *The Essence of Christianity*, trans. M. Evans (London: Trübner & Co., 1843).

Finamore, Steve, "The Gospel and the Wrath of God in Romans 1," *Understanding, Studying and Reading* (1998): 137–154.

Forde, Gerhard O., *On Being a Theologian of the Cross: Reflections on Luther's Heidelberg Disputation, 1518* (Grand Rapids: Eerdmans, 1997).

—, *Justification by Faith: A Matter of Death and Life* (Mifflintown, PA: Sigler Press, 1990).

Fretheim, Terence E., "Theological Reflections on the Wrath of God in the Old Testament," *Horizons in Biblical Theology* 24(2) (2002): 1–26.

—, *Exodus*, Interpretation (Louisville: John Knox Press, 1991).

Gathercole, Simon J., "Justified by Faith, Justified by His Blood: The Evidence of Romans 3:21–4:25," in *Justification and Variegated Nomism, vol. 2: The Paradoxes of Paul*, eds D.A. Carson, P.T. O'Brien, M.A. Seifrid (Grand Rapids: Baker Academic, 2004), pp. 147–184.

Gerrish, Brian A., "Tradition in the Modern World: The Reformed Habit of Mind," in *Toward the Future of Reformed Theology: Tasks, Topics, Traditions*, eds D. Willis, M. Welker, M. Gockel (Grand Rapids: Eerdmans, 1999), pp. 3–20.

—, "Theology within the Limits of Piety Alone: Schleiermacher and Calvin's Notion of God," in *The Old Protestantism and the New: Essays on the Reformation Heritage* (Edinburgh: T&T Clark, 1982), pp. 196–207.

—, *Tradition and the Modern World: Reformed Theology in the Nineteenth Century* (Chicago: University of Chicago Press, 1978).

Gowan, Donald E., *Theology in Exodus: Biblical Theology in the Form of a Commentary* (Louisville: Westminster John Knox Press, 1994).

Graesser, Carl, "Righteousness, Human and Divine," *Currents in Theology and Mission* 10 (1983): 134–141.

Gregersen, Niels Henrik, "Guilt, Shame, and Rehabilitation: The Pedagogy of Divine Judgment," *Dialog* 39(2) (2000): 105–118.

Gregory of Nyssa, "On the Soul and the Resurrection," in *Nicene and Post-Nicene Fathers of the Christian Church*, ser. II, vol. 5, eds P. Schaff, H. Wace (Grand Rapids: Eerdmans, 1983).

Grenz, Stanley J., *The Named God and the Question of Being: A Trinitarian Theo-Ontology* (Louisville: Westminster John Knox Press, 2005).

Grosse, Sven, "Der Zorn Gottes: Uberlegungen zu einem Thema der Theolgie bei Tertullian, Laktanz und Origenes," *Zeitschrift fur Kirchensgeschichte* 112(2) (2001): 147–167.

Gundry, Robert H., *Matthew: A Commentary on His Handbook for a Mixed Church under Persecution* (Grand Rapids: Eerdmans, 1994).

Gunton, Colin E., *Act and Being: Towards a Theology of the Divine Attributes* (Grand Rapids: Eerdmans, 2002).

—, "The Being and Attributes of God: Eberhard Jüngel's Dispute with the Classical Philosophical Tradition," in *The Possibilities of Theology: Studies in the Theology of Eberhard Jüngel in His Sixtieth Year*, ed. J.B. Webster (Edinburgh: T&T Clark, 1994).

—, *The One, the Three and the Many: God, Creation and the Culture of Modernity* (Cambridge: Cambridge University Press, 1993).

—, "Trinity, Ontology and Anthropology: Towards a Renewal of the Doctrine of the *Imago Dei*," in *Persons, Divine and Human: King's College Essays in Theological Anthropology*, eds C. Schwöbel, C.E. Gunton (Edinburgh: T&T Clark, 1991), pp. 47–61.

Gutenson, Charles E., *Reconsidering the Doctrine of God* (London: T&T Clark, 2005).

Haerle, Wilfried, "Die Rede von der Liebe und vom Zorn Gott," *Zeitschrift für Theologie und Kirche, Beihefte* 8 (1990): 50–69.

Hagner, Donald A., *Matthew 14–28*, Word Biblical Commentary, vol. 33B (Dallas: Word Books, 1995).

Hanson, Anthony T., *The Wrath of the Lamb* (London: SPCK, 1957).

Hays, Richard B., *Echoes of Scripture in the Letters of Paul* (New Haven: Yale University Press, 1989).

Heppe, Heinrich, *Reformed Dogmatics: Set Out and Illustrated from the Sources* (London: Allen & Unwin, 1950).

Herion, Gary A., "Wrath of God (OT)," in *The Anchor Bible Dictionary*, ed. David Noel Freedman, vol. 6 (New York: Doubleday, 1992), pp. 989–996.

Heschel, Abraham J., *The Prophets* (New York: Harper & Row, 1962).

Hill, William J., "The Historicity of God," *Theological Studies* 45 (1984): 320–333.

Holmes, Christopher R.J., "The Theological Function of the Doctrine of the Divine Attributes and the Divine Glory, with Special Reference to Karl Barth and his Reading of the Protestant Orthodox," *Scottish Journal of Theology* 61(2) (2008): 206–223.

—, *Revisiting the Doctrine of the Divine Attributes: In Dialogue with Karl Barth, Eberhard Jüngel, and Wolf Krötke* (New York: Peter Lang, 2007).

Holmes, Stephen R., "The Attributes of God," in *The Oxford Handbook of Systematic Theology*, eds J.B. Webster, K. Tanner, I.R. Torrance (Oxford: Oxford University Press, 2007), pp. 54–71.

—, "Trinitarian Missiology: Towards a Theology of God as Missionary," *International Journal of Systematic Theology* 8(1) (2006): 72–90.

—, "The Upholding of Beauty: A Reading of Anselm's *Cur Deus Homo*," in *Listening to the Past: The Place of Tradition in Theology* (Grand Rapids: Baker Academic, 2002), pp. 37–49.

—, "Something Much Too Plain to Say: Towards a Defense of the Doctrine of Divine Simplicity," in *Listening to the Past: The Place of Tradition in Theology* (Grand Rapids: Baker Academic, 2002), pp. 50–67.

Hubbard, Robert L., "Dynamistic and Legal Processes in Psalm 7," *Zeitschrift für die alttestamentliche Wissenschaft* 94(2) (1982): 267–279.

Hughes, Gerard J., *The Nature of God* (London: Routledge, 1995).

Hultgren, Arland J., *The Parables of Jesus: A Commentary* (Grand Rapids: Eerdmans, 2000).

Hunsinger, George, "*Mysterium Trinitatis*: Karl Barth's Conception of Eternity," in *Disruptive Grace: Studies in the Theology of Karl Barth* (Grand Rapids: Eerdmans, 2000), pp. 186–209.

—, *How to Read Karl Barth: The Shape of His Theology* (New York: Oxford University Press, 1991).

Irenaeus of Lyon, "Against Heresies," in *The Ante-Nicene Fathers: Translations of the Writings of the Fathers Down to A.D. 325*, vol. 1, eds A. Roberts, et al. (Edinburgh: T&T Clark, 1986).

Jaeger, Werner W., *Early Christianity and Greek Paideia* (London: Oxford University Press, 1969).

Jans, Jan, "Neither Punishment Nor Reward: Divine Gratuitousness and Moral Order," in *Job's God*, ed. E.J. van Wolde (London: SCM Press, 2004), pp. 83–92.

Jenson, Robert W., *Systematic Theology*, 2 vols (Oxford: Oxford University Press, 1997).

Jeremias, Jörg, *The Book of Amos: A Commentary*, The Old Testament Library, trans. D.W. Stott (Louisville: Westminster John Knox Press, 1998).

Jersak, Brad, M. Hardin, eds, *Stricken by God?: Nonviolent Identification and the Victory of Christ* (Grand Rapids: Eerdmans, 2007).

Jewett, Robert, R.D. Kotansky, E.J. Epp, *Romans: A Commentary*, Hermeneia (Minneapolis: Fortress Press, 2007).

Jüngel, Eberhard, *Justification: The Heart of the Christian Faith*, trans. J.F. Cayzer (Edinburgh: T&T Clark, 2001).

—, "Theses on the Relation of the Existence, Essence and Attributes of God," *Toronto Journal of Theology* 17(1) (2001): 55–74.

—, "The Last Judgment as an Act of Grace," *Louvain Studies* 15 (1990): 389–405.

—, *God as the Mystery of the World: On the Foundation of the Theology of the Crucified One in the Dispute between Theism and Atheism*, trans. D. Guder (Grand Rapids: Eerdmans, 1983).

Kaiser, Otto, *Isaiah 1–12: A Commentary*, Old Testament Library (London: SCM Press, 1983).

Kant, Immanuel, "Religion with the Boundaries of Mere Reason," in *Religion and Rational Theology*, eds A.W. Wood, G. DiGiovanni (New York: Cambridge University Press, 1996), pp. 39–215.

Käsemann, Ernst, *Commentary on Romans*, trans. G.W. Bromiley (Grand Rapids: Eerdmans, 1980).

Kaufman, Gordon, *Systematic Theology: A Historicist Perspective* (New York: Scribners, 1968).

Kelly, J.N.D., *Early Christian Doctrines*, 5th ed. (New York: HarperCollins, 1978).

Kitamori, Kazō, *Theology of the Pain of God* (London: SCM Press, 1966).

Koch, Klaus, "Gibt es ein Vergeltungsdogma im AT?" *Zeitschrift für Theologie und Kirche* 52 (1955): 1–42.

Koyama, Kōsuke, *Mount Fuji and Mount Sinai: A Critique of Idols* (Maryknoll: Orbis Books, 1985).

—, "The 'Wrath of God' and the Thai Theologia Gloriae," in *Christ and the Younger Churches: Theological Contributions from Asia, Africa, and Latin America*, ed. G.F. Vicedom (London: SPCK, 1972), pp. 42–50.

Krötke, Wolf, *Gottes Klarheiten: Eine Neuinterpretation der Lehre von Gottes 'Eigenschaften'* (Tübingen: Mohr Siebeck, 2001).

Lactantius, "De ira Dei," in *The Ante-Nicene Fathers: Translations of the Writings of the Fathers Down to A.D. 325*, vol. 7, eds A. Roberts et al. (Edinburgh: T&T Clark, 1986).

LaCugna, Catherine M., *God for Us: The Trinity and Christian Life* (San Francisco: HarperSanFrancisco, 1991).

Ladd, George E., *A Commentary on the Revelation of John* (Grand Rapids: Eerdmans, 1972).

Lane, Tony, "The Wrath of God as an Aspect of the Love of God," in *Nothing Greater, Nothing Better: Theological Essays on the Love of God*, ed. K.J. Vanhoozer (Grand Rapids: Eerdmans, 2001), pp. 138–167.

Luther, Martin, *Luther's Works*, 55 vols, eds J. Pelikan, H.T. Lehman (Philadelphia: Fortress Press, 1955–1986).

Luz, Ulrich, *Matthew 8–20: A Commentary*, Hermeneia (Minneapolis: Fortress Press, 2001).

—, *The Theology of the Gospel of Matthew*, trans. J.B. Robinson (Cambridge: Cambridge University Press, 1995).

Macgregor, G.H.C., "The Concept of the Wrath of God in the New Testament," *New Testament Studies* 7 (1961): 101–109.

MacKinnon, Donald M., " 'Substance' in Christology: A Cross-Bench View," in *Christ, Faith and History: Cambridge Studies in Christology*, eds S.W. Sykes, J.P. Clayton (Cambridge: Cambridge University Press, 1972), pp. 279–300.

Mackintosh, H.R., *Types of Modern Theology: Schleiermacher to Barth* (New York: Charles Scribner's Sons, 1937).

Macquarrie, John, *Principles of Christian Theology* (London: SCM Press, 1977).

—, *Twentieth-Century Religious Thought: The Frontiers of Philosophy and Theology, 1900–1960* (London: SCM Press, 1963).

Marion, Jean-Luc, *God without Being: Hors-Texte* (Chicago: University of Chicago Press, 1995).

Marshall, I. Howard, *Beyond the Bible: Moving from Scripture to Theology* (Grand Rapids: Baker Academic, 2004).

McCormack, Bruce L., "The Actuality of God: Karl Barth in Conversation with Open Theism," in *Engaging the Doctrine of God: Contemporary Protestant Perspectives*, ed. *idem* (Grand Rapids: Baker Academic, 2008), pp. 185–242.

—, "Not a Possible God but the God Who is: Observations on Friedrich Schleiermacher's Doctrine of God," in *The Reality of Faith in Theology: Studies on Karl Barth Princeton-Kampen Consultation, 2005*, eds *idem*, G.W. Neven (New York: Peter Lang, 2007), pp. 111–139.

McGrath, Alister E., *Iustitia Dei: A History of the Christian Doctrine of Justification* (Cambridge: Cambridge University Press, 1986).

McKnight, Scot, "A Loyal Critic: Matthew's Polemic with Judaism in Theological Perspective," in *Anti-Semitism and Early Christianity: Issues of Polemic and Faith*, eds C.A. Evans, D.A. Hagner (Minneapolis: Fortress Press, 1993), pp. 55–79.

McNicol, John, "The Righteousness of God in the Epistle to the Romans," *Evangelical Quarterly* 6(3) (1934): 302–311.

Micka, Ermin F., *The Problem of Divine Anger in Arnobius and Lactantius: A Dissertation* (Washington D.C.: Catholic University of America Press, 1943).

Miggelbrink, Ralf, *Der Zornige Gott: Die Bedeutung einer Anstössigen Biblischen Tradition* (Darmstadt: Wissenschaftliche Buchgesellschaft, 2002).

Minns, Denis, *Irenaeus* (London: Geoffrey Chapman, 1994).

Moberly, R.W.L., "Whose Justice? Which Righteousness? The Interpretation of Isaiah 5:16," *Vetus Testamentum* 51(1) (2001): 55–68.

Molnar, Paul D., *Divine Freedom and the Doctrine of the Immanent Trinity: In Dialogue with Karl Barth and Contemporary Theology* (London: T&T Clark, 2002).

Moltmann, Jürgen, *The Trinity and the Kingdom of God: The Doctrine of God*, trans. M. Kohl (London: SCM Press, 1981).

—, *The Crucified God: The Cross of Christ as the Foundation and Criticism of Christian Theology*, trans. R.A. Wilson, J. Bowden (New York: Harper & Row, 1974).

Moo, Douglas J., *The Epistle to the Romans*, The New International Commentary on the New Testament (Grand Rapids: Eerdmans, 1996).

Morris, Leon, *The Gospel According to Matthew*, The Pillar New Testament Commentary (Grand Rapids: Eerdmans, 1992).

Morris, Thomas V., *Our Idea of God: An Introduction to Philosophical Theology* (Downers Grove: InterVarsity, 1991).

Muller, Richard A., *Post-Reformation Reformed Dogmatics: The Rise and Development of Reformed Orthodoxy, ca. 1520 to ca. 1725: Volume 3, the Divine Essence and Attributes* (Grand Rapids: Baker Academic, 2003).

—, *Dictionary of Latin and Greek Theological Terms Drawn Principally from Protestant Scholastic Theology* (Grand Rapids: Baker, 2001).

Murray, Stephen Butler, "Reclaiming Divine Wrath: An Apologetics for an Aspect of God Neglected by Contemporary Theology and Preaching" (unpublished Ph.D. dissertation; Union Theological Seminary, 2004).

Newbigin, Lesslie, *Foolishness to the Greeks: The Gospel and Western Culture* (Grand Rapids; Eerdmans, 1986).

Niebuhr, Reinhold, *The Nature and Destiny of Man: A Christian Interpretation*, 2 vols. (New York: Charles Scribner's Sons, 1943).

Niesel, Wilhelm, *The Theology of Calvin*, trans. H. Knight (London: Lutterworth Press, 1956).

Norris, Richard A., *God and World in Early Christian Theology: A Study in Justin Martyr, Irenaeus, Tertullian and Origen* (London: Adam & Charles Black, 1966).

Oakes, Robert A., "The Wrath of God," *International Journal for Philosophy of Religion* 27(3) (1990): 129–140.

Oberdeck, John W., "Speaking to Contemporary American Culture on Sin and the Wrath of God," *Concordia Journal* 31(4) (2005): 398–410.

O'Donovan, Oliver, *The Ways of Judgment* (Grand Rapids: Eerdmans, 2005).

Otto, Rudolf, *The Idea of the Holy: An Inquiry into the Non-Rational Factor in the Idea of the Divine and its Relation to the Rational* (London: Oxford University Press, 1958).

Owen, John, "A Dissertation on Divine Justice," in *Works of John Owen*, vol. 10 (Edinburgh: Banner of Truth, 1967), pp. 481–624.

Pannenberg, Wolfhart, *Systematic Theology*, 3 vols. (Grand Rapids: Eerdmans, 1991).

—, "The Appropriation of the Philosophical Concept of God as a Dogmatic Problem of Early Christian Theology," in *Basic Questions in Theology II*, trans. G.H. Kehm (London: SCM Press, 1971), pp. 119–183.

Paul, Shalom M., *Amos: A Commentary on the Book of Amos*, Hermeneia (Minneapolis: Fortress Press, 1991).

Peels, H.G.L., *The Vengeance of God: The Meaning of the Root NQM and the Function of the NQM-Texts in the Context of Divine Revelation in the Old Testament* (Leiden: Brill, 1995).

Pelikan, Jaroslav, *The Christian Tradition, vol. 1: The Emergence of the Catholic Tradition (100–600)* (Chicago: University of Chicago Press, 1971).

—, *Development of Christian Doctrine: Some Historical Prolegomena* (New Haven: Yale University Press, 1969).

Pohlenz, M., *Vom Zorne Gottes: Eine Studie über den Einfluss der Griechischen Philosophie auf das Alte Christentum* (Göttingen: Vandenhoeck und Ruprecht, 1909).

Price, Robert B., " 'Letters of the Divine Word': The Perfections of God in Karl Barth's Church Dogmatics" (unpublished Ph.D. dissertation, University of Aberdeen, 2007).

Pseudo-Dionysius, *Pseudo-Dionysius: The Complete Works*, trans. Colm Luibhéid, ed. P. Rorem (New York: Paulist Press, 1987).

Quash, Ben, *Theology and the Drama of History* (Cambridge: Cambridge University Press, 2005).

Rahner, Karl, *The Trinity*, trans. J. Donceel (New York: Herder & Herder, 1970).

Reeling-Brouwer, Rinse H., "The Conversation between Karl Barth and Amandus Polanus on the Question of the Reality of Human Speaking of the Simplicity and the Multiplicity in God," in *The Reality of Faith in Theology: Studies on Karl Barth Princeton-Kampen Consultation, 2005*, eds B. McCormack, G.W. Neven (New York: Peter Lang, 2007), pp. 51–110.

Rehnman, Sebastian, "Theistic Metaphysics and Biblical Exegesis: Francis Turretin on the Concept of God," *Religious Studies* 38(2) (2002): 167–186.

Reumann, John, "Righteousness (NT)," in *The Anchor Bible Dictionary*, vol. 5, ed. D.N. Freedman (New York: Doubleday, 1992), pp. 745–773.

—, "The Gospel of the Righteousness of God: Pauline Interpretation in Romans 3:21–31," *Interpretation* 20 (1966): pp. 432–452.

Richards, Jay W., *The Untamed God: A Philosophical Exploration of Divine Perfection, Immutability, and Simplicity* (Downers Grove: InterVarsity Press, 2003).

—, "Schleiermacher's Divine Attributes: Their Coherence and Reference," *Encounter* 57(2) (1996): 149–170.

Ripley, Jason J., "Covenantal Concepts of Justice and Righteousness, and Catholic-Protestant Reconciliation: Theological Implications and Explorations," *Journal of Ecumenical Studies* 38(1) (2001): 95–108.

Robbins, Jerry K., "God's Wrath: A Process Exposition," *Dialog* 33 (1994): 252–258.

Rowe, William L., *The Cosmological Argument* (Princeton: Princeton University Press, 1975).

Rowland, Christopher C., *The Book of Revelation*, The New Interpreter's Bible (Nashville: Abingdon, 1994–2002).

Sanders, Fred, "The Trinity," in *The Oxford Handbook of Systematic Theology*, eds J.B. Webster, K. Tanner, I.R. Torrance (Oxford: Oxford University Press, 2007), pp. 35–53.

Schleiermacher, Friedrich, *Brief Outline of Theology as a Field of Study*, trans. T.N. Tice (Lewiston: E. Mellen Press, 1990).

—, *Servant of the Word: Selected Sermons of Friedrich Schleiermacher*, trans. D. DeVries (Philadelphia: Fortress Press, 1987).

—, *On the Glaubenslehre: Two Letters to Dr. Lücke*, AAR Texts and Translations 3, trans. J. Duke and F. Fiorenza (Atlanta: Scholars Press, 1981).

—, *The Christian Faith*, eds H.R. Mackintosh, J.S. Stewart (Edinburgh: T&T Clark, 1928).

Schroeder, Christoph, "Standing in the Breach: Turning Away the Wrath of God," *Interpretation* 52(1) (1998): 16–23.

Schweizer, Eduard, *A Theological Introduction to the New Testament* (London: SPCK, 1992).

—, *The Good News According to Matthew* (London: SPCK, 1976).

Schwöbel, Christoph, *God: Action and Revelation* (Kampen: Kok Pharos, 1992).

Seifrid, Mark A., "Righteousness, Justice and Justification," in *New Dictionary of Biblical Theology*, eds T.D. Alexander, B.S. Rosner (Leicester: InterVarsity Press, 2000), pp. 740–745.

Seitz, Christopher R., *Isaiah 1–39*, Interpretation (Louisville: John Knox Press, 1993).

Sherman, Robert J., *King, Priest, and Prophet: A Trinitarian Theology of Atonement* (London: T&T Clark, 2004).

Silberman, Lou H., "You Cannot See My Face: Seeking to Understand Divine Justice," in *Shall Not the Judge of All the Earth Do What is Right?: Studies on the Nature of God in Tribute to James L. Crenshaw*, eds D. Penchansky, P.L. Redditt (Winona Lake: Eisenbrauns, 2000), pp. 89–96.

Smith, D. Moody, *The Theology of the Gospel of John* (Cambridge: Cambridge University Press, 1995).

Snodgrass, Klyne R., "From Allegorizing to Allegorizing: A History of the Interpretation of the Parables of Jesus," in *The Challenge of Jesus' Parables*, ed. R.N. Longenecker (Grand Rapids: Eerdmans, 2000), pp. 3–29.

Sokolowski, Robert, *The God of Faith and Reason: Foundations of Christian Theology* (Notre Dame: University of Notre Dame Press, 1982).

Sonderegger, Katherine, "The Absolute Infinity of God," in *The Reality of Faith in Theology: Studies on Karl Barth Princeton-Kampen Consultation, 2005*, eds B. McCormack, G.W. Neven (New York: Peter Lang, 2007), pp. 31–49.

—, "Anselm, *Defensor Fidei*," *International Journal of Systematic Theology* 9(3) (2007): 342–359.

—, "On the Holy Name of God," *Theology Today* 58(3) (2001): 384–398.

Spence, Alan, *The Promise of Peace: A Unified Theory of Atonement* (Edinburgh: T&T Clark, 2007).

Stählin, G., "orgē," in *Theological Dictionary of the New Testament*, 9 vols, eds G. Kittel, G. Friedrich, G.W. Bromiley, vol. 5 (Grand Rapids: Eerdmans, 1985), pp. 422–447.

Stead, Christopher, *Divine Substance* (Oxford: Clarendon Press, 1977).

Steussy, Marti J., "The Problematic God of Samuel," in *Shall Not the Judge of all the Earth do what is Right?: Studies on the Nature of God in Tribute to James L. Crenshaw*, eds D. Penchansky, P.L. Redditt (Winona Lake: Eisenbrauns, 2000), pp. 127–161.

Stuhlmacher, Peter, *Gerechtigkeit Gottes bei Paulus* (Göttingen: Vandenhoeck & Ruprecht, 1965).

Sweet, J.P.M., *Revelation*, TPI New Testament Commentaries (London: SCM Press, 1990).

Tanner, Kathryn, "Incarnation, Cross, and Sacrifice: A Feminist-Inspired Reappraisal," *Anglican Theological Review* 86(1) (2004): 35–56.

—, *Jesus, Humanity and the Trinity: A Brief Systematic Theology* (Edinburgh: T&T Clark, 2001).

—, "Creation and Providence," in *The Cambridge Companion to Karl Barth*, ed. J.B. Webster (Cambridge: Cambridge University Press, 2000), pp. 111–126.

—, "Justification and Justice in a Theology of Grace," *Theology Today* 55(4) (1999): 510–523.

—, *God and Creation in Christian Theology: Tyranny or Empowerment?* (Oxford: Blackwell, 1988).

Tasker, R.V.G., *The Biblical Doctrine of the Wrath of God* (London: Tyndale, 1951).

Taylor, Charles, *Sources of the Self: The Making of the Modern Identity* (Cambridge: Harvard University Press, 1989).

Tevel, J.M., "The Labourers in the Vineyard: The Exegesis of Matthew 20:1–7 in the Early Church," *Vigiliae Christianae* 46 (1992): 356–380.

Tillich, Paul, *Systematic Theology*, 3 vols. (Chicago: University of Chicago Press, 1976).

Torrance, Thomas F., *The Christian Doctrine of God: One Being, Three Persons* (Edinburgh: T&T Clark, 1996).

Tracy, Thomas F., *God, Action, and Embodiment* (Grand Rapids: Eerdmans, 1984).

Travis, Stephen H., "Wrath of God (NT)," in *The Anchor Bible Dictionary*, ed. D.N. Freedman, vol. 6 (New York: Doubleday, 1992), pp. 996–998.

—, *Christ and the Judgment of God: Divine Retribution in the New Testament* (Basingstoke: M. Pickering, 1991).

Trueman, Carl R., "John Owen's *Dissertation* on Divine Justice: An Exercise in Christocentric Scholasticism," *Calvin Theological Journal* 33 (1998): 87–103.

Tucker, Gene M., *The Book of Isaiah 1–39*, The New Interpreter's Bible (Nashville: Abingdon Press, 1994).

—, "Sin and 'Judgment' in the Prophets," in *Problems in Biblical Theology: Essays in Honor of Rolf Knierim*, ed. H.T.C. Sun (Grand Rapids: Eerdmans, 1997), pp. 373–388.

Turretin, Francis, *Institutes of Elenctic Theology*, 3 vols, trans. G.M. Giger, ed. J.T. Dennison (Phillipsburg: P&R, 1992).

van der Kooi, Cornelis, *As in a Mirror: John Calvin and Karl Barth on Knowing God—A Diptych* (Leiden: Brill, 2005).

Vanhoozer, Kevin, "Human Being, Individual and Social," in *The Cambridge Companion to Christian Doctrine*, ed. C.E. Gunton (Cambridge: Cambridge University Press, 2003), pp. 158–88.

Velde, H. te., *Seth, God of Confusion: A Study of his Role in Egyptian Mythology and Religion*, trans. G.E. van Baaren-Pape (Leiden: E. J. Brill, 1967).

Volkmann, Stefan, *Der Zorn Gottes: Studien zur Rede vom Zorn Gottes in der evangelischen Theologie* (Marburg: Elwert, 2004).

—, "Zorn Gottes: Theologiegeschichtlich und dogmatisch," in *Religion in Geschichte und Gegenwart: Handwörterbuch für Theologie und Religionswissenschaft*, 8 vols, ed. H.D. Betz, 4th ed., vol. 8 (Tübingen: Mohr Siebeck, 1998), pp. 1905–1906.

von Balthasar, Hans Urs, *Theo-Drama: Theological Dramatic Theory*, vol. 4, trans. G. Harrison (San Francisco: Ignatius Press, 1994).

von Rad, Gerhard, *Old Testament Theology*, 2 vols. (Edinburgh: Oliver and Boyd, 1962).

Watts, John D.W., *Isaiah 1–33*, Word Biblical Commentary (Waco: Word Books, 1985).

Weaver, J. Denny, *The Non-Violent Atonement* (Grand Rapids: Eerdmans, 2001).

Weber, Ferdinand, *Vom Zorne Gottes: Ein biblisch-theologischer Versuch* (Erlangen: Andreas Deichert, 1862).

Weber, Otto, *Foundations of Dogmatics*, 2 vols, trans. D.L. Guder (Grand Rapids: Eerdmans, 1981).

Webster, John, "Principles of Systematic Theology," *International Journal of Systematic Theology* 11(1) (2009): 56–71.

—, "Life in and of Himself: Reflections on God's Aseity," in *Engaging the Doctrine of God: Contemporary Protestant Perspectives*, ed. B.L. McCormack (Grand Rapids: Baker Academic, 2008), pp. 107–124.

—, "God's Perfect Life," in *God's Life in Trinity*, eds M. Volf, M. Welker (Minneapolis: Augsburg Fortress Press, 2006), pp. 143–152.

—, *Barth*, 2nd ed. (London: Continuum, 2004).

—., "The Holiness and Love of God," in *Scottish Journal of Theology* 57(3) (2004): 249–268.

—, "The Immensity and Ubiquity of God," in *Denkwürdiges Geheimnis: Beiträge zur Gotteslehre, Festschrift für Eberhard Jüngel zum 70. Geburtstag*, eds I.U. Dalferth, J. Fischer, H.-P. Grosshans (Tübingen: Mohr Siebeck, 2004), pp. 539–556.

—, *Holiness* (London: SCM Press, 2003).

—, *Barth's Moral Theology: Human Action in Barth's Thought* (Edinburgh: T&T Clark, 1998).

—, *Barth's Ethics of Reconciliation* (Cambridge: Cambridge University Press, 1995).

Weinandy, Thomas G., *Does God Suffer?* (Notre Dame: University of Notre Dame, 1999).

Welch, Claude, *Protestant Thought in the Nineteenth Century, Volume 1: 1799–1870* (New Haven, Yale University Press, 1972).

Welker, Michael, "God's Eternity, God's Temporality, and Trinitarian Theology," *Theology Today* 55(3) (1998): 317–328.

Wendel, Francois, *Calvin: The Origins and Development of his Religious Thought* (London: Collins, 1963).

Westerholm, Stephen, *Perspectives Old and New on Paul: The "Lutheran" Paul and His Critics* (Grand Rapids: Eerdmans, 2004).

Westermann, Claus, *The Parables of Jesus in the Light of the Old Testament*, trans. F.W. Golka, A.H.B. Logan (Edinburgh: T&T Clark, 1990).

Whitehead, Alfred North, *Process and Reality: An Essay in Cosmology*, corr. ed, The Gifford Lectures, 1927–1928, eds D.R. Griffin, D.W. Sherburne (London: The Free Press, 1978).

Wildberger, Hans, *Isaiah 1–12: A Commentary*, A Continental Commentary, trans. T.H. Trapp (Minneapolis: Fortress Press, 1991).

Williams, Robert R., *Schleiermacher the Theologian: The Construction of the Doctrine of God* (Philadelphia: Fortress Press, 1978).

Williams, Sam K., "The 'Righteousness of God' in Romans," *Journal of Biblical Literature* 99 (1980): 241–290.

Willis, David E., *Notes on the Holiness of God* (Grand Rapids: Eerdmans, 2002).

Wolterstorff, Nicholas, "Justice of God," in *For Faith and Clarity: Philosophical Contributions to Christian Theology*, ed. J.K. Beilby (Grand Rapids: Baker Academic, 2006), pp. 179–197.

Yeago, David S., "The New Testament and the Nicene Dogma: A Contribution to the Recovery of Theological Exegesis," in *The Theological Interpretation of Scripture: Classic and Contemporary Readings*, ed. S.E. Fowl (Cambridge: Blackwell, 1997), pp. 87–100.

Young, Edward J., *The Book of Isaiah*, 2 vols, The New International Commentary on the Old Testament (Grand Rapids: Eerdmans, 1965).

INDEX OF SCRIPTURE REFERENCES

New Testament

INDEX OF NAMES

INDEX OF NAMES

Made in the USA
Middletown, DE
19 March 2023

27129588R00135